Bob Zuppke

D1643274

For Jane

LIBRARY OF CONGRESS CATALOGUING-IN-PUBLICATION DATA

Brichford, Maynard J.
    Bob Zuppke : the life and football legacy of the Illinois
coach / Maynard Brichford.
        p.   cm.
    Includes bibliographical references and index.

    ISBN 978-0-7864-4301-7
    softcover : 50# alkaline paper ∞

    1. Zuppke, Robert C. (Robert Carl), 1879–1957
    2. Football coaches — United States — Biography.
    3. University of Illinois at Urbana-Champaign — Football —
History. I. Title.
    GV939.Z8B75   2009
    796.332092 — dc22
    [B]   2009014694

British Library cataloguing data are available

On the cover: Bob Zuppke, 1912; the 1923 national championship Illinois football team (both photographs from the University of Illinois)

Manufactured in the United States of America

*McFarland & Company, Inc., Publishers
    Box 611, Jefferson, North Carolina 28640
    www.mcfarlandpub.com*

Bob Zuppke

*The Life and Football Legacy
of the Illinois Coach*

MAYNARD BRICHFORD

McFarland & Company, Inc., Publishers
Jefferson, North Carolina, and London

Table of Contents

Preface

As a youth, I was exposed to football mania in northeastern Ohio. When I was seven, I read about the University of Illinois football team that played Army in the new municipal stadium in Cleveland. In the seventh grade, the boys in my class were photographed as the North Madison Grade School football team. Lacking the ability and time to play on the high school team, I described interscholastic games for the school newspaper. As a college freshman, I played in one game against the local seven-man high school team. In the Navy in World War II, we played flag football and watched professionals and amateurs play for military teams. After playing "horizontal guard" on a college intramural team, I went to the University of Michigan in the fall of 1948 and watched the Rose Bowl team play in the Big House. There I witnessed crowd behavior, which my roommate likened to a Nuremberg Rally. In the Alan Ameche years at the University of Wisconsin, we saw more "big time" football and lived next door to a dedicated "Packer Backer." When we moved to Urbana, Illinois, in 1963, we purchased a home on Eliot Drive, at the end of Mills Street, a block east of Zuppke, three blocks from George Huff, four blocks from Harding and six blocks from Grange. At Memorial Stadium, the football team won the Big Ten title and the Rose Bowl game.

As University Archivist at the University of Illinois, I soon discovered that President Edmund James had honed his administrative skills in the Stagg years at William R. Harper's University of Chicago and that his successor, David Kinley, was a product of Yale University in the Walter Camp era. Surrounded by the evidences of the importance attached to intercollegiate football in a land-grant university, I began to notice significant gaps in understanding the role of public higher education in developing intercollegiate football. Most literature published by sports historians, publicists and administrators was related to the origins of intercollegiate sports in eastern and private universities. Biographies of coaches featured greats such as Knute Rockne of Notre Dame and Amos Alonzo Stagg of Chicago. Many of the volumes on sports in public universities were devoted to statistics and photographs supplemented by legends and lore. Media coverage of athletic contests tended to emphasize sensational highlights and newsworthy scandals. The gradual acquisition of the Robert Zuppke Papers by the University Archives revealed that not all coaches were sports heroes, sideline generals, or migratory specialists. The documents indicated that Zuppke was a talented artist, a popular spokesman for the university, an active participant in the development of extracurricular programs and a vigorous defender of intercollegiate sports.

Academic critics have been nearly unanimous in their condemnation of college football. Their studies have often contained lengthy recitations of abuses, corruption, crises, hypocrisy, hysteria, problems, professionalism, recruitment of unqualified students, reform failures, scams, scandals, unethical acts, and questions about the relevance of athletics to higher education. Less attention has been paid to collegiate football as public entertainment, a vehicle for alumni outreach and a public relations program. Many secondary sources have focused on specific themes, institutions, events and individuals and avoided the context of institutional policies and politics, financial strategies and public relations. Critics of athletics in academic institutions frequently adopted a patronizing tone in discussing physical education and intercollegiate sports, and viewed athletic competition as a means for students to let off steam between lectures and laboratory sessions. They deplored college sports as an overemphasized and commercialized entertainment business that was unrelated to the business of higher education. Other scholars have applied broad social concepts to their analyses of the popularity of intercollegiate athletics. They have read cultural significance into public entertainment at nine seasonal competitive performances by eleven uniformed representatives of the university. Cultural dysfunction, male hegemony, consumption societies, hostile symbolisms and the financial exigencies of higher education have been identified as paramount issues and influences in college sports. Many of the "evils" that critics have found in college football dated from its origins in the nineteenth century. When spectators outnumbered players, the game became entertainment. When gate receipts exceeded operating expenses, it became a commercial property. When professional administrators directed the seasonal productions, it became a performing art. When advertising revenues and media coverage brought extensive publicity, it became a primary public relations program for colleges and universities.[1]

Considered as a performing art, both football wins and losses and the scores were less significant than the quality of the performers' play in relation to their abilities. Bob Zuppke coached high school and university teams that played 287 games and won 187 of them. He earned the respect of rival coaches and players on both his winning and his losing teams. The performances at athletic contests before spectators were measured and scored to determine the winners and losers. Detailed statistical tables recorded the team's effectiveness and provided evidence for the evaluation of the coach's abilities. Many persons viewed the won-loss records and scores as the measure of the success of the football program. In this study, the results of games are cited to provide a quantitative basis for the more important themes of Zuppke's impact on players, spectators, the university community and the public.

Zuppke, the "Dutch Master"at the University of Illinois, was a leading football coach in the first half of the twentieth century. This was a period of nationwide changes affecting American higher education. Between 1912 and 1941, Americans were involved in two world wars, a major economic depression, the urbanization of cities, the cultural assimilation of substantial immigrant populations, and the rapid development of public land-grant universities. These institutions responded by offering new curricula for the professional education of engineers, businessmen, entertainers and educators. In this period, there was a dramatic increase in interest in sports as a competitive performance and public entertainment. The 1920s were often hailed as the Golden Age of sports. Publicity in newspapers, magazines, books, motion pictures and radio broadcasts marketed intercollegiate football. Public interest and participation in baseball, football and basketball symbolized the emergence of a unique American sports culture.

Zuppke's career paralleled the story of the rise, prosperity and survival of big-time intercollegiate football. He was head football coach at the University of Illinois from 1913 to 1941. During this period, the Illini won or tied for seven Big Ten conference championships and two national championships. Collegiate football profits paid for huge stadiums and recreational facilities. While academic critics waged a continuing campaign against overemphasis on football, the sport prospered. In writing about University of Chicago football, Robin Lester noted the remarkable ability of the intercollegiate football industry "to survive each new reform binge and emerge with a firmer hold on institutions and market."[2] This biography of Zuppke is a study of his passion for football, his advocacy of its educational value and his ability to promote and market the game to the academic community and the general public. It places him in the context of multiple themes, including the development of interscholastic, intercollegiate and professional football, presidential support and public relations, sports psychology, coaching schools, stadium building and commercial football, academic criticism, the fraternity system, boosters and football in a state-supported public university.

1

The "Sport" from Milwaukee

The foundations for Zuppke's career were laid in his youth as a son of immigrant parents in Milwaukee. When the twentieth century began on January 1, 1901, Robert Carl Zuppke was a twenty-one-year-old student at Milwaukee Normal School in Wisconsin. The eldest son of Franz Simon Zuppke and Hermine Bocksbaum Zuppke was born in Berlin, Germany, on July 2, 1879. The Zuppkes and their two sons had been among the 210,485 Germans who left the Second Reich in 1881 for the opportunities of a new life in America. A jewelry designer in Berlin, Franz Zuppke settled in a German neighborhood on the south side of Milwaukee. In 1880, twenty-seven percent of the population was German-born and Milwaukee looked like Germany. Its 115,587 residents supported three Turner Halls and four jewelry establishments, which employed eighteen people. In 1884, the circulation of the three German-language newspapers was twice as much as that of the three English-language papers. In 1890, 12,000 citizens marched in the German Day parade. The leading industries were meat processing and iron working. Close behind them were flour milling and brewing.[1]

Franz Zuppke ran a jewelry store on Grand Avenue. German was taught in grammar school, but his family usually spoke English. Franz did not join any of Milwaukee's many German societies and said "where you fare well, that is your fatherland." Art, music and poetry were part of the atmosphere of the Zuppke home. Robert regarded his mother as very kind and gentle, but described his father as a strict disciplinarian and a snarly idealist. As an adult, he would draw upon both the idealistic perfectionism of his father and the supportive compassion of his mother.[2]

Robert, and his younger brothers, Paul and Herman, attended kindergarten and grade school in Milwaukee. He did well in drawing and mathematics and Paul excelled in scholarship. The boys joined a German gymnastics institution, as there was not enough physical training in the grade school. After a few years at 701 Forest Home Avenue, the Zuppkes moved to 1515

Sixth Street. Franz applied for citizenship on October 13, 1890, and became an American citizen on October 7, 1896. An impatient thirteen-year-old, Robert left school in 1892 to be an apprentice in a sign writer's shop, where he earned fifty cents a week. His first commercial artwork was a campaign banner for Republican presidential candidate Benjamin Harrison. In 1890, Milwaukee had 3,417 retailers, 1,592 teachers and about 60 artists. His father discouraged him from becoming an artist because he did not believe that his son could earn a living by his art. After a year as an apprentice, Franz obtained Robert's release and he "again appreciated" school.[3]

In 1895, Robert walked two and a half miles to Milwaukee's new West Division High School, where he studied drawing and took a gymnastics class. Short of stature, but physically mature at sixteen, he learned about the popular game of football. He saw his first forward pass in a game between Milwaukee West and Minneapolis Central High School. When West Division lost a 69–0 game with Fond du Lac and Bob's collarbone was among the casualties, the high school principal banished football. This decision forced young Zuppke to organize and play on the amateur "West Ends" football team. A classmate, who became a mathematics teacher, recalled that he was very popular and attributed his later football success to his skills in mathematics and chess. Milwaukee West had an excellent faculty and modern facilities. The principal was tutoring young Douglas MacArthur in preparation for his West Point examinations. The Zuppke brothers were in the English course and Robert illustrated the school yearbook. He sketched busts of Schiller and Goethe for the German Literary Society article. From a friend who was a sign writer, he learned to letter and use oils in painting. His friend Chris Steinmetz recalled that Mrs. Zuppke had "the patience of a saint to sit for a fellow like you," who "daubed paint on the canvas."[4]

When he was a high school junior, Robert passed the Normal School entrance examination. In the fall of 1898, he and Paul entered Milwaukee Normal School. Robert took American, English and Greek history courses. At a teacher training institution, the few male students were outnumbered ten to one by the girls. Robert made some "serious attempts at flirtation," but was checked by his colleagues. Robert was fourteen months older, but his apprenticeship had enabled Paul to catch up with his brother. Paul was assistant editor of the 1900 yearbook. Robert contributed twenty illustrations. Both Zuppkes belonged to the Young Men's Lyceum and the Epicureans Boarding Club's Coffee Club. In their second year at Normal, Paul was editor of the yearbook and Robert contributed a dozen pen-and-ink illustrations. Robert also had a role in the senior play. Oratorical contests were often associated with athletic games. He was a member of the inter–Normal debating team that defeated Whitewater Normal in a debate on building the Panama Canal.

Paul led the team and held several oratorical association offices. At Whitewater Normal, the all-male Milwaukee team was regarded as "so many curiosities." In the yearbook, Robert was described as being so practical that he believed that man had been created first and that women were "a sort of recreation." In the yearbook he proclaimed he was "a plain blunt man that loves my friends." In 1901, he graduated from the Normal School in social science. His teacher training had prepared him for a career of instructing athletes, coaches and the public. [5]

Robert's academic activities were supplemented by his enthusiasm for sports. In 1898, "Contrary Rob" played quarterback on the Normal School football team that lost most of its games. The yearbook listed "overwork, lack of good material, prejudice and financial difficulties" as problems. Robert recalled that his football career at Normal didn't amount to much as he recovered from his broken collarbone, but he remembered that his distinctive coach, Ike Carroll, had been a star back on the Wisconsin team. Bob was a center fielder on the Normal School baseball team, which lost three games, and a guard and forward on the basketball team, which had a 13–3 record. He recalled basketball games on the "kerosene circuit" in arenas with hot stoves in the corners and oil lamps that were changed from one end to the other whenever the home team made a try for a basket. Some of the basketball floors included parts of two rooms, and the teams would be playing around the corner from the crowd, and also away from the officials.[6]

A Normal School diploma enabled Robert to get a teaching position to earn money for further education. In 1901–02, he taught in a rural school in Milwaukee County, where he earned $45 a month. The following year, he taught a fifth grade class in the city of Milwaukee. His Normal School training provided an opportunity to attend a National Education Association meeting in Milwaukee, where an eminent educator pointed to grandstands seating 6,000 people as an indication that football caused the decay of academic institutions. His Normal School years provided him with both the didactic skills for coaching and an enthusiasm for the educational merits of extracurricular activities. While teaching, he also worked as a financial reporter for the Dun and Bradstreet Company and applied his artistic talents as a sign writer. In his spare time, he organized a football team known as the North Side Apaches. In the warm summer months of 1903, Zuppke and Chris Steinmetz played baseball and swam in the Milwaukee River and Okauchee Lake. They also dined occasionally on beer, rye bread and limburger cheese. At the Zuppke house, these refreshments were consumed in the woodshed, as Bob's mother did not like the limburger odor.[7]

With the money earned from teaching and other jobs, twenty-four-year old Bob Zuppke entered the University of Wisconsin in Madison in September 1903 as a junior. In two years at Madison, he received excellent instruction from an outstanding faculty, such as history professors Carl R. Fish and Dana Munro, who became leading figures in American and medieval history. His academic work included eleven semester courses in history with a standing of 87, seven in German with a standing of 90, five in education or pedagogy with a standing of 90, three in philosophy with a standing of 81, two in psychology with a standing of 93 and one in political science with a standing of 93. He decorated the margins of his meticulous course notes with sketches of locomotives, teachers and young ladies. Professor Joseph Jastrow taught his abnormal and comparative psychology courses, where he read some of the works of William James and Edward Thorndike. In 1903, Jastrow was ranked as a psychologist just behind John Dewey as tenth in order of distinction.

While attending the university, Zuppke continued to work as a sign painter to earn money for expenses. In 1904, he painted a portrait of presidential candidate Theodore Roosevelt for a Milwaukee political banner. Seven of his illustrations appeared in the 1905 Wisconsin *Badger* and eleven in the 1906 edition of the yearbook. Bob also served on the editorial board of *Sphinx*, the college humor magazine. On June 22, 1905, he graduated from the College of Letters and Science with a Ph.B. The commencement addresses were delivered by Carl Schurz, the leading nineteenth-century German-American politician, and the university's new president, Charles Van Hise.[8]

During Zuppke's two years in Madison, academics were lamenting "excessive student interest" in football. When Wisconsin history professor Frederick J. Turner criticized the game as a business run by professionals, students burned him in effigy. Zuppke studied football, participated in football practices and attended the games, but he did not make the team. He was a "tackling dummy" who imitated the next week's opponents. As a slow, 142-pound quarterback, he competed with the second team against Ripon, Lawrence and the teacher's colleges. In the fall of 1903, he watched Amos Alonzo Stagg coach the University of Chicago team against the Wisconsin varsity. A short, rugged man dressed in collegiate style and hatless, Stagg used Walter Eckersall's field goals, the T formation and a delayed fullback plunge in defeating the Badgers, 15–6. President William R. Harper had brought Stagg from Yale to Chicago as the first permanent coach in the Midwest. Harper and Stagg had promoted the development of student enthusiasm for alumni-controlled athletics under Yale president Timothy Dwight. Zuppke also observed Minnesota's team coached by Henry Williams, another Yale graduate, who had influenced Stagg's tactics and used direct center passes to the backfield. He also watched Michigan's famous point-a-minute team coached by Fielding Yost as they shut out the Badgers. In the fall of 1904,

Bob had an opportunity to apply his football knowledge. A fraternity member asked him to coach the football team at Mount Horeb High School. The school was located twenty miles west of Madison, so the young coach rode the caboose of a freight train to and from practices. He held two or three practices a week, but never saw the team play a game. The players were enthusiastic and cooperative. While there was no "burning bush," the coach enjoyed every minute of his Mount Horeb experience.[9]

In collegiate basketball, Bob was a substitute in 1903–04 and a guard on the 1904–05 team. Milwaukee's Chris Steinmetz was the star forward. He persuaded the coach to try Zuppke at guard. Bob became a starter and the team had successful seasons with an 19–11 record. The schedule included colleges, YMCAs and city teams. The games were played in makeshift gymnasiums under variable rules. On basketball trips, he sketched waitresses on the tablecloth and added sketches of the way they would look in bathing suits. Chris said that he had a wonderful imagination. In Bob's senior year, the team's 1–0 record enabled them to claim a conference championship. They made an eastern invasion, playing nine games in ten nights. Zuppke and Steinmetz played every minute of the games, and Wisconsin defeated Chicago and Rochester, but lost to Columbia and Ohio State. Returning to Milwaukee with his basketball letter on his sweater, he recalled that a lady cautioned her children about associating with that "sport."[10]

2

Coaching at Muskegon and Oak Park

Bob's enthusiasm for sports and his informal coaching experience at Mount Horeb led him toward a coaching career. However, at twenty-six, his interest in painting again inspired him to test his skills in a leading market for artistic talents. With thirty-four dollars in his pocket, the aspiring painter left Milwaukee for New York City. He recalled that this was "the greatest year of my life from the point of view of developing self-reliance." He painted wall signs, drew sketches for a Hartford poet, worked over Broadway on a swinging scaffold, and visited the Metropolitan Museum of Art. He also watched Yale football practices and games in New Haven. In 1906, he returned to the Midwest for a position as a furniture illustrator for the Shaw-Torey advertising firm in Grand Rapids, Michigan. When he converted the shop into an athletic gym, the offending employees were fired. The University of Wisconsin notified him about a position at the Muskegon High and Hackley Manual Training School as football coach and gymnasium director. He took the electric train from Grand Rapids to Muskegon for an interview, where he asked for and received a salary of $1,000 a year.[1]

At Muskegon, the coach found a large new gymnasium for instruction in physical education. Zuppke organized fourteen classes into small competitive groups with distinctive names and supervised twenty-two basketball teams. He evaluated students in the gym classes and selected players for his interscholastic football, track, swimming and basketball teams. He also taught two history classes and was an ex-officio member of the student Athletic Association Board of Control, which was required to ratify his actions. Students were impressed by their new history teacher, who compared the Roman armies with football teams. In 1908–09, he sent his track stars to Stagg's National Interscholastic meet in Chicago. In 1909, they won interscholastic meets in Ann Arbor and Lansing and claimed a state championship. A track man recalled that Zuppke had motivated a "scraggly bunch of kids" by "bull about not cutting our hair" to gain the "strength of Samson." The student annual boasted about their "sound and clean" athletic program and the thorough training program of "our great coach." In 1910, he was involved in clarifying the status of a high school track athlete accused of competing with a Michigan Agricultural College team. Former player Fred Jacks recalled that Zup would paint at the beach and that then they would swim a couple miles, but all he would talk or think about was football. Coach Zuppke's ambition was also fired by Fielding Yost's 304-page *Football for Players and Spectators* with its section on the prestige and popularity of football in American colleges and high schools, descriptions of the offensive and defensive styles employed at major universities, illustrations of huge crowds at college games, analyses of position play, diagrams of formations, and rules.[2]

Muskegon's coach was a drillmaster. He introduced uniforms and shoulder pads and experimented with punt formations, spiral passes from center and the "flea-flicker" passes. The flea-flicker was a forward pass followed by a lateral pass to a running back. The Muskegon Big Reds were drawn from the Beidler Street Gang, the Gas House Gang and the secret Mule Delts. From 1906 to 1909, his team compiled a 29-4-2 mark. In 1906, they outscored eight opponents 289 to 6. Local fans would compare Muskegon with Yost's Michigan team, which had outscored their thirteen opponents 495 to 2 in 1905. Two Muskegon players became stars for Stagg at Chicago. In 1908, after holding favored Saginaw to a 0–0 tie in a seventy-minute game, Muskegon claimed a state championship. Saginaw fans stoned them. Zuppke's teams consistently defeated Muskegon's greatest rival, Grand Rapids Central High School. In 1909, with an open type of game that featured passes, reverses and spinner plays, Zuppke's "bunch of ragamuffins" held the Hope College team to a scoreless tie.[3]

The success of Muskegon's "great little coach" attracted attention in the region. In 1910, Zuppke announced that he would take a position as athletic director at a Cleveland technical high school. However, as the school year ended, fellow teacher Joe Tallman contacted his brother who taught at Oak Park High School in Illinois. When Oak Park principal John Hanna visited Muskegon to check on Zuppke's work, he found the coach directing classes scattered over a large field. When the coach blew his whistle, the well-disciplined students rushed over like an army. Hanna hired Zuppke to coach five teams and teach five Greek and Roman history courses and three gymnasium classes for $2,000 a year. Located in west suburban Chicago, Oak Park had a strong sports tradition. The Boys' Athletic Association of Oak Park and River Forest Township High School was a booster organization that promoted sports. After defeating Crane Tech in 1911, Zuppke protested the exclusion of

Oak Park from the major section of the Cook County High School Baseball League.[4]

Zuppke's track teams won two out of three National Interscholastic meets held at the University of Chicago. Coach Amos Stagg was an expert salesman for Chicago's athletic program. He secured national prominence in 1902 by bringing the very best high school athletes from six midwestern states to the campus and showing them the advantages of an education at his university. Following meets, he passed out medals. Silver cups and Maroon blankets added to the color of the occasion. Several Oak Park football players missed one of the team's practices and were found at a University of Chicago tryout wearing green practice jerseys. There were no rules against tryouts, but their coach made sure that they did not go again.[5]

Interscholastic football had gained in popularity as fast as the college game. Increasing numbers of secondary schools and rising enrollments in physical education classes led to expanded athletic programs, which became sources of community pride and provided players with the academic qualifications for college work. In 1890, 204 Illinois high schools enrolled 14,120 students. Three decades later, 651 high schools enrolled 112,557 students and more than eighty percent of them had football teams. The University of Illinois had begun state interscholastic track meets in 1893. From 1907 to 1920, Oak Park High School won most of the state meets held at the University in Urbana. Zuppke organized Oak Park's gymnasium work and assembled a talented football team. In 1910, he supervised physical education for 355 boys, of whom forty-two played football. The second team was nearly as good as the starting team. One player recalled that his coach designed an aluminum brace for an injured shoulder that he received in his first game and then had him tackle the dummy. In determining whether he could take the pain, the coach gave him "something then that no one can take away." The school board questioned how he could maintain discipline when the students called him "Zup." He explained that the coach-student relationship was a benevolent dictatorship in which mutual confidence and sympathy led to "infectious enthusiasm."[6]

The 1909 Oak Park football team had been a tailender in its division of the Cook County football league. By November 1910, using Zuppke's open game with speedy and tricky offensive and defensive formations, the team had won six games by overwhelming scores. Guards dropped back to protect Zuppke's aerial game, which featured multiple passes to speedy receivers. After a 21–0 warm-up win over Maywood YMCA on November 5, they defeated Lane High School 17–0 on November 6 for the league championship. With a line averaging 160 pounds and a 150-pound backfield, Zuppke's team was one of the lightest to win the title. His teams won twenty-seven straight games at Oak Park. Upon graduation, several of the Oak Park players continued their football careers at Chicago, Dartmouth, Illinois, and Washington and Lee universities. A few played on professional teams.[7]

Under Zuppke, the Oak Park season did not end with the league championship. The parents and the board of education approved a post-season western trip. On December 1, 1910, the high school announced that the football team would go to the Pacific Northwest for two regional championship games. Stagg's 1894 university team had made a West Coast trip, but lengthy post-season excursions for high school teams were unusual and sometimes controversial. In 1902 and 1903, Chicago high schools won intersectional games in Brooklyn. In 1906 and 1908, they lost games in Seattle and Denver. While intersectional games brought strong criticism as well as travel problems, they also provided publicity for football and the schools. After two days of practice, the Oak Park team boarded "Petoskey," a special railway car, and left Chicago on December 20. Before their departure, the Sunday *Chicago Tribune* featured a photograph of Coach Zuppke and his fourteen players on the front page of its sports section. "Prep" reported that Zuppke was confident that the Orange and Blue were fit for an invasion of the Northwest. Whenever the train stopped on its four-day trip to Seattle, the coach held workouts or had the team run around the train. As the Seattle school board had banned games with out-of-state schools, Oak Park's opponent would be Wenatchee High School. Chicago men looking for money at any odds in Seattle sought Wenatchee backers. A grueling practice on December 24 and rest on Christmas day preceded a 22–0 Oak Park victory on December 26. After three quarters, disappointed Wenatchee backers opened a supply of free apples, which led to a crowd riot and suspension of the game with eight minutes left to play. Back in Oak Park, students celebrated by singing school songs at the Intersorority Dance. Fifty boys overturned furniture at the YMCA. After two days of rest and practice, the team left for a game with Washington High School in Portland, Oregon. The field, soaked by three days of rain, was made playable by covering it with wood shavings and sawdust. Portland scored first, but Oak Park won 6–3 by a vigorous defense that caused fumbles and a third-quarter thirty-yard run after a triple pass. Oak Park's speed and passing had produced two victories. The weary and mud-covered team boarded the North Coast Limited for the return trip to Chicago. They soon encountered a blizzard with heavy snow and frigid temperatures reaching thirty-five degrees below zero. The weather slowed the train and the engine broke down a hundred miles west of Minneapolis. The team spent five hours in their cars until a relief engine brought them to the Twin Cities. The tired party reached Chicago at 3 A.M. on January 5. Zuppke lauded the team, which gave him credit for the wins. The long season ended with a football banquet at the Parkside Hotel and a theater party.[8]

Soon after the return of the football champions, Oak Park athletics were involved in controversies. In February 1911, five of the best athletes were suspended by the principal for joining a Delta Sigma Phi fraternity. Coach Zuppke was discouraged, but the boys withdrew from the fraternity before the major track meets. In May, Zuppke lost an appeal for entry into the Cook County High School baseball league. Neither problem had a lasting impact on the high school's athletic program.[9]

In 1911, seven of Zuppke's thirty-five players returned from the 1910 squad. The coach handed out a rigid set of training rules and switched Bart Macomber from the line to the backfield. A faculty member and an alumnus assisted in the drills and scrimmages. At the end of the season, Oak Park again defeated rival Lane High School by a 23–0 score in the championship game. Concerned about the long trips in bad weather during the holiday season, the Oak Park School Board banned out-of-county games on November 14. The team had already planned a Thanksgiving Day game in Cleveland. When a reconsideration petition failed, the Oak Park Athletic Association sought to schedule a Massachusetts team for another championship game. Everett High School was tied in a late season game, so the Oak Park group contracted for a game with St. John's School in Danvers. With an 8–0 record, St. John's arrived in Chicago on December 1. They were greeted by the Loyola Band and a welcoming committee that included a number of priests. On December 2, Oak Park employed an aggressive offense in defeating St. John's 17–0. Eight thousand fans attended the game on the University of Chicago's Marshall Field, which was refereed and reported by Chicago's football star, Walter Eckersall.[10]

The 1912 season started with a game against the alumni, which was played under the new rules that provided four downs for the offense and governed the kickoffs and touchbacks. In their first ten games, Oak Park outscored opponents from Elgin to Culver Military Academy in Indiana by 518 to 3. Lane, Englewood and Hyde Park high schools gave up 162 points to Oak Park and failed to score. Before losing 33 to 3, Wendell Phillips High School spoiled a perfect season with a forty-yard dropkick field goal in the opening period. For the game with Evanston Academy, Zuppke augmented his trick plays by adding the "Bearcat" and "Flying Dutchman" to his "Gee-Haw," "Flea-Flicker" and "Whoa Back" plays. Oak Park met undefeated Lake Forest Academy in its final game. A fast and heavy backfield, a home-field advantage and teamwork based on several years' practice between units carried the day. The Lake County team was "bewildered and puzzled by the most complicated plays ever engineered by a local high school team." The Gee Haw and Flying Dutchman plays produced a 49–0 victory. Four days later Oak Park students and citizens gave Zuppke and his sixteen players a rousing send-

Zuppke's Oak Park champions, who defeated Boston's Everett High School, 33-14, 1912. Top row, left to right: Coach Bob Zuppke, Howe, Paul Trier, Joseph P. Carolan, Harry Goelitz, Reynold Craft, Thalman, Manager Bingham; middle row, left to right: Maize, Gloss, unknown, Caron, Burton, Royal; front row, left to right: Ralph Shiley, Johnny Barrett, Buelos, Bart Macomber, Voight. Courtesy University of Illinois Archives.

off as they left for a national title game with Everett High School in Boston. The team had a signal drill in Buffalo and practiced at the Brookline Playgrounds when a final practice at Boston's Fenway Park was canceled because the field was covered with snow. Zuppke's charges also spent time shopping and attending motion pictures. Gamblers in the "big pools" favored Oak Park, 10 to 8. A private wire transmitted a play-by-play report to the Oak Park High School assembly room. On November 30, the weather improved and Oak Park crushed Everett, 32–14. A Boston sportswriter described Oak Park's varied passing game as resembling basketball. It was a revelation of what an "open play" offense could accomplish when executed by a skilled and well-drilled team. Everett's passing game was nullified by Oak Park's strong defense and Bart Macomber's fifty-yard punts. Boston mayor John F. Fitzgerald, former Oak Park mayor Frank Macomber and Oak Park principal John Hanna were in the large crowd at the game and the post-game banquet at the City Club. The Oak Park faculty manager said that his school did not play a "western" type offense, but played "Zuppke football." Zuppke said that Everett outplayed his line and that he learned that he should change his method of coaching the offensive line. After the coaches' exchange of complimentary remarks, Mayor Fitzgerald praised the Chicago boys for their American spirit, urged that every great city should provide a stadium in which schoolboys can play, and led the boys in two verses of "Sweet Adeline." Following a banquet, which included oysters and lobsters, the Everett "rooters" escorted Zuppke and the Oak Park team to their hotel and the train station.[11]

In his three years at Oak Park, Zuppke's teams had won three consecutive Cook County football championships and obtained national publicity. In 1912, they also won championships in heavy- and lightweight football, swimming, soccer, and outdoor and indoor track. His football coaching record of fifty-six wins, four losses and two ties in seven years against major competition in two states attracted the attention of administrators, students and alumni clubs at several universities. Northwestern fraternity members voted for Zuppke as their next coach. A week and a half after the Everett game, Zuppke signed a contract with the University of Illinois.[12]

Zuppke's gridiron success and academic workload at Muskegon and Oak Park did not interfere with his social life. In Muskegon, he married Fannie Tillotson Erwin on June 27, 1908. Bob was twenty-nine and Fannie was thirty-four. Five feet tall, she was a head shorter than Bob. She was a talented music teacher and vocalist, who had studied at conservatories in Chicago and New York. Her father, Daniel Erwin, was a prominent lawyer and a director of banks and public utilities in Muskegon. His family came from Rushville, Illinois. Grandfather Louis Erwin was a friend of Stephen A. Douglas and had served in the state legislature. Fannie's mother, Florence Tillotson Erwin, was the daughter of a Muskegon mill operator. After their marriage, the newlyweds moved into the Erwin house. Fannie was listed as a milliner in the city directories. She handled their financial affairs and was a loyal supporter of Bob's football career and artistic activities. An Oak Park player remembered that Mrs. Zuppke had prepared "some real cold cuts" for team members who came to their Grove Avenue apartment for Sunday night suppers. Players recalled a "keen appreciation" of the part she played in her husband's plans.[13]

3

Higher Education and Football in 1913

The high school coach from Oak Park moved to a bigger stage when he took the job at Illinois. The public university in the nation's third most populous state had doubled its enrollment in the previous decade. American public and higher education had undergone rapid expansion in the five decades after the Civil War. The population trebled and nearly fifteen percent were foreign born. Illinois businessmen and farmers were prospering. Railroads, automobiles, hard roads, typewriters and telephones were binding the nation together. Industry and technology were creating demands for educated men and women. High schools and land-grant state universities began to supply thousands with the education required for business, industry and agriculture. The proliferation of academic specialties was accompanied by rising enrollments and increased employment opportunities for college graduates. Specialized engineering and commercial education supplemented, and often displaced, traditional academic disciplines in the curriculum. Instruction in the academic community was both curriculum and extracurricular. It included formal classroom lectures and discussions, laboratory work, tests, field trips and physical education. Extracurricular instruction occurred in activities such as concerts, dances, dramas, campus shows, and intramural and intercollegiate athletic competitions. The extracurriculum proved to be as attractive to many students as the traditional curriculum.[1]

The institutional setting for Zuppke's coaching career differed from that of coaches at elite private universities. At a public land-grant university, he participated in the popularization, nationalization and democratization of higher education. Taxpayers financed the "people's university" and voters elected its Board of Trustees, which had final responsibility for the intercollegiate athletics program. In the five decades after 1891, the University of Illinois had grown from a small land-grant institution on the prairie to a major

17

state university. Founded as the Illinois Industrial University in 1867, it was renamed in 1885. The 1887 legislature provided for the popular election of the trustees. In practice, the Alumni Association nominated slates of three people for both the Democratic and Republican tickets. Political shifts usually resulted in the election of three members of the party of the governor and the general assembly majority. On the whole, the popular electoral system produced well-qualified trustees with a personal interest in the university. Six-year terms provided continuity. In 1913, the Board of Trustees included nine elected members and three ex officio members — the governor, the superintendent of public instruction and the director of agriculture. The statewide election of trustees and a system of county and legislative scholarships confirmed the university's position as the people's institution of higher learning. The Alumni Association's direct involvement with both the Board of Trustees and the university's Athletic Association strengthened support for a developing program of intercollegiate athletics.[2]

Illinois was an attractive situation for a talented thirty-three-year-old football coach from Milwaukee. Zuppke's career had paralleled the emergence of intercollegiate sports from the early-barnstorming days, which publicized private universities such as Chicago and Notre Dame. Under the aggressive leadership of President Edmund James, the state university was undergoing rapid growth in its academic standing, enrollment, physical facilities and national reputation. American intercollegiate athletics had originated in eastern private institutions, such as Yale, Harvard, Princeton and Pennsylvania. Alumni controlled the governing boards, where presidents were hired and athletic policies were formulated. By 1900, presidents and alumni in midwestern state universities were committed to the development of athletic programs and the public entertainment of spectators. Football was also generating extensive publicity for both the state universities and their political sponsors. Alumni clubs and peer-group pressure from other universities were major factors in the rapid development of intercollegiate athletics. The coach's successes attracted the support of loyal alumni, dependent sports journalists and leading politicians. His triumphs and his failures would be reported in newspaper columns, magazines, motion picture theaters and telegraphic reports to assembled fans. They were discussed by critics, or "wolves," in alumni clubs, businessmen's organizations, public meetings and the state legislature. The political dynamic for athletics at the people's universities and state colleges began with the state legislature, which chartered the institutions, provided for their governance, and appropriated funds for their operations. In Illinois, the state university was dependent on biennial legislative appropriations. Growing numbers of alumni provided an influential bipartisan political constituency. Graduates with degrees in law, business and engineering also tended to become active in political affairs. Legislators awarded university scholarships in their districts, toured the campus on annual legislature visits, and received free tickets to athletic events. These contacts served to cultivate interest in, and loyal support of, the state universities and their football teams.[3]

The American sporting public embraced sports legends and legendary figures. Community and institutional loyalties encouraged them to accept the achievements and dedication of football coaches and gridiron heroes as symbols of virtue and common values in a democratic republic. The casual recreational activities of an agricultural society were replaced by community sports for an urbanized America. High schools and colleges responded by incorporating gymnasium work in their curricula and promoting interscholastic,

Bob Zuppke, the thirty-three-year-old coach from Muskegon, Michigan, and Oak Park, Illinois, 1912. Courtesy of University of Illinois Archives.

intramural and intercollegiate competition. Spalding's *Official Guides*, Walter Camp's publications and extensive newspaper coverage promoted football as an attractive part of American student life and culture and an educational experience. The games were a performing art with weekly exhibitions and seasonal awards. At the intercollegiate level, most students were involved as spectators, rather than players. The rapid growth of state universities also stimulated institutional competition. In 1908, the chorus of the Illinois version of "College Days" caught the spirit of undergraduates:

> Sing me a song of college days, Tell me where to go;
> Northwestern for her pretty girls, Wisconsin where they row;

Michigan for chappies, Purdue for jolly boys;
Chicago for her Standard Oil, for good fellows, Illinois!

College students had a long history of pranks and riots. With growing enrollments, faculty members were alarmed by riotous behavior involving hundreds or thousands of students. Organized class contests such as push ball, flag rushes and sack rushes resulted in injuries. After several injuries and two fatalities resulting from the 1915 sack rush, Illinois discontinued all class contests in 1916. Athletic victories or favorable weather also tended to produce periodic vandalism at local businesses. After a 1912 win over Indiana, a student mob broke up a political meeting in Champaign's Gazette Square and attacked the Walker Opera House. Athletics director George Huff dispersed the students by warning them that they were killing football by just such actions.[4]

Midwestern intercollegiate football competition began around 1890. Illinois played its first game on October 2, 1890. On February 8, 1896, the presidents of Chicago, Illinois, Michigan, Minnesota, Northwestern, Purdue and Wisconsin formed the Intercollegiate Conference of Faculty Representatives. The conference established rules for eligibility and scheduled competitions. It became known as the Western Conference and, later, with the addition of

George Huff, the Illinois athletic director who hired Zuppke and organized the Coaching School, 1912. Courtesy University of Illinois Archives.

Indiana and Iowa in 1899 and Ohio State in 1912, as the Big Ten. By 1903, football was a well-established part of university life, and Chicago, Illinois and Michigan were scheduling twelve to fourteen games every year. The athletic program at Illinois was the responsibility of the student Athletic Association, which with faculty supervision, was incorporated on February 21, 1890.[5]

As the popularity of football increased, control passed from the student managers to the faculty and administration. Actually, the "pass" was deflected by the administrators and intercepted by professional athletics directors. Initially, the faculty took a more active role in management, but they gradually realized that the management of athletics was "not the faculty's business." The students became alumni, joined the Alumni Association, and became boosters and financial supporters of the athletic program.

While administrative responsibilities were being established, football tactics were also being developed. The flying wedge, similar to a moving rugby scrum, was a favorite formation in the early 1890s. The resulting scores were either lopsided victories for the heavier and stronger team or low-scoring defensive struggles between evenly matched opponents. Illinois had successful seasons in 1901–02, 1904, and 1908–10, but experienced difficulty in attracting talented football players to a location more than a hundred miles from a metropolitan area. In 1901, it also trailed Michigan, Chicago, Minnesota, Northwestern and Wisconsin in student enrollment.

In 1905-06, prompted by a national outcry that resulted from publicity concerning football injuries, and deaths, the nine Western Conference universities reduced their schedules to five games. The crisis was a major factor in the creation of the National Collegiate Athletic Association and expediting the development and standardization of the rules of the game. It was Zuppke's good fortune that he began his coaching career in 1906 when the Western Conference began implementing its new reform rules. From 1905 to 1910, the rules for intercollegiate football were revised to open up the game by expanding the use of the forward pass and specifying legal formations. The changes led to the open game that was Zuppke's specialty. Schedule limitations reflected concerns about injuries and new player eligibility requirements were intended to control professionalization.[6]

After 1890, there was a steadily increasing demand for news of university athletic teams. Many male voters were regular readers of seasonal feature articles in the sports section and reports and scores of baseball, football, track and field, and basketball games. As sports claimed a major presence in urban life, the print media met popular demands for increased sports coverage. Illinois was served by several metropolitan daily newspapers in Chicago, which had extensive downstate circulations. The larger cities also had dailies and most counties had weekly newspapers. Extensive coverage of athletics in newspapers and magazines provided ample evidence of both the excessive glorification of intercollegiate athletics and the failures to resolve its problems. Sensitive to the effects of "good" and "bad" publicity, public university administrators issued press releases and kept scrapbooks to document institutional achievements. Public relations offices issued news of student accomplishments, local interest items, research reports, extension bulletins, and announcements of awards and honors. In 1912, the Illinois Alumni Association began publication of the *Alumni Quarterly and Fortnightly News*, which had statewide circulation and excellent coverage of academic, alumni and sports affairs.[7]

The popularity and expense of intercollegiate sports created a demand for professional supervision. On March 23, 1901, the deans serving on the Illinois Council of Administration adopted a resolution against employing eastern professionals at large salaries to coach football teams. However, the Athletic Council or Board, composed of faculty and alumni, acquired policy responsibilities and began to hire a professional staff to manage intercollegiate athletics. In 1906, a faculty conference recommended the evaluation of the university's system of part-time graduate coaches. The effectiveness of professional sports administrators and coaches at Western Conference universities became evident in the dominance of Michigan with Fielding Yost and Chicago with Amos Stagg. By 1903, Chicago and Michigan were locked in a recruiting battle for Chicago's high school football players. From 1895 to 1912, Michigan won 82 percent of their games and 89 percent of its games with Western Conference opposition. Chicago won 81 percent of all games and 72 percent in the conference. The corresponding record at Illinois was 67 percent and 49 percent. With highly successful baseball and track programs, Illinois presidents, alumni and trustees were impressed by the publicity given to intercollegiate sports and the 26,000 paying spectators who watched the 1905 Chicago-Michigan football game. From 1904 to 1912, the Illinois team was coached by alumni and part-time coaches, and compiled a 1–7–1 record against Chicago. In 1906, Illinois suffered a 63–0 loss to Stagg's Chicago team, which featured the passing of Walter Eckersall. In 1912, part-time coach Arthur Hall resigned.[8]

Illinois found its athletics administrator at home. George Huff was a Champaign native and member of the university's first football team in 1890. After playing football at Dartmouth, he returned to Illinois in 1895 as Coach of Athletic Teams. In 1901, he was appointed director of the Department of Physical Training. His success as a baseball coach and developer of a physical education program brought pay increases from $1,800 in 1901 to $3,000 in 1912. He was active in the Alumni Association and personified high standards of sportsmanship and amateur athletics. When the autumn football games gradually replaced spring baseball in popularity, Huff sought a promising young coach. In 1909 and 1912, riotous post-game celebrations of football victories also provided an additional incentive to stimulate and direct student interest toward a successful football program. Illinois alumni Robert F. and George C. Carr of Oak Park brought Zuppke's coaching record to Huff's attention. At a meeting in Robert Carr's office, Huff and Zuppke favorably impressed each other. On December 12, 1912, the Athletic Board of Control recommended a three-year appointment of Zuppke as full-time football coach at $2,700 a year. President Edmund James placed a few telephone calls to Chicago and Zuppke was hired. On the following day, he signed a contract with George Huff for $2,750, beginning September 20, 1913. His duties included assisting in basketball and baseball and extended from September 15 to June 1. While he was appointed at the lowest academic rank as an associate, the base salary for full professors was $3,000. Zuppke recalled that he had offers of $3,500 from Northwestern and Purdue but believed that Illinois had better material, so he "euchred" them up from $2,500 and signed. His coaching qualifications were unusual. Most university coaches had been outstanding football players and were often alumni of the institutions where they coached. They usually had coaching experience at other colleges. Zuppke had a impressive record as a high school coach and seven years of experience in classroom teaching of academic subjects in addition to physical education.[9]

4

Zuppke Installs the System

As a normal school graduate and high school teacher, Zuppke was at home in an academic setting. The physical location was a new experience. Arriving at their apartment on Oregon Street in Urbana, Bob and Fannie found a small town bordering a rapidly expanding state university with 4,369 students. The Illinois Central railroad, running from Chicago to New Orleans, passed through Champaign a mile west of the campus. William McKinley's traction line afforded rail connections from the campus to the Illinois Central, St. Louis and Indianapolis. The surrounding great swamp was being drained and becoming the fertile "Grand Prairie" envisioned by early land promoters and bankers. Muddy streets were being paved with bricks, but the football team still practiced in a mudhole near the Boneyard Creek. In 1915, an Oak Park football player, with a poor academic record at the University of Chicago, came to Illinois and said it was "like darkest Africa" compared to Chicago. And when his Urbana landlady found that Zuppke was a football coach, she threatened to move out, but changed her mind when she saw how "small and meek" the Zuppkes were.[1]

The timing of Zuppke's arrival at Illinois was fortuitous. By 1912, football rules had stabilized with a 100-yard field, fifteen-minute quarters, four downs to gain ten yards for a first down, a seven man line, free forward passing and six points for touchdowns. His appointment was welcomed by alumni and students eager to back the football program. In the January 1913 *Alumni Quarterly*, George Carr introduced "Pepper" Zuppke as the most popular man in Oak Park. He described the new coach as a student of football since childhood, who had made a scientific study of the game. Zuppke stipulated that he be "given absolute sway." He used his spring vacation to drill the football team in Urbana. A large crowd turned out in the Armory to watch his thirty-seven players at their first night of practice on March 28, 1913. The players had begun fitness training on February 1 and commenced regular suited practice on March 29. On April 18, he discussed college sport's with alumni in

Peoria. On April 25, he explained football psychology for Springfield alumni. On May 16, he returned with his Oak Park track team to win the state interscholastic meet. On June 11, Zuppke mentioned the championships won between 1910 and 1913 in his farewell speech at Oak Park. Official fall practices began on September 29, and he announced the schedule: "Morning, afternoon and evening. Rest Sunday." After the first heavy scrimmage in the fall, one exhausted freshman left for Stagg's Chicago camp. Four linemen did not report for the fall practices, but Zuppke and line coach Justa Lindgren found capable replacements.[2]

In the October issue of the campus literary magazine, the new coach stated that football would develop the physical and moral courage of a man by overcoming pain and increasing self-possession. Football ability was determined by a vital brain, executing the dictates of an aggressive mind. Noting that green men were creatures of habit, he observed that the advice of a coach must be pounded into them in practice by constant repetition so that it became a part of their character. He never swore at players and maintained that an aggressive mental attitude was the best assurance of victory. He conceded that football was not a trade or a profession, but a helpful incident in college life and of secondary importance. It was a game "of the soil and near the soil," with medieval ideals that every healthy man should possess. He praised the spirit at Illinois and invited strong young men to try out for the team. The football captain hailed a new era in Illini football due to the persistency and dogged determination of the new coach and "the willingness of the men to be driven."[3]

The Illinois schedule would require fight and determination to overcome a lack of weight and speed. The university's football record since 1895 had placed it in the middle of the seven-member Western Conference. After the withdrawal of Michigan in 1908, Henry Williams' Minnesota Gophers and Amos Stagg's Chicago Maroons were the dominant teams. Chicago had organized its alumni recruiters in 1904. The third position belonged to the Wisconsin Badgers. Following Illinois, with winning percentages from 23 percent to 26 percent, were Indiana, Iowa and Purdue. Ohio State had finished its first year in the conference without playing another conference team. Zuppke won his first three games against Kentucky, Missouri and Northwestern, but closed the season by tying Purdue and losing to Chicago and Minnesota. At a rally before the Homecoming game with Purdue, he said that his team was very green. While they were big boys and had scored 77 points against the freshmen, they were not good tacklers. He found that Stagg's teams were feared and that the adulation of the Chicago coach was at its peak, so he "set to work to push Stagg from that throne as far as Illinois was concerned." On November 1, 1913, Illinois lost to Chicago 28–7 before 19,000 fans on Stagg's home field. On the Monday after the game, Zuppke took his team to a cornfield several miles from Champaign. His brief message was "Notice the weeping skies and that the corn is down, but it will be up next year — just like you!" Two weeks later, Zuppke said that the game "still sticks in my crop." Following a 4-2-1 season, he contributed a statement for the university yearbook. He wrote that the team did well considering they were slow afoot and made "costly, spiritless relaxations." He further predicted that if they maintained their scholastic standing, possessed determination, and underwent intelligent training and arduous preparation throughout the year, it would help make them better men and contribute to future success.[4]

Hailed as a hard worker with a forceful personality and inexhaustible energy, Zuppke coached his team to a Western Conference championship in 1914. He had a versatile backfield that included transfer student George "Potsy" Clark at quarterback, 142-pound sprinter Harold Pogue at halfback, Oak Park's Bart Macomber as kicker, and Gene Schobinger at fullback. Pogue and Schobinger were track stars. Schobinger had been on the 1912 American Olympic track and field team. Forty-two years later, he recalled the many facets of Zuppke's complicated mind. "There was rare intelligence, humor, sarcasm, irony, kindliness, ready wit, philosophy, but above all a dynamic energy radiating from him to spark his every action and his teams." The team used the single wing, I and T formations, with wide halfbacks and ends. Spread and deep punt formations also allowed an open style and an array of forward and lateral passes that gave an advantage to faster and smaller players. Zuppke's experience as a Wisconsin basketball player contributed to his use of a multiple pass offense. After a 37–0 win over Ohio State, the alumni reported that Zuppke's "machine ... runs in the most thrilling ways." Two trainloads of Illinois fans went to Evanston to see a 33–0 win at Northwestern.[5]

The big game pitted the Illini against Stagg's unscored upon Chicago Maroons. The lead editorial in the November "Victory" issue of the *Siren*, a campus humor magazine, began with these words: "We must have a victory ... over Chicago." The editor included two cartoons. One showed Zuppke driving an I car over Indiana, Ohio, Northwestern and Minnesota, heading for Chicago. The other was a full-page sketch of "Zup, the First" dressed as Napoleon standing over the deflated footballs of four conference opponents. On November 14, 1914, Illinois defeated Chicago 21–7. The fans threw so many straw hats on the field that "it looked like a wheat threshing." On November 21, Zuppke returned to Madison, where his squad completed an undefeated season and claimed the conference championship with a 24–9 victory over Wisconsin. The Chicago alumni club celebrated the victorious season with the coach and his team as they were returning to Urbana. In retrospect, Zuppke rated this as "the best college football team I ever saw." On December 16, Huff signed him to a new five-year contract at $4,000 a year. In the spring of 1915, Harvard coach Percy Haughton met him in Chicago for a discussion of ball-handling techniques, which contributed to Harvard's 1915 win over Yale. Haughton invited Zuppke to come to Harvard on August 1 to study eastern football.[6]

Before the 1915 season, Zuppke warned of overconfidence. He cautioned that champions often tended to overlook football rules, training and conditioning. Other campuses also had their own talent and heroes. Despite a green line and a string of injuries, Illinois had a strong nucleus of men with proven ability. Led by Captain John W. Watson at center, the Illini compiled a 3–0–2 record for a shared conference championship. The ties were 3–3 with Ohio State and 6–6 with Minnesota. Before the final game in Chicago, Zuppke took the team to Comiskey Park for a baseball game. On November 20, Illinois defeated Stagg's Maroons 10–0 while the American Pathe News cameras recorded the action. After the season, Clark, Macomber, fullback Bernard Hallstrom and end George Squier were chosen for Walter Camp's All-Western team. A player recalled that, to put it mildly, he "was entirely out of sympathy with his football coach," but that in later years he came to realize the value of discipline and hard work, which Zuppke so ably expounded. "You worked the tail off of us but we did not lose any games in 1914 and 1915 — which seems to indicate that you knew better than we did what was good for us."[7]

Football's popularity gave rise to legends and lore about the game. Zuppke was skeptical about claims for the invention of football formations and plays. His offense was a deft combination of passing and running from several formations. He varied it with trick plays and surprises selected for the opponent, location and situation. Many sports writers credited him with inventing the spiral pass from center, the multiple passes of his flea-flicker play, and the screen pass. He claimed that he had introduced the spiral pass from center at Muskegon in 1906. The only claim of a football invention that he defended with vigor was his regular use of the huddle for calling plays. In 1924, he declared that Illinois was the first to use the huddle "as a principle and method" in an October 1921 game with South Dakota. He noted that the crowd noise in the new stadia also encouraged the use of the huddle. Glenn "Pop" Warner claimed that he had used the huddle in 1896. Rutgers claimed its use in 1914. Zuppke used plays developed by Warner and praised Michigan's Fielding Yost, Chicago's Amos Stagg, Minnesota's Henry Williams and Ohio State's John Wilce as his mentors. His multiple lateral and screen pass plays required a skilled quarterback and exact timing. For those who credited Notre Dame's Knute Rockne and Gus Dorais with the invention of the forward pass in 1913, his response was that "there were 70,000 passes completed in the Midwest in 1906 — when Rock was in knee pants." Zuppke attributed the rapid development of the forward pass in the 1906 –12 period to the new rules, which allowed only three plays to make a first down. Since it was most difficult to negotiate the ten yards in three tries without the aid of a forward pass, college and high school boys all over the country soon learned to throw the ball forward in baseball fashion.[8]

While Zuppke would not recruit players, he was available when they visited the campus. He advised alumni and friends who knew of football prospects that the players should write him concerning admission and that they should contact fraternities about invitations to visit the campus. Hired as an assistant in basketball and baseball, his services in these sports were provided after the football season and spring practices had ended. Coaching the freshman basketball team until 1919 and joining the baseball team for southern tours in the 1920s enabled him to meet athletes who might also play football. In May, the gala interscholastic weekends were the most effective and important sites for recruiting students and student athletes for the football teams. Students hosted visiting high school pupils. In addition to the high school track meet, the entertainment included dual college track meets, baseball games, varsity versus alumni and freshmen track meets, Maypole dances, regimental parades, movies, musicals and a final Fraternity Interscholastic Circus with vaudeville acts and skits. Players received complimentary tickets to football games at home and in Chicago and were advised and assisted in finding employment and housing. For the 1916 Chicago game played in Urbana, they received ninety-nine complimentary tickets worth $250. Fifty-three tickets went to the press, forty-eight to trustees and twenty-nine to the coaches. Football players were excused from military drill. On campus, George Huff awarded game concessions to needy players, and a booster provided motion picture passes. Zuppke never missed a practice and stressed team effort. He was less interested in following strict training rules as long as players performed well on the field. Ernie Lovejoy, quarterback on the 1919 championship team, recalled that he was scared of Zuppke and doubted that "any of his players really loved the guy, but their respect and affection were tremendous, and their production prodigious."[9]

Dean of Men Thomas A. Clark '90 stated the predominant administrative and faculty view of football in his book of homilies on undergraduate life. He did not agree with the many respectable people who thought that a championship football team was more important than a library or a distinguished faculty, but did agree that a good football team was a worthwhile asset. After watching three of Zuppke's teams, he noted that their training was most severe and that the coach was not polite and kind as he drove his men to their utmost capacity with words that were often brutally goading. He suggested that the glory and the hero worship the players received was not commensurate with the bruised muscles, wrenched tendons, fractured bones and sore bodies they sustained in three hours of practice. Despite the many adverse criticisms of the game, he concluded that "there is no other single influence which does so much in a big institution like ours to foster democracy, to place undergraduates of all classes upon the same footing, to develop a feeling of loyalty to the university, and to unify the whole undergraduate body as does the football team."[10]

Faculty and administrators views of football were soon overshadowed by the interests of alumni. The increasing popularity of the game and the first Homecoming in 1910 provided new incentives for the promotion of alumni loyalty and association with fellow graduates. Zuppke's arrival at Illinois coincided with the reorganization of the university's Alumni Association. Before his move to Urbana, the Association paid for his April 13 trip to speak to graduates in Peoria. In the spring of 1913, Chester Fischer toured the state and found twenty-two active alumni clubs. Members enjoyed publications, which carried campus news, reports of speakers and banquets, and accounts of the homecoming celebrations. By 1915, they were complaining about alumni seating at football games. During World War I, their campaign for a Gregory Memorial Building, to honor the university's first regent, was put on hold. In 1919, membership had increased from 2,500 to 3,224 and a War Memorial Committee replaced the Gregory Memorial Committee. Athletics Director George Huff was a member of the Class of 1892. He received his baccalaureate degree in 1917 and became president of the Alumni Association in 1919–20. His form letters and personal visits brought in 600 new members and increased the number of clubs to eighty-eight. One of his letters mentioned that Michigan alumni recruited high school athletes and that Illinois had defeated their football team in 1919. In December 1920, Huff secured Alumni Association approval of precedence for a Stadium and War Memorial Drive.[11]

5

The War Years

The 1914 outbreak of the Great War in Europe brought the traditional response of neutrality from the U.S. government. The European-American public followed the news as their relatives fought in the old country. The war also brought increased propaganda campaigns by the belligerents, military actions and public movements for preparedness. By the fall of 1916, a stalemate in France led to unsuccessful negotiations for peace. The threats of American involvement in the war gradually increased after the 1916 presidential election and war news filled the city and campus newspapers. Collegiate football publicity became an attractive alternative to the news of slaughter and revolution in Europe. Football's conditioning, drills and teamwork matched goals of the preparedness movement in the United States.

After undefeated 1914 and 1915 seasons, Zuppke had warned St. Louis alumni that dark days were bound to come and suggested that Stagg and Williams knew a lot more about football coaching than he did because they had been at it longer. Faced with the task of preparing a new team in practices after classes, he used secret practices and a lighted field. When the practices "by searchlight" began, Deans Kendrick Babcock and Thomas Clark investigated and reported to the Council of Administration that the sessions ended at 6:15 P.M. and the lights were only used when it was dark. In 1917, ghost footballs were used in night practices. The 1916 season began with a 30–0 win over visiting Kansas. The dark days began with a 15–3 home loss to Colgate and a 7–6 defeat by Ohio State, whose Chic Harley scored a game-wining fourth-quarter touchdown. Captain Bart Macomber produced a 14–7 Illinois win at Purdue. On November 4, 1916, Illinois traveled to Minneapolis to play an undefeated Minnesota team, which had tied them for the 1915 championship. Preparing the players for the defeat predicted by the press, the coach responded with a week of heavy scrimmages and celebrated with a dinner and show on the evening before the game. A spread formation and a pass interception gave Illinois a two-touchdown lead in the first half. Zuppke directed tenacious defensive formations that nullified Minnesota's offensive shifts and ordered stalling tactics by Bart Macomber that earned a 14–9 victory. Recovering from the October 5 "Colgate Illinicide," thousands of fans at Illinois Field followed telegraphic reports of the Minnesota game by watching a sliding gourd on a wire and responded with a "roar that crashed over the prairie" and a two-day celebration. Two weeks later an overconfident Homecoming crowd saw the Chicago Maroons upset Illinois, 20–7. The 2–2–1 Big Ten season ended with a 0–0 tie at Wisconsin. Inspired by Zuppke's combative personality in a tough season, the Illinois Indians became the Fighting Illini. Writing to Walter Camp, Zuppke selected four Minnesota players and three Illini for a Middle-Western conference team. He considered Minnesota "by far the best team in the West" and explained that their upset by Illinois was due to their overconfidence. He concluded that the upsets in a peculiar season were due partly to the variety of offenses that required special defenses.[1]

American entry into World War I in April 1917 provided new opportunities to arouse popular enthusiasm for football. A diverse nation composed of many competing ethnic and religious groups regarded sports as distinctive activities for the Americanization of young men. In 1916, Zuppke gave the Fourth of July oration in Mahomet and spent the summer in Muskegon. In January 1917, he spoke on "Athletics" at a Bloomington High School dedication. The War Department's hearty approval of physical education and sports exposed many prospective students to football. The war also provided advocates of physical education and fitness training in universities with data on the necessity for physical education in the public school systems.[2]

In 1917, after a summer in Muskegon, Zuppke guided Illinois to decisive wins over Kansas, Oklahoma, and Purdue and a 7–0 win against Wisconsin. In November, the early success was followed by a 0–0 tie with Chicago and losses to Ohio State and Minnesota. On Thanksgiving Day, the Illinois football team won a 28–0 game with Camp Funston in Kansas before an estimated hillside crowd of 30,000 soldiers. At the December 12 football banquet, Zuppke urged the letter winners to become advertisers of the university.[3]

Wartime brought new public service opportunities. Zuppke urged investors to buy war stamps as a loan to the government. Travel restrictions prompted Zuppke and track coach Harry Gill to stage a mass athletics competition on May 25, 1918. Chanute Field airmen from nearby Rantoul participated and six midwestern universities telegraphed their results to the other participants.[4]

Wartime manpower needs had a major impact on Big Ten football. As higher education was mobilized for the war effort, the government encouraged the continuation of college football. From September to December 1918, the Western Conference tendered its services to the War Department. Most of the university players were in military service or war industries or were waiting for military calls. The 1918 Illinois Student Army Training Corps football team practiced from seven to eight each morning before beginning their military training. The football company drilled Tuesday and Thursday evenings. Illinois had many potential players. Eighty candidates for the varsity produced a final squad of thirty-seven. A freshman team of 50 was chosen from 245 hopefuls, who had responded to a February invitation to participate in light workouts. On October 12 and 26, Zuppke took his team to Chicago, where they lost 7–0 games to more experienced teams at Great Lakes Naval Training Station and Navy Pier. In November, they scored 83 points and shut out Iowa, Wisconsin, Ohio State and Chicago. With four victories, Illinois shared the conference title with Michigan, which won two conference games, and Purdue, which defeated Chicago. Rated by Stagg as the best Illinois team, they joined the 1910 squad as the only two Illinois teams unscored upon in conference games.[5]

As the nation mobilized for war, a strong anti–German sentiment spread across the nation. Citizens of German origin were watched for any evidence of disloyalty. Champaign-Urbana had its spy mania. The Boy Scout movement served as a focal point for the Americanization of youth and grew rapidly during the war. Its American membership jumped from 32,929 in 1913 to 636,536 in 1926. In 1919, banker Benjamin F. Harris recruited Zuppke to serve as president of the Champaign County Boy Scout Council. In this capacity, he appointed leaders and talked to scouting groups. His major contribution was the attraction of his celebrity status in recruiting the men and boys who organized and joined the scouts. The German-born coach served the patriotic Boy Scouts organization until 1921, when he resigned because of the demands of the Stadium drive. In March 1922, Zuppke and Rev. James C. Baker spoke at a Kiwanis-Rotary dinner that raised $2,000 for the Boy Scouts. Scouting taught that playing the game was physical, intellectual and ethical preparation for the development of young men. The militaristic origins of the English scouting movement were modified in the United States by Ernest T. Seton's *How to Play Indian* (1903) and *The Birch-Bark Roll of the Woodcraft Indians* (1910), which incorporated the Native American motif into the movement. The Scouts' *Handbook* contained ten pages on Indian handicrafts. It proclaimed that the adoption of Indian lore into their program produced the highest type of Scouting. The authors acknowledged that "no white man can dance like an Indian, but he can try, thereby … coming in closer understanding with our Red Brothers." A four-page "getting on the team" article by Fielding Yost with scattered references to the sterling qualities required for making the Michigan football team may have provided an additional incentive for Zuppke's scouting activities.[6]

Illini postwar prospects in 1919 were bright because of the returning veterans who had played on the 1915, 1916 and 1917 teams. In all, 225 young men had tried out for the freshman team. After a 14–7 win on a wet field at Purdue, Illinois defeated Iowa when Laurie Walquist recovered an onside kick and ran for a touchdown. On October 25, the Illini lost two backs and a lineman to injuries and lost to Wisconsin, 14–10. Following the game, they sang "Illinois Loyalty." The November 1, 1919, homecoming game with Chicago signaled the postwar return of football mania. After the traditional senior Hobo Parade and controlled contests between paint-smeared freshmen and sophomore warriors, 7,000 Illini filled the Gym Annex for a Friday night rally. Encouraging words from All-American Ralph Chapman '15, a Marine war hero, opened the rally. Speeches by congressman William B. McKinley and Purdue's George Ade followed. Zuppke then ... snapped out his song of hate ... and the crowd responded with ... thundered amens.... Introduced as the ... next president of the United States ... by acting university president David Kinley, Governor Frank Lowden concluded the rally. The following afternoon, 18,000 Illini packed Illinois Field to watch Zuppke's queer formations and fancy emergency plays produce an upset 10–0 victory over Chicago. The governor greeted the record crowd at halftime, and a wing-walker flew over the field during the game. Walquist's passing and Ralph Fletcher's placekicking brought a 10–6 victory at Minnesota's homecoming. At home for State Day on November 15, the "homegrown, simon-pure, and 100 percent products of Illinois" trounced Michigan, 29–7. In their first year after returning to play a full Big Ten schedule, the Wolverines could not stop a well-balanced team "trained by a wizard coach." Chicagoan Paul Des Jardiens reported that Illinois mixed its style with deadly effect and that some players thought that Zuppke used telepathy in directing the calls of his quarterbacks.[7]

With the championship at stake, Illinois closed its season on November 22 at Ohio State's homecoming in Columbus. Chic Harley, the undefeated All-American halfback, and the Buckeyes had a 7–6 lead. Four of the best Illinois players were on the bench with injuries. The powerful defensive line of Illinois, the team's mastery of the fundamentals of blocking and interference, Zuppke's last-minute time-out and substitution, and a field goal by Bob Fletcher halted Harley's twenty-game winning streak, 9–7. A special edition of the *Daily Illini* announced that the returning champions would each receive a piece of angel food cake decorated with orange and blue frosting upon their return to Champaign. The championship was celebrated at a rally in the Auditorium. Like the 1914 champions, the 1919 squad were all from Illinois. While the squad had no individual stars, it included Ed "Dutch" Sternaman, future co-owner of the Chicago Bears, and Burt Ingwersen, future coach at Iowa. In 1916, 1917 and 1919, Sternaman had academic eligibility problems in Mechanical Engineering. Tutoring and special examinations enabled him to win letters.[8]

Winning or sharing four conference championships in seven years brought rewards for the coach and the team. In achieving the last-minute win at Ohio State, Zuppke won a conference championship and secured a new five-year contract. To achieve success, he had moved five players to new positions. Only one of them was chosen for an All-Western team that included six men from Wisconsin, Iowa and Ohio State. The student newspaper congratulated Zuppke for placing the Illinois football machine at the top of western football. At the first Rotary Club football banquet, Zup talked at the top of his voice for fifteen minutes. He praised his coaching assistants and the captain, who had been replaced at fullback. The program carried the lyrics for the Rotarians' musical rendition of "Good evening, Mr. Zup, Zup, Zup, with your team that always crosses the line." It also listed his winning records against all conference teams in his first seven years. At the Chicago Illini Club banquet, Avery Brundage introduced the invited Cook County high school football players to coach Zuppke and the alumni. The attendance at seven conference games was 45,000 for four home games and 47,000 for three road games. With six Big Ten games on its 1920 schedule, Illinois was unable to accept an offer for an intersectional game with Harvard.[9]

In his first sixteen years from 1913 to 1928, Zuppke's teams became a major force in the Big Ten. They won 75 percent of their games. Ohio State won 68 percent and Chicago won 58 percent. Michigan also won 75 percent, but did not play a Big Ten schedule from 1913 to 1918. In conference games before 1919, Illinois won 73 percent compared to Ohio State's 62 percent and Chicago's 52 percent. The composition of the teams that won or shared Big Ten championships in 1914–15, 1918–19, 1923 and 1927–28 demonstrated the wisdom of hiring a well-known coach from Chicago. Most of the players on the undefeated 1914 and 1915 squads were from the Chicago area. Two were from his Oak Park team. Northern Illinois and downstate provided an additional 34 percent of the players. Their academic majors were engineering 43 percent, agriculture 38 percent and commerce 11 percent. The eighteen members of the 1919 championship squad included eight from Chicago and two each from Rockford and Morris. Five others were from northern Illinois and one was the son of an 1886 graduate from Decatur, who had moved to Pasadena, California. Seven players majored in commerce, five in engineering, and two each in agriculture and pre-medicine.[10]

The wartime Big Ten championships stimulated demands for Zuppke as a speaker and established the annual cycle of post-season alumni banquets in Champaign and Chicago followed by a schedule of speeches for the university in other cities. In 1917, he promoted the value of college and high school athletics at a Bloomington P.T.A. meeting. On February 26, 1920, he spoke at the Southwestern Alumni Association's annual banquet in Kansas City about the necessity of increasing the Illinois mill tax from one half to one mill. After talking about university problems, he discussed his Boy Scout work and drew upon his "footballatory" to include incidents in recent games. He gave similar speeches to the Cleveland Illini Club on March 27 and the Detroit club on April 10. On April 2, he spoke to alumni in Sterling, Illinois about the university's financial needs. The next day, he addressed Oak Park Rotarians at a mass meeting in the high school auditorium. The primary purpose of the gathering was to call attention to the university's serious financial condition. Talks by Chicago lawyer Dick Garrett and building contractor Avery Brundage and the Alumni Association's motion picture completed the program. On April 22, he addressed the Chicago Chamber of Commerce on "Championship Spirit." He claimed that Illinois was probably the fastest-growing public university in the nation. Its population had doubled since 1913, but its revenue had remained the same. Citing a per-pupil expenditure of $259 in 1913 and an adjusted for inflation figure of $123 in 1920, he concluded that the students were cheated. His concluding appeal cited football as a symbol of human nature and a civilizing agent, in contrast to physical education. It developed a sense of sportsmanship and the instinct of youth. In his fifteen years of coaching, he had learned to respect every nationality "from the dark skin up the line to the whitest skin." He claimed that the body was away ahead of the brain and should be respected. On April 28, he spoke at the Urbana Hi-Y on the importance of developing personality, reading worthwhile authors and a knowing of art and music. On May 22, he addressed the Champaign Rotary Father and Son banquet.[11]

Aside from the public relations and entertainment values of the games, intercollegiate athletics provided financial support for sports programs that did not generate revenue. Football profits enabled the Athletic Association to assume responsibility for the intramural sports. In 1918, the Physical Welfare Department developed an intramural program to supplement interclass and intercollegiate athletics. Most of the 1,700 students who participated were from the 3,000 enrolled in the Student Army Training Corps (SATC). The SATC unit at Illinois fielded sixteen football teams. In 1919, a decision by Zuppke enabled the juniors to win the intramural football championship game. By 1921, 3,990 students participated in basketball, swimming, track and field, baseball, soccer, tennis, wrestling, boxing, golf and water basketball. Speaking in 1922 to a hundred representatives of intramural basketball teams, Zuppke urged them to "stick in the game" as "we all have a certain number of losses allotted to us in our lives and the sooner we work off these losses, the sooner we will gain our victories." The large Armory built in 1913 and a new gymnasium in 1925 provided ample facilities and space for the growing student body.[12]

The popularity of intercollegiate and intramural sports programs also led to their incorporation into the university's academic structure. In 1919, the university trustees designated Huff's physical training departments as the Departments of Physical Education for men and women in a fledgling College of Education. Sixty-five men were enrolled in the athletic coaching curriculum. Fifty of them were freshmen. Ten male and twelve female students comprised the rest of the College of Education. By 1920, 82 of the 137 Education students were in athletic coaching. Forty-five of the aspiring coaches were freshmen and twenty-one were sophomores. In the summer of 1922, Zuppke lectured on college sports at the American College of Physical Education in Chicago.[13]

6

Presidential Support and Professionalism

The viability of intercollegiate football was sustained by its base in the public schools, the physical fitness movements, and the popularity of competitive sports. Its success was also due to the strong support of university administrators. University presidents were enthusiastic supporters of the popular game and the publicity generated by successful seasons and victories over rival institutions. Public interest in football aided the presidents in becoming the center of the relationships with the university's external constituencies and other institutions of higher education.[1]

Zuppke's choice of Illinois was fortunate because his coaching skills were both needed and appreciated by the university's presidents. Like Zuppke, Edmund J. James was a five-foot-six ball of fire. An Illinois native with graduate education at Harvard and Halle in Germany, he had obtained valuable administrative experience at Pennsylvania, Chicago and Northwestern. Both Pennsylvania and Chicago had strong football programs. Arriving in 1904, he attacked the problems of increasing the visibility and reputation of a large state university in a small prairie town. James was an aggressive builder of the university and particularly adept in securing publicity and organizing a growing institution. He was also a dedicated exponent of enlarging the scope of higher education to include "new callings" and professional educators. He secured financial support from the state legislature and hired the talented faculty required by a developing research university. While Zuppke did not have the cozy relationship that Amos Stagg had with Chicago president William R. Harper, he could devote his full attention to football, whereas Athletics director George Huff cultivated close relationships with Illinois presidents. In the winter of 1913–14, James sent Huff to study physical training in eighteen eastern normal schools and large universities. In advising Huff to revise the listing of a coach in a university publication, he admired the coach's vigor but counseled that "we always have to consult somewhat the prejudices" of our academic colleagues.[2]

James' promotional skills had born fruit in 1911. The passage of a two thirds of a mill tax yielded $4,500,000 per biennium and provided a precedent for regular increases in legislative appropriations. By 1919, the enrollment had jumped from 2,674 to 6,602. With the corresponding increases in income, buildings, faculty and library holdings came the school spirit, entertainment and publicity of a successful football program. James perceived intercollegiate athletics as an extracurricular activity that would generate favorable publicity. Growing numbers of alumni provided spectators for football games, as well as contributors and supporters for improved athletics facilities. The popularity of the games made them a commercial entertainment property, which yielded an annual football profit. Among the primary community beneficiaries of intercollegiate athletic contests were local businesses, such as railroads, hotels, boarding houses, restaurants, motion picture houses, newspapers and stores selling sporting goods and college paraphernalia.[3]

David Kinley succeeded James as acting president in 1919 and told alumni that the prospects for football were encouraging. He had high hopes that "the Illinois eagle will scream in victory in the homecoming game with our old rivals of Chicago." He was a five-foot-six Scotsman who graduated from Yale four years after Walter Camp, the "father of American football," and four years before Amos Stagg, the first full-time college coach. In the early eighteen nineties, he played on a faculty football team at Illinois. In 1916, Dean Kinley joined Zuppke for the first I-Night awarding of letters. He hailed the coach as a "great theorist" who was making Illinois famous from coast to coast.[4]

At the conclusion of a successful season in 1919, Kinley wrote an open letter to Zuppke, which was published in the *Urbana Courier*.

I have watched with pleasure and pride the splendid progress of the football team under your direction this fall and have rejoiced with all other Illini in its great success. I want to congratulate you on what you have done for the team and the University, and I want to congratulate the team for its excellent achievements under your guidance.

"Late last Saturday afternoon, I walked down Pennsylvania Avenue in Washington to find a newspaper bulletin and learn the score. In my mind I saw our fine boys and those of Ohio matching their wits, their knowledge and their strength in a fine contest. Of course I could not help seeing, even in advance, that we were to win, and I was glad that another triumph was to be added to our team's great season. Yet I could not help thinking that in turning out so excellent a team you had done more than bring rejoicing to the hearts of the past and present members of the University, and that the team has done more for their Alma Mater this season than only win the championship. I pictured you as a leader of men, fusing their individual wills, merging their characteristics, combining their activities into one complex unit of force for the accomplishment of your purposes. That is an educational achievement of no small moment. It is the training of character. You were teaching self-control, obedience to orders, respect for authority, surrender of self-seeking, cooperation, and unity of purpose. The development of these traits is a large part of the making of men.

The team "has done more for the University than to win the championship. They have done much for themselves in accepting and benefiting by the training I have just described. They have done much, too, for all the rest of us. There is abroad in the world a spirit of insubordination and disrespect for constituted authority, both in and out of universities.

The names of your team and their coach will go down in Illinois athletic history as an inspiration not only to the athletes of the future but to all Illini. I am sure that the more imponderable influence of the team...will also be felt among the collegiate generations and will go far to make a University of Illinois student a man of character and a dependable member of the community.

Zuppke responded with thanks for Kinley's interest "in this by-product of the university, which we call sportsmanship and feeling with us that our work is necessary." When Zuppke missed an opportunity to speak at the 1926 Freshman Welcome, Kinley responded, "The sight of you and a dozen words mean so much to our young people."[5]

Kinley believed that the university of ancient Athens regarded physical training as part of its curriculum and that American universities would place athletics and physical education in a position to regulate them and eliminate evils. His support of intercollegiate athletics led to the approval of a four-year course for athletics coaches. On May 21, he read the Athletic Association's financial statement to the deans in his Council of Administration. The 1920 football program had an income of $162,600 and performed before 125,500 spectators. At a rally of 6,000 students before the 1922 Iowa game, Kinley shouted that "we are sounding forth the trumpet that will never call retreat." In 1923, he explained that he had integrated athletics into the general educational program of the College of Education so that they would have a definite status and not be exposed to criticism and attack by people prejudiced against athletics. Citing problems at Michigan, he opposed the Board of Trustees oversight of athletics. Formalizing Huff's relationship to the College of Education also provided a safeguard against increased alumni involvement in the affairs of the Athletic Association. Bringing the physical education and coaching instruction into the College of Education conferred a modicum of academic respectability. Unfortunately, the college was an educational backwater, due in part to Kinley's doubts about the academic status of professional education as a social science.[6]

In 1923, Kinley brought Yale professor Charles Foster Kent to speak at an Illinois convocation. A scholar of biblical history, Kent declared that Illinois was the most typically American university and strongly democratic. He

praised Gerorge Huff for stamping out athletic professionalism and for taking his stand for real sportsmanship and clean living. He noted that the state
university was "encompassed by vast prairies, highly cultivated, studded with
farmsteads and villages from which come the great majority of its 10,000 students" and characterized it as "an oasis of intellectuality in a desert of fertil-
ity." The oasis was nurtured by appropriations from legislators who awarded
scholarships and received football tickets. Under Kinley's presidency, the university continued the construction of athletic facilities, which had begun in
the James administration. A huge Armory in 1914, the 60,000-seat stadium
in 1923, a 7,000-seat gymnasium in 1925, and a women's gymnasium and an
ice rink in 1931 attracted students and provided brick-and-mortar symbols of
the university's growth. Construction contracts and the crowds attending athletic events also had direct benefits for the local economy. When the stadium
was completed in 1923, the President's Office began the distribution of 700
free football tickets to trustees, legislators, elected state officers, and other
distinguished guests.[7]

The presidents of Illinois' land-grant university realized the value of
sports in reaching governors and legislators, attracting new students, promoting institutional recognition and cultivating alumni loyalty. World War I had
tended to stimulate, disrupt, expedite and revise college education. Both the
nation and the alma mater tended to cultivate loyalty. After 1906, football
spectators at each Illinois football game sang "Illinois Loyalty."

> We're loyal to you Illinois, we're "Orange and Blue," Illinois
> We'll back you to stand 'Gainst the best in the land
> For we know you have sand, Illinois, Rah! Rah!
> So crack out that ball Illinois, We're backing you all, Illinois
> Our team is the fame protector; On boys, for we expect a
> Victory from you, Illinois Chehee, cheha, che-ha-ha Go Illini Go!

Presidential support was complemented by student enthusiasm. In 1922,
they dedicated the 1922 *Illio* to Zuppke. In honoring the man who brought
three conference championships and one tie in eight years and had spread the
story of Illinois achievements throughout the land, they cited his "rare qualities of sportsmanship in which the spirit of fight-to-win may be fused in the
ability to accept defeat generously and gracefully." They praised his fair play
and alert, vigorous personality, which produced a "finer edge on what we call
Illinois spirit."[8]

The popularity and profitability of intercollegiate football led to
increased interest in professional football and the commercial possibilities of
the college game. As Civil War veterans had popularized professional baseball, many men returning from military service in World War I began playing for professional and semiprofessional football teams. In 1919, George

Halas, a 1918 Illinois graduate, who had played on the Great Lakes Naval Training Station team in the Rose Bowl, moved to the Hammond Pros. In 1920, he organized the Decatur Staleys and was active in the new American Professional Football Association. The Staleys were one of the original midwestern franchises. In 1922, they became the Chicago Bears in the National Football League.[9]

While the Decatur Staleys compiled a 10–1–1 record in 1920, Halas's alma mater defeated Iowa, Michigan, Minnesota and Chicago. Following a 20–3 win over Iowa, Zuppke went to an Intercity Rotary meeting. After an ovation, he was asked to tell about the victory. The coach said that he didn't know anything about it, as the team pulled a lot of plays that they had "not let him in on" and "got away with it." The largest crowd of the season attended Michigan's homecoming and witnessed a 7–6 Illinois victory. The defense gave up only sixteen points in the first five games, but allowed twenty-one in the last two. The Illini lost late season games at Wisconsin's homecoming and Ohio State. The last-minute 7–0 loss to Ohio State deprived them of another conference championship.[10]

Succesful seasons stimulated demands for tickets. By 1921, football tickets between the thirty-yard lines cost $2.50 and tickets for the South Dakota and DePauw games and general admission cost a dollar. Hampered by preparing new men for competition and minor injuries, the Illini were not a championship contender. Regardless, Zuppke's team was again able to score a major upset. On November 19, 1921, Illinois had lost its last six Big Ten games. The coach was preoccupied with the Stadium drive as they prepared to play Ohio State, which needed a win for the conference title. On a muddy, hay-covered field, a spirited pass defense stymied the Buckeye offense. Zuppke installed a huddle at an angle from the ball so that the Ohio defense could not anticipate his formations. A deflected screen pass from Don Peden was snatched by Laurie Walquist, who scored for a 7–0 victory for the team that Harvey Woodruff of the *Chicago Tribune* called the "Fighting Illini." Zuppke described the biggest upset of his coaching career with an assessment that "you should be able to get one lemonade out of a bunch of lemons."[11]

Returning from Columbus, Zuppke told a howling, cheering mob in Champaign that the Illini were creating "an imperishable, undying tradition." Unfortunately, the players were soon involved in two other traditions, which were speculative investments and compensation for services rendered, also known as gambling and professionalism. Betting on the hometown team was a cultural tradition in central Illinois. The coal-mining towns of Carlinville and Taylorville had teams in an independent semi-professional league. They often included former college players in their lineups. Taylorville had hired quarterback Charley Dressen from George Halas's Decatur Staleys. Carlinville agreed to a November 27 Sunday afternoon football game with Taylorville. They had won in 1920, but sought to improve their chances in a road game at Taylorville. A Notre Dame player from Carlinville invited several teammates to join him in the game for $200 each and expenses. Word of heavy wagering spread among local and regional gamblers. Reports of Carlinville's Notre Dame players reached Taylorville. Illinois sophomore Roy Simpson from Taylorville invited several teammates to join him for the game, including Laurie Walquist and Joe Sternaman. Reports of gambling caused Chicago men to accumulate a pool to wager against an Illinois basketball team that would be weakened by the anticipated suspension of the football players who also played basketball.[12]

By game time on November 27, Taylorville backers assured Carlinville fans they would cover all the money that Carlinville might bring. The 2,200 spectators included passengers on Carlinville's special train, which made intervening stops on the forty-mile trip to Taylorville. While the visitors dominated the first half, Dressen's end run had given Taylorville a 7–0 lead. The Illinois players entered the game in the second half and preserved the lead. After the game, cheerleader Billy Larkin led a black jackass labeled "Carlinville" in a victory parade to Milligan's Smoke House. An estimated $50,000 had changed hands.[13]

The joy in Taylorville's victory was not shared at the university. In January 1921, faculty representative George Goodenough, on behalf of the NCAA, had undertaken an investigation of proselytizing and the growth of gambling in sports. On December 11, George Huff received an anonymous letter alleging that Illinois players received a percentage of the gambling take. On January 25, 1922, Huff, Zuppke and Goodenough interrogated the Illinois football squad. On the following day, ten players had a formal hearing. On January 31, the faculty banned nine of them from athletic competition. Four were seniors who had used their football eligibility. Three juniors would have been likely starters in 1922. Simpson was one of two sophomores. Captain Laurie Walquist and Joe Sternaman continued their football careers with George Halas and Ralph Jones of the Chicago Bears. Sternaman said that he was offered no money to play for Taylorville and that he was "persuaded to make the trip as a lark." He knew that the game was sponsored by the American Legion and didn't know that he was violating a conference rule. Notre Dame players joined the Chicago Cardinals. Illinois received unwanted publicity in urban newspapers and lost five players. Zuppke denied wire service quotes in which he accused other teams of playing professionals. As a result of the continuing concerns about eligibility and proselytizing and the expanding semi-pro and professional market for talented college players, the Big Ten hired John Griffith as its first commissioner.[14]

It was more difficult to fix a football game and there have been few major scandals in college football. Nevertheless, increased publicity and gate receipts stimulated betting on the home team. Local semi-professional football provided an attractive place for gambling. A 1919 game between Arcola and Decatur had been canceled because Arcola had recruited a roster of college stars. In the wake of the 1919 Chicago Black Sox scandal in professional baseball, Huff had been a leader in the anti-gambling fight at Illinois. He condemned the practice in speeches to students and alumni clubs and assigned a graduate student to study methods of controlling betting on college sports. In reporting the November 22, 1919, Big Ten championship game between Ohio State and Illinois, a Columbus newspaper stated that "Ohio State was backing her team to the limit, as thousands of dollars were lost in the last eight seconds of play." Kenneth Wilson, president of the Illinois Student Union and later Big Ten commissioner, had assisted his Delta Upsilon fraternity brothers in matching a $500 wager proffered by a representative of the Ohio State chapter. Attending the game, he found police guarding a gambling table in the lobby of the Deschler-Wallick Hotel.[15]

A Chicago paper read by the wagering public took a dim view of the antiquated collegiate rules forbidding participation in professsional sports. *Collyer's Eye* editorialized that if a professional athlete met residency and scholastic requirements, he should be permitted to play with the college team.

> The abolition of camouflaged jobs during the school term, the removal of the off-season restrictions and the recognition that education is the thing...would make impossible such so-called "scandals" as now fill the press, would give the poor athlete a chance with the rich and would purge this nation of those snobbish amateur regulations we inherited from the European nobility who had nothing else to do but indulge in sports while their feudal subjects supported them. College athletics need reformation..., but not so much of the athletes as of the antediluvian faculty controlling them.[16]

George Huff had played football for both Illinois and Dartmouth before a brief stint as manager of professional baseball's Boston Red Sox in 1907. He believed that the colleges had no monopoly on football and that men should be able to play and watch games on Sunday. In 1913, he had favored allowing student athletes to play professionally in the summer. While he was a zealous defender of amateurism in college football, Zuppke denied press reports that he had accused other conference teams of playing professional athletes, but conceded that there was no clear boundary between amateurism and professionalism.[17]

George Halas, Red Grange and other football players who Zuppke taught played major roles in the commercial development of professional football. Of the several professional teams that Illinois football players organized or joined upon their return from military service, the Chicago Bears were the most successful. Two Illini, George Halas and Edward "Dutch" Sternaman, were co-owners. Halas often quoted Zuppke's 1917 remark, "Just when I teach you fellows how to play football, you graduate and I lose you," as the inspiration for his professional football career. Walquist and Joe Sternaman were the seventh and eighth Illini to join the team. They would soon be followed by a dozen others. By 1924, seven of the sixteen Bears had played football at Illinois. In Red Grange's first year with the Bears, there were eleven former Illini on the team. Halas appreciated Zuppke's coaching and was a lifelong admirer of his coach.[18]

The professional game steadily gained popularity in the 1920s and 1930s. When the money was right, players made the transition. By 1932, thirty-three former Illini players had played professional football. The National Football League championship game featured five Illini. To avoid the winter weather, Halas arranged for the game to be played before 11,000 fans on an eighty-yard field in the enclosed Chicago Stadium. Coach Ralph Jones' Chicago Bears defeated George "Potsy" Clark's Portsmouth Spartans and Red Grange scored the only touchdown. Jones had been Zuppke's freshman coach, and Bears tackle Lloyd Burdick lettered at Illinois in 1927–29. The Bears lost $18,000 in 1932, whereas the Illini had a $34,000 profit. Zuppke watched the Bears defeat the New York Giants in 1933 and declared that it was great entertainment, but thought that Michigan, Ohio State and Minnesota were as good as the professionals. By 1940, nineteen Illinois players had played football for the Chicago Bears, and nine had played for the Chicago Cardinals. After 1927, with only eight to twelve National Football League teams, relatively few collegians found opportunities as professionals. Positions as coaches, athletics directors, or officials remained the major markets for college football talent. Name recognition also increased the possibility of their employment as journalists, insurance salesmen, correspondents at games and business and investment representatives.[19]

7

Organizing and Staffing the Football Program

A successful football program required more than training eleven young men to execute plays. Zuppke's ability to evaluate player skills carried over in his work with George Huff as they assembled an outstanding group of athletics staff members. Achievements in athletics, as in politics and science, were usually cooperative and cumulative. A large part of Zuppke's success at Illinois was the result of strong administrative organization and staff support. His close and harmonious relationship with Athletics Director George Huff was a major factor. The striking physical differences between the six-foot, 240-pound Huff and the five-foot-seven, 160-pound Zuppke were accompanied by mutual confidence and a strong commitment to collegiate athletics and good sportsmanship. For Huff, sportsmanship was "saying the golden rule with one word." Illinois was noted for press reports on its "simon-pure" athletic programs and seldom incurred warnings or penalties from the conference. The university's Athletic Association administered intercollegiate and intramural sports and reported to the Board of Trustees via the President's Office. The wartime concern for physical training and student sports, and the financial problems and possibilities resulting from the building and use of a huge stadium all contributed to the prestige and independent status of the Association. As intercollegiate sports became a thriving business in 1922, the Association's statutes were amended to provide for three faculty and two alumni board members. Huff remained a dominant force. He was an effective prairie politician and skilled lobbyist with the state legislature. From 1921 to 1929, he had the complete confidence of President David Kinley and was a key figure in contacting alumni and legislators in university campaigns for appropriations. On behalf of the president, he urged alumni to organize Illini Clubs and lobby state legislators. Once organized, the clubs might book Zuppke as a "drawing card" for their meetings.[1]

Early business operations at the Athletic Association were informal. Students elected the officers and managed activities. George Huff took the proceeds of events home and counted the money in the evening. Before World War I, students hired a train for $250 to attend a road game. A full train meant a big profit. In 1923 Frank Murphy moved from providing scholastic advice to athletes and coaching school students to business manager for the association. He found the unsold tickets in a bathtub in an apartment in the YMCA building that was used as the Athletic Association office. A shrewd administrator, Huff hired Charles "Chilly" Bowen in 1927 as the Association's ticket manager to handle the distribution and sale of tickets for games in the new stadium. The nephew of Mary Busey, a prominent local member of the university's Board of Trustees, Bowen served as business manager from 1930 to 1942. He managed the association's budgets, receipts and expenditures and helped in securing talent for the football team. Zuppke would not compete with other schools in offering inducements for players, but Bowen and Shelby Himes, a local sports store owner, were known as friends of the athletes. They secured job offers, and the players worked for their pay.[2]

An excellent judge of personnel, Zuppke hired a series of able assistant coaches. His most valuable assistant was Justa M. Lindgren who won four football letters as a tackle before graduation in 1902. He earned a master's degree in 1907 and combined a career as a chemical engineer and a staff position with the Department of Chemistry with coaching from 1904 to 1947. He was the line coach from 1912 through 1944. Zuppke had a high regard for Lindy's also ability to concentrate on essential skills in the limited practice times. The strong lines that he developed were instrumental in complementing Zuppke's offensive and defensive strategies. "Lindy" was a Phi Delta Theta advisor and distributed the letters to the players at the annual football banquets.[3]

Successful coaches depended on assistants and position coaches for information on players trying out for the large varsity and freshman teams. Zuppke drew upon former players for the assistant coaches who worked with the backfield and freshmen. They often accompanied him on trips to speak to alumni and civic groups. Ralph Jones, Burt Ingwersen, Ernest Bearg, Milt Olander, Frank Rokusek, Doug Mills, and Ray Eliot were outstanding members of his coaching staff. Ingwersen, who coached the freshman Red Grange, later coached at Iowa and Northwestern. He recalled that Zuppke was fiery and unpredictable ... and that one never knew what he would say. The coach was sarcastic if a player didn't work hard. While they couldn't get very close to him personally, they respected him as a great psychologist and strategist.[4]

Physical conditioning and injuries were continuing concerns of the coaches. Trainer David M. "Matt" Bullock handled conditioning, injuries

Zuppke (left) and line coach Justa Lindgren, who served throughout Zuppke's years at Illinois, September 1938. Courtesy University of Illinois Archives.

and menus from 1914 to 1941. In 1919, Huff and Zuppke sent him to New York to learn massage and training work. He advised coaches and players on training, provided first aid to the injured, and carried the coach's messages to and from players on the field. He collaborated with Zuppke and Lindgren in designing football equipment. They designed jerseys with adhesive material on the front, and Bullock patented an improved design for padded pants. In 1929, the Bailey and Himes store advertised Bullock's Rubbing Oils in the football programs. Red Grange rated him tops among trainers, as he dealt with "a lot of prima donnas" and not only massaged the muscles but the mind. A fast-talking Kentucky horse trainer with a talent for fictional stories and country humor, Bullock complemented Zup's driving the team in practice with training room jokes and stories. He related fictional accounts of the exploits of Herkimer Hobbs, Joe Nucleus and his Kentucky relatives He instructed a guard who missed tackles or blocks to say "Oh, feces!" In the 1930s, his budget request included twelve pairs of crutches. He advised Zup when players should be removed from the game. In 1933, he was joined by team physician Dr. Leland Stillwell. By 1937, Bullock had three assistant trainers and an interest in a family pharmacy in Champaign.[5]

Football required mental as well as physical preparation. Zuppke drew upon his coaching experience and knowledge of applied psychology in coaching his teams. He defined his football psychology as the employment of knowledge, tact and energy to instill morale and loyalty. He had kept his detailed course notes for the psychology courses that he took at Wisconsin.

From 1920 to 1922, a young psychology professor, Coleman Griffith, attended football practices and discussed the applicability of psychological testing and measurement to football. They discussed testing reaction time, memory, emotionalism, mental alertness, emotional steadiness, habit formation and courage. A pioneer in sports psychology, Griffith developed a growing respect for Zuppke's "extraordinary knowledge of human nature and of the fundamental facts of psychology." He admired his ability to apply psychology to football and football campaign strategy. He thanked Zuppke for the instruction he had received and the privilege of seeing psychology as a "science of actual human beings." Zuppke appreciated the compliment and liked to see him on the field. With the aid of sportswriter Westbrook Pegler, Red Grange recalled that Griffith went around talking with players during practice "disguised as a common human being" and "prepared a special psychological serum" for each athlete on the freshman squad. He said that the prescriptions worked for him and teammate Earl Britton. Grange was "gentled and encouraged." Britton, a "reckless kid," who "had no sense of awe nor appreciation of the solemn immensity of his responsibilities," was constantly targeted by the coach. Grange remembered that Zuppke's favorite pre-game story was the 1916 Minnesota upset, which he used to warn against overconfidence and to inspire a team facing a favored opponent. In later years, Grange said that he was a cog in Zup's machine and that the coach was "the best psychiatrist I ever met in my life." Coincidentally, the Zuppke-Griffith collaboration contributed to the national championships the Illini won in 1923 and 1927.[6]

Griffith brought a knowledge of the current professional literature to teaching Psychology 25, which applied the facts of psychology to athletic competition. The topics that he covered were taken from Zuppke's system, which included learning the signals system, developing a spirit of determination or fight, maintaining pep or morale, devising and executing trick plays, selecting men for special positions, and keeping a good spirit between the team and the coach. He incorporated them into his course and published *The Psychology of Coaching* in 1926. In addition to his work with Zuppke, Griffith contacted Knute Rockne about preparing teams for games. Rockne avoided getting players "keyed up" for games. He wanted an alert team and regarded a recent trip to play Stanford in California as pleasurable, educational and profitable. By 1935, Griffith and Zuppke had compiled a manuscript on "The Psychology of Football," which called for the study of reaction time, memory, learning, attention, emotional balance and perception. These topics formed the bases for many of the coach's witticisms. Zuppke was also skillful in using humor and superstitions to inspire players, for example, the number 13, the 77 on Red Grange's jersey, Yost's bad luck penny being thrown out of the Illinois locker room, his brother Herman's lucky necktie being put in a bank vault, and his finger rings being changed to find a lucky combination.[7]

In the 1920s, intercollegiate football became the "central pillar" of the university's public relations program. It was the most publicized and measurable competitive activity between institutions of higher education. Students, faculty, alumni and the public knew the team names, colors and songs. Press and radio coverage provided detailed accounts, scores, photographs, point spreads and analyses of the big games. Extensive press coverage and an expanding market for sports publications stimulated the public interest in competitive sports. Newspapers and magazines met the seasonal market for football news. The competitive aspect of a seasonal schedule produced a flood of publicity from August to December, which stimulated alumni loyalty and ticket sales, and attracted gamblers. Students, alumni and faculty used new technologies to follow sports by watching motion pictures and listening to radios. Sports publicists in university athletic departments provided much of the narrative and statistical information that stimulated ticket sales. They also found that alumni and sports fans provided ready markets for legends and lore publications that extolled the achievements of great teams and individual stars. Press releases touted prospects for success in Homecoming games against old rivals. Produced for the use of sports journalists, they were loaded with illustrations and statistics. Official histories based on these accounts seldom rose above the level of the pre-season promotional releases from the sports information offices.

One of Zuppke's witticisms was that it took a "poet" in the press box to make an All-American. Talent in the press box was also an important asset for a successful football coach. Both the adulatory and promotional reporters and the critical reporters were dependent on the sports they covered. With the beginning of radio broadcasting in 1921,"live" accounts of football games reached several midwestern states. From 1919 to 1922, Major John L. Griffith was an athletic organization instructor in the Illinois coaching school and publicity director for the Athletic Association. When Griffith left to become Big Ten commissioner in 1922, he was succeeded by Louis M. "Mike" Tobin. With the opening of the stadium in 1923, Tobin prepared statistics and press

Zuppke (left) and publicist Mike Tobin, August 1939. Courtesy *The News-Gazette.*

releases for the media, distributed several hundred complimentary tickets to the press, composed tributes for ceremonial occasions, edited publications for the athletic coaching and football programs, and collaborated with Zuppke on articles for *Liberty* and the *Saturday Evening Post*. Zuppke typed and edited letters and dictated articles. Tobin was particularly zealous in publicizing Red Grange. One of his challenges was interpreting the coach to the media. Reporters covering Illinois complained that in early September Zuppke never seemed to know the names of new players and talked about green peas, clod-hoppers and puddle jumpers. He referred the frustrated scribes to Tobin for their names, but he knew which ones were capable of playing intercollegiate football. Tobin ran the press box until Zuppke retired.[8]

Zuppke also maintained close relationships with public relations staff, local editors and sports reporters. In 1916, he appeared in a motion picture on Illinois and Champaign-Urbana. By 1920, the university public relations program was circulating motion pictures of football games with Minnesota, Chicago and Ohio State, as well as a Kinogram projection on the coaching school. The visiting "poets" in the press box received his personal attention.

He cultivated the friendship of the leading national and regional sports columnists and provided the press with lively copy for their readers. After a losing season in 1921, a reporter depicted Zuppke as "a truly magnetic, dynamic personality — the personification of pep and fight" and "the creator of the Fighting Illini — a clean fighter — a lover of the strong and a terrible taskmaster," who bullied and drove his men through endless hours of practice. Grantland Rice, Christy Walsh and Arch Ward publicized his football program throughout the country. Zup also fraternized with sportswriters in Chicago, Columbus, Milwaukee, Detroit, New York and Los Angeles. He read the newspapers and kept the clippings sent by friends, alumni and relatives. Writers have lamented the fact that magazines gave more publicity to coaches than to players. Coaches provided both strategies and continuity in intercollegiate football programs, where as the exploits of star players were news for a year or two.[9]

Coaches also used the press as a vehicle for psychological motivation. Opinions communicated to reporters were read by rivals. In December 1920, Zuppke considered dropping Iowa from the schedule because a hard battle at the beginning of the season was harmful to the development of the squad. A year later, the *Daily Iowan* declared that the "doctor of psychology" was up to his old tricks. It cited Zuppke's extravagant praise of Duke Slater and Lester Belding reported before the 20–3 Illinois win in 1920. After the game, the *Iowan* alleged that Zuppke said that Iowa was easy to beat as he sent plays around Slater and Belding. The Iowa account bore fruit in a 14–2 victory for the Hawkeyes in 1921. The *Iowan* also criticized the *Chicago Tribune*'s Walter Eckersall for partiality toward Illinois and Zuppke's stories about crippled players, who would be replaced by players of equal ability.[10]

The development of the Athletic Association as an office for the administration of intercollegiate and intramural sports increased interest on the part of the growing Alumni Association. The popularity of George Huff, director of physical education, signaled a decline in faculty involvement. Before 1910, the Illinois faculty had taken an interest in the development of athletics programs for students. The rapid growth of the student body and the large number of specialized faculty appointments to new academic departments also contributed to diminished faculty interest. Most faculty were not interested in competitive sports, although many attended the games and a few served on athletics committees. After 1913, the principal faculty involvement in intercollegiate athletics was through the Senate Athletics Committee. Sixty-nine percent of the appointments to this committee were from the colleges of Liberal Arts and Sciences, Engineering, and Education. Eleven percent were from the College of Law. The most active faculty were often from the colleges of Commerce, Engineering, Education, Agriculture, and Law. The Engineering, Commerce and Law alumni were particularly interested in the construction contracts, annual profits and political appeal of intercollegiate football. The Big Ten rules, as revised in 1925 and 1930, called for full and complete faculty control of athletics and provided that faculty representatives must not be connected with physical education. From 1908 to his death in 1929, civil engineering professor George Goodenough served as the Illinois faculty representative to the Western Conference. His successors as Illinois representatives from 1930 to 1941 were mining engineering professor Alfred Callen and Frank Richart, who specialized in concrete construction research. Goodenough's successor as senior member of the Intercollegiate Conference of Faculty Representatives was Ralph Aigler of the University of Michigan Law School.[11]

In practice, the important decisions relating to budgets and coaches were made by the Athletic Association officers, especially director George Huff. Coaches cleared schedules with Huff, who, in turn, cleared them with the university's Council of Administration. Faculty and students serving on the Athletic Board of Control elected managers and distributed awards. The system was based on Huff's administrative ability and reputation for honesty and sportsmanship. Avery Brundage, a zealous defender of amateur athletics in the American Athletic Union and the American Olympic Committee, was the university's alumni representative on conference boards and advisory committees. In 1931, the trustees recommended that the Association "be associated more closely with the University." The creation of the School of Physical Education in 1932 placed Intercollegiate Athletics in the Department of Physical Education for Men and designated the Athletic Coaching program as a "Professional Curriculum in Physical Education." By 1935, 453 coaching school graduates held posiitions in forty states. Seventy-six percent worked in high schools and fifteen percent in colleges. Forty-seven percent were in Illinois, sixty-eight percent in the Midwest and fifteen percent in the northeastern states. After Huff's death in October 1936, the Board of Trustees refused to enlarge the Association's Board of Directors to include the Director of the School of Physical Education. On February 25, 1937, the trustees created a separate Department of Athletics. These actions provided some protection from alumni intervention in intercollegiate athletics, but it did little to increase faculty control of athletics policies and finances.[12]

8

Zuppkeisms

As intercollegiate football became popular entertainment, Zuppke was in demand as a speaker at banquets, alumni gatherings and media interviews. He preferred oral communication to writing and excelled as an after-dinner speaker. He used brief, quotable sentences in discussing the values, strategies and techniques of football. With a staccato delivery, he drew upon Nietzsche in combining humor and criticism in pithy prose. His oratorical and public relations styles were laced with one-liners that were well received by audiences. Ted Ashby of the *Des Moines Register* described the coach as a "gymnastic conversationalist" who could be extremely funny and employ sarcasm with "an edge on it like a new razor blade." For one who claimed that he was expelled from West Division High School when he refused to get on his feet and give a talk and who disliked banquets, he found these talents as a coach. His reputation as a "hard, distant man" in his first decade at Illinois was softened as he regaled audiences with stories and mixed with the players. He impressed hearers with his sincerity, ability to inspire the players and devotion to football. As a featured speaker at sports and civic dinners, he delivered his messages in an hour, glanced at his watch and had the audience clamoring for more. Students were also impressed by his direct, rapid-fire style.[1]

Collections of "Zuppkeisms" drawn from speeches and press conferences were in print from 1920 until his retirement years. They form his most cohesive statement on the theory and practice of college football. In this chapter, they are presented in Zuppke's language with a few introductions and transitions. Quotation marks have been eliminated as distractions in conveying Zuppke's style. Most of his apothegms, aphorisms, axioms, maxims and witticisms related to football. He said that the sport was not good for physical exercise, but that it toughened the mental and moral fiber of players. It taught self-restraint and developed character. Its training and play was a physical expression of a mental exercise. He noted that other performing artists, such as singers, pianists, violinists, dancers, painters and speakers, all expressed their thoughts physically. The physical nature of the game taught self-control. Like good color in paintings, football made college life throb and vibrate. Men played college football with imagination and spirit because of a hero urge. The intensity and enthusiasm of the game stimulated sportsmanship and bred courtesy in the form of respect for rivals. Although it was a brutish game, brutes could not play it. The football had a funny shape and took funny bounces. Inches often counted for more than yards. The tremendous interest in, and success of, intercollegiate football made it a target for both praise and persecution. Zuppke accused its persecutors of having never played the game. He also held that the football experience, while enduring, was only a series of starts toward a goal. It was the finish that counted the most.

For Zuppke, victory in football was forty percent ability and sixty percent courage and that courage was the athlete's greatest asset. Championships demanded accurate and courageous men. Moral and physical courage were closely associated. Brains and nerves and body and muscles functioned together. He warned against allowing imagination or fear overcome courage. Worry was a disease that destroyed harmony. Fear made us fail. In games, courageous players may lack ability, but they maintain their moods. The better players were able to stretch at critical periods. He maintained that no poet ever sings about your guts, yet that is what holds you up and is the most important thing to have. A second asset was grace. A good player performs without lost motion — the same as a dancer, who is graceful and relaxed. In his sayings, Zuppke referred to the rattled player who tries to run in all directions at once, the timid soul who has a lot of ghosts hanging to his shirttail, the tough mug who has a trembling knee, the soft player who puts an air cushion between himself and the opponent he hopes to block or tackle, and the green candidate who dares because of ignorance and who will wilt after the first bump. The real disappointment was the man with ability who but half tried. He pointed out that the other man may be just as afraid as you were in spite of his cocky demeanor. Gamble and hope were united by greed. Other positive values of football were poise and perseverance. Poise enabled the athlete to perform at top speed within the rhythm of the environment. Endurance and tenacity were essential for success. Here are of his favorite epigrams: He makes good who is game enough to come back. Never stop with the horn. Its not the start that counts, its the finish; Never let hope elude you; that's life's biggest fumble.

The era of Theodore Roosevelt and Bob Zuppke's youth was a time when masculinity and virility were esteemed as popular values. From 1920 to 1940, male undergraduates at Illinois outnumbered women 70 percent to 30 percent. Alumni and sports fans were also predominantly male. Zup proclaimed that the environment of football was clean, hardy and masculine. He contrasted the patriarchy of football with the matriarchy of the school, and said that football was the only masculine note in college. Football was a safer channel for heroes who strove to fight and excel. Only the old and dilapidated talked about recreation and exercise. Morality caused a negative attitude in older persons. He contrasted youths who developed straight-arming tactics by warding off tacklers with those who pushed sorority porch swings. Even necking strained the muscles of a lounge lizard.[2]

Football was a mental exercise expressed physically. A man who can't do college work can't play good football. Like any good artist, a football player must learn to express himself with alert abandonment. Three monkeys could be taught to execute a triple pass or hit the line, but they could not play the game, as they had the muscle, but not the mind. Be prejudiced only in favor of motion, quickness and courage. The greatest athlete was the one who could carry a nimble brain faster than anybody else to the place of action and execution. Thinking may be too slow for a fast game and habits must be stimulated into speedy activity. Successful players tapped their second wind physically and mentally. Matter made mind, but mind controlled the things that mattered. The best physical specimens did not always harbor the best spirits. Self-control is important. Control your moods. You can fumble the game away mentally and morally as well as physically. A Phi Beta Kappa pin does not ensure the possessor of a control of his wits. You may talk hardly at all, yet say too much. Be stubborn to avoid being stepped on, but also be willing to compromise. An honest man is easier to get along with on the field. Envy loses as many touchdowns as the opposition stops. Courtesy is necessary for harmony on the squad. Vulgarity breeds more contempt than familiarity. There is one man you can never get away from — yourself! You cannot shake off your shadow, which should remind you that you cannot run away from yourself.[3]

Physical ability complemented mental ability. Youth expresses itself better physically, and football players are trained to assimilate punishment. Lost motion in an athlete is a waste of energy and a drag on time. A football candidate who was as slow as a mud turtle had better learn to clip coupons. A team with too many oversized feet may have too much traction. Zuppke's personal experience prompted "Don't despise the little fellow. Champions come in all sizes." Good little men brought home the bacon for Illinois. There are few men over six feet who have not some physical defect. In the world of motion, the man of economical build is usually superior to the one of surplus tissue. The tough mug may have a trembling knee. Many a weak-chinned man has a fighting heart. Positive thought and the exact movement are two of the factors that create expert executions. He observed that in athletics, every joint was a hazard. His humor was evident in the admonition that players should not drink the liniment and in the statement that while big nostrils often indicated good lung power, a big nose interfered with peripheral vision and often drew more tears, as it is easily hit.

Morale or spirit was the major problem of competitive athletics. Most games are lost or won before they are played. Young men play because of the desire to excel or win a gold football championship medal. The goal of an athlete was touchdowns, not first downs, or the goal line and not headlines. The difference between champions and near-champions was the ability to play for something outside of self— teamwork. The size or strength of opponents was unimportant as long as they're human beings. The other fellow is bound to quit if you keep after him long enough unless he knocks you out in the meantime. Neutrality is being afraid of one side and ashamed of the other. A famous player has less freedom, as freshmen may observe him go wrong. There is nothing more difficult to endure than a series of easy victories. A team with too many gold footballs is apt to list. An unearned victory due to the opponent's mistakes is not a great accomplishment. Poor morale causes a team to wilt near the goal line. We have to lose to appreciate winning. A good loser is no good. All quitters are good losers. A player must have a fear and horror of losing. A team that always has an alibi is never beaten. The man who has no alibi is hopeless. A good fighter is not a good loser, although he may have appeared to be one as a social necessity. The mock modesty of the good loser may develop into the whine and wail of those who have acquired the habit of defeat. The hard loser can be a greater sportsman and has more sympathy and regard for his opponent. The less said in victory or defeat the better. A good loser is a sign of a dying spirit, and it is immaterial whether his skill is developed. An indispensable player of superior ability is dangerous as he may get an exaggerated sense of importance and hamper the development of his substitute. The ability to stretch at critical periods shows the difference between mediocrity and success. He makes good who is game enough to come back and tap superhuman energies held in reserve. Those who do this are in accord with Plato's Divine Afflatus.

He stressed timing and rhythm in practices and scrimmages. For him, symmetric form and rhythmic motion were indications of athletic success. Theory should lead to practice and practice to more theory. He preferred fifteen minutes of scrimmage every Wednesday during the season. He always hoped that the other coach wouldn't scrimmage enough. Scrimmage should be balanced with drills and signal practice to prevent the loss of enthusiasm for physical competition. He emphasized fundamentals and plays that would be practicable against the best opponent on the worst field and the wettest day. Too much attention to fundamental skills might hamper the development of competitive spirit and limit players' ability to put them into practice. It was difficult to persuade players to improve upon their weaknesses by practice, as they loved to practice that which they could do well. Soft players preferred signal practice to scrimmage. Practice games developed the most important fundamental, the game sense. Intelligent teamwork required that the left hand knew what the right hand was doing. Too much practice against equipment was a waste of time and energy, as a tackling dummy was not a football player. Some players loved to prepare; others played well in practice, but not in games. Don't leave the game on the practice field.[4]

His coaching success depended as much on his strong defenses as on his publicized offensive plays. A good offense is a good defense provided the team has a good defense. Defense contradicted the offense — the offense talks and the defense answers. A good defense steers the offense into its grasp. If every man is alert, charges and stays in front of the play, no offense can gain. Expect any kind of play at any time. When the ball is snapped, every man should play to excess, even beyond his ability. Defenders should first crack their opponents strongest attack. A team of eleven good tacklers is hard to beat. The team that controls the first yard beyond the line of scrimmage ... should win. Back up the play. It is better to play safe than to be sorry. If you run harder than the other team, you will win. A slow starter often makes a good defensive lineman because he is unable to commit himself too quickly. The Lord is generally on the side of the team with the biggest tackles. Hit a man and make his ribs squeak. Defenses must stop both running and forward-passing attacks. On pass defense, play the man until you see the ball — then play the ball. The punt is the transition between defense and offense. With a punt, one team gets forty yards and the other gets the ball — a fair exchange. When in doubt, punt. When it rains, it rains on both teams, fifty-fifty. On a wet day, a smart team lets the other one splash about and slip in the mud with the ball. Mud and rain favor the team on defense. Many fumbles are caused by hard tackles, which alert players can anticipate. A loose ball belongs to everybody. Those who profit from a fumble may perish by a fumble.

On offense, If every man carries out his assignments no defense can stop the play. An offense should be constructed so as to educate the defense to be fooled. Touchdowns were the goal. Remember the play that is gaining. Don't repeat plays that are not working. Don't assume that you can push a good team off the field by mass attack. Too much system destroys the initiative; too many plays, exactness. Men and plays are more important than signals. Insist that your plays be used early in the season. No matter what style of offense a coach is using, if he is losing he wishes he had another. Never prophesy a great football future for any back until he has gained his first yard and taken his first bump. Championship football demands accurate and exact men, not careless signals and fumbles. Rhythmic offensive signals may enable the defense to time them and nullify the advantage. Play for a touchdown on the first two downs and a first down on the third. A good open-field runner is to football as a good left is to a prize fighter. A good back should keep his feet as long as he can and must never lose his head. Some backs run very fast on one spot. A player must adapt his rhythm to the opponents' movements. When about to block or tackle, go through. The laws of leverage aid or hamper human movements. The best forward pass is the one thrown by the best thrower to the highest jumper who has the rhythm to time his jump and can hang on to the ball. He who falters at the goal line will not enter football's kingdom of heaven, the end zone.

A keen observer of coaches, Zuppke counseled students to keep your coaching simple and your English plain. The coach should be perfectly impartial with his men and bury or hide any prejudices he has about his players. Look at a candidate with your eyes, and then do not warp him out of shape with your mind. Like a painter, the coach must see with the eye only; all things of the mind in time become prejudices and biases. He must keep young mentally and handle players differently according to their backgrounds. The coach should be impersonal in criticisms to the whole squad and make his direct criticisms to the player in private. He should be sincere and truthful and introduce a little whimsy at a ratio of about three to ten. Collegiate coaching is a fight against time, but the coach must not neglect details. In a crisis, few coaches can think on the bench. Coaching a green team required more creativity than holding an experienced one in form. A losing squad needed more help than a winning team. The true test of a coach was how he handled a team that lacked the talent and ability to compete with a bigger team. Many coaches grumble merely because their ideal standards are much too high for student athletes even to approach. Insisting that athletes improve upon their weaknesses makes the coach temporarily unpopular. The coach must conquer the element of fear of the unknown in football players. Don't over-exaggerate the ability of your opponents, or your players will think that they are up against superhuman men. Always assume that the rival coach knows at least as much as you do. Coaches of athletic teams are the only college professors who test each other's metal. A coach is in direct contact with the vital part of the school, is the center of gossip and takes the abuse. Zuppke's service on rules committees produced: A considerable part of life is a gamble. Rulemakers must not divorce the athletic games from life. The laws of chance lend color to the games. If the committee keeps on tampering with the rules, we may soon have a round field with rubber goal posts.[5]

Publicity and spectators also received Zup's attention. All players look good in newspaper publicity before the season starts. Yards of paper did not produce yards of ground. The hero of a thousand perfect plays becomes a bum after one error. A coach developed the Four Horsemen, but weak opposition and a poet in the press box immortalized them. A coach is responsible to an irresponsible public and learns to enjoy the vociferous irresponsibilities of the enthusiastic spectators. Movie stars may be God's gift to women, but the second guess is God's gift to the football fan. Football was a great kicking game; however, the kickers are in the stands at three dollars a seat. If the team wins all its games, the alumni are loyal.

Zuppke maintained that there should be no conflict between the cloister and the athletic field, but he resented attacks on football and stated that its lessons in self-control had pedagogical value and that it made the nation college conscious. A major aim of a university should be to unfold personality. Athletes learned from their labor and athletics was the most important extracurricular activity. Football had an indirect disciplinarian force, as students saw crowds passionately in love with a game restrain from rioting although the causes may be there. Opining that information doled out in the classroom was not always elevating, he said that it was better to worship a football hero than a fiddling Nero. Intercollegiate athletics helped to destroy provincialism, had a broadening influence and furnished outside contacts. Students who couldn't make the ball teams tried for the debating team and then went down the line to campus politics, the lowest form of collegiate endeavors. Both a Phi Beta Kappa pin and a gold football represented achievement based on endurance, tenacity and intelligence. The United States added the intercollegiate idea to the European university. Illinois was a university of the people where there was no vestige of snobbery, and the only way to raise your head above the level of the crowd was to be a better person. It stood for courage and fair play and was not fat, soft, self-satisfied, or too old to grow. It was eager to be in harmony with the times.

For Zuppke, football also had a civilizing force. Civilization followed the ball and depended on the controlled mood of the individual. Football developed the individual's ability to control moods and turn the other cheek. The code of sportsmanship must be everlastingly propounded as untutored; nature squawks when it loses and crows when it wins. Sportsmanship helps to soften the rough spots in life. Conduct on the field may influence thousands. Be courteous and congratulate the victor as civilization decrees. The Roman Empire may have vanished because it never taught the multitude how to play. The world is continually changing. No man who ever lived was necessary. To eat, to love, and to fight are the fundamentals of life. Learn to do some one thing well. Up to fifty, you earn and save money; after that, you spend your life trying to keep everybody from stealing it from you. Zuppke was fifty in 1929.

9

The Coaching Profession

Zuppke brought academic experience as a normal school and university graduate and a high school teacher to the task of teaching college football. He was more interested and effective in talking about football than writing about it, but he was aware of the market for sports journalism and sports publications. *New York Times* reporter John Kieran wrote that he would talk about football "or any other subject under the sun and pour out his ideas for hours, thirteen words to the dozen, with gestures." Red Grange recalled that Zuppke was never at a loss for words and that he would say anything to inspire the team or create a good story for reporters. He used his distinctive personal style in contacts with the media and alumni and was a master at motivating student athletes. He was a leading figure in the development of coaching schools and a lifelong educator at schools in the United States and Cuba. He enjoyed travel and speaking to prospective coaches. Highly respected as a coach and teacher by Amos Stagg, Fielding Yost and Knute Rockne, he was the third president of the American Football Coaches Association and the first from the Big Ten and the Middle West. He was a vigorous defender of college athletics and sportsmanship. Acclaimed for adapting and designing plays that made the game an attractive and profitable form of mass entertainment, he applied psychology in preparing and drilling his teams for aggressive defensive and innovative offensive plays. In teaching football in the coaching school and training his players, he emphasized visual perception and game performance. In the *Chicago Tribune*, Walter Eckersall observed that Zuppke was a "stickler for tackling and blocking teams" and that he had originated the huddle system. He also found that they were well drilled in defensive tactics and had a large assortment of plays. His success as a coach contributed to his security in a profession noted for its high turnover. During his twenty-nine years as the head coach at Illinois, the average tenure of coaches at the other Big Ten state universities was four and a half years.[1]

By the 1920s, athletic coaching had become an attractive profession.

Zuppke's involvement in coaching schools and his work in promoting football as a popular student activity helped to fill stadiums and publicize universities. Five Big Ten football championships between 1914 and 1923 brought national recognition and personal financial security. As a student of coaching, he was aware of market conditions. In December 1919, he broke off negotiations with Northwestern when he signed a five-year renewal of his contract with Illinois. By 1924, his salary reached $8,000 a year, of which came $1,600 from the university, $1,500 from teaching in the Athletic Coaching School and $4,900 from the receipts of the Athletic Association. In response to criticism, Huff wrote that Zuppke stayed at Illinois at a "considerable financial sacrifice" and that another conference university had offered him a five-year guaranteed contract at a salary $3,000 greater than that paid at Illinois. Huff also demonstrated the need for higher salaries for coaches by listing Kenneth Wilson, George Clark, Burt Ingwersen, Ernest Bearg and John Griffith, who left Athletic Association salaries at Illinois from $2,400 to $4,500 for positions with salaries from $3,800 to $6,000. Like Knute Rockne and Amos Stagg, Zuppke used California job offers to leverage his earnings at Illinois. In 1929, his salary was increased to $10,000.[2]

Late in 1913, the Big Ten faculty representatives had gazed into the future and condemned professional coaches. At the same time, George Huff toured eastern universities and found a big demand for coaches. President Edmund James approved Huff's plan to teach physical training and athletic coaching. In 1914, Zuppke began teaching a summer session football course to forty-five high school and college teachers. In six weeks, he taught Physical Training 13, or "Football." The course covered the rules from the standpoint of coach, players and officials; offense and defense; generalship and strategy; training, conditioning and players' equipment; punting, dropkicking, placekicking, kick off, and forward passing; tackling dummy and practice sled; special drills for linemen, ends and backs; interference, team work and following the ball; fundamental plays, freak plays and signal systems. George Huff taught baseball, Ralph Jones taught basketball and Harry Gill taught track. Summer registration increased from 122 in 1914, to 265 in 1921 to 473 in 1924. Summer coaching schools provided excellent contacts with high school and college coaches. In the first decade, 1,200 coaches from across the country came to Illinois for the summer course. George Little, who attended the 1916 summer school, quoted Zuppke many times to his team, which won a championship in the following fall. Little later assisted Yost and was a head coach at Miami, Michigan and Wisconsin. In 1922, Zuppke hired professional football's Frank McCormick to teach in his coaching school. In 1923, 1924 and 1925, Cornell coach Gil Dobie joined Zuppke in teaching the Illinois summer course. In 1923, 330 students registered for courses, 236 took basketball taught by Craig Ruby, 203 took football taught by Gil Dobie, 193 took track taught by Harry Gill, 189 took football taught by Zuppke, 117 took baseball taught by Carl Lundgren, 115 took athletic training taught by Matt Bullock, and 85 took swimming taught by W.S. Brown from Massachusetts. By 1924, 1,500 coaches had attended the summer sessions. By 1925, Illinois, Michigan, Minnesota, Wisconsin, Iowa, Indiana and Notre Dame were among the eleven universities advertising summer coaching schools. In 1926, Zuppke conducted a four-week athletic coaches conference at Washington State University, while Dobie and Milt Olander taught the Illinois school. Zuppke's football books and a national championship in 1927 were factors in attracting fifty-four coaches who attended a July 1928 School for Coaches at Bucknell University. Zuppke and Glen "Pop" Warner were the instructors.[3]

The success of the summer school courses led Huff to propose the first four-year program in athletic coaching and physical education in 1916. Course requirements included fifty-two credit hours of athletics and coaching, fifty hours of electives, seventeen hours of education, thirteen hours of psychology, four hours of military service and two hours of public speaking. Approved and publicized in 1919, enrollment in the four-year program increased from 68 in 1919 to 356 in 1925. Aided by funding from the Athletic Association, the coaching school had twenty-one staff members in 1926. The thirteen college championships in baseball won by George Huff's teams, the nine Big Ten championships won by Harry Gill's track teams and the seven championships of Zuppke's football teams attracted both students and employers. In the 1923–26 period, there were 167 graduates. A third were from Illinois and 51 percent came from the Midwest. The other half came from twenty-six states. Seventy-four percent obtained high school positions. A coaching school bulletin issued in 1925 claimed that more than 2,000 coaches reflected Zuppke's football strategies and methods. In the1920s, the Department of Athletic Coaching and Physical Education provided most of the enrollment in the College of Education. Most students majoring in secondary school education attended the five Illinois state teachers colleges. By 1930, 440 of the 539 Education students were in the Athletic Coaching and Physical Education program. A substantial part of the salaries of Huff and Zuppke was paid by the Athletic Coaching program, which produced athletics directors and coaches from 1923 to 1932. Registration peaked in 1924–27. In 1929, the university restricted admissions to the coaching course. George Huff explained that many Illinois graduates could not be placed because of the coaching schools that had opened at other universities.[4]

The coaching schools required textbooks. In 1922, Zuppke and Assistant Coach Ernest Bearg published twenty-two summer lectures as *Football Techniques and Tactics,* in which they diagrammed plays and addressed the moral obligation of the coach to further the principle of good sportsmanship by respecting and following the rules of the game. Stagg in1893, Yost in 1905 and Warner in1912 had published football books before World War I. Zuppke's book and Charles Daly's *American Football* were the first postwar contributions to football literature. Based on his 1914 summer school lectures, the book contained chapters on offensive and defensive tips for each position, formations, signals, diagrams and practices. Fielding Yost of Michigan, John Wilce of Ohio State and Glenn Thistlethwaite of Northwestern praised it as the best book on football fundamentals on the market. Chapters were read on WRM, the University's radio station. From 1921, his lectures were supplemented by motion picture films of games.[5]

In 1924, Bailey and Himes sporting goods store published a second edition of *Techniques and Tactics* with photographs, added notes and suggestions gathered in the 1922 and 1923 seasons. Studded with aphorisms, Zuppke's textbook covered tackling and blocking; line play by the center, guards, tackles and ends; ten basic backfield plays; three defensive formations; the punt and placekick; seventeen forward pass plays and six screen pass plays; development of the coach's system of guiding the quarterback and captain; signals and signals practice; and scouting. About 7,000 copies were sold.[6]

By the time the second edition was published, Zuppke was one of eleven coaches who were selling football books. In 1930, he published *Coaching Football*, which included thirteen chapters with photographs and diagrams. One chapter covered the practices and scrimmages of the 1928 championship season. He observed that coaching was a fight against time that required courage, tact, perseverance and dynamic inspirational qualities. He advised his readers to keep a respectful distance from players and to praise sparingly, but not to be unduly aloof. The coach should be a developer of men and encourage loyalty — win or lose. He applied psychology in preparing players for their roles in the games. While his 1935 collaboration with Coleman Griffith on "The Psychology of Football" was unpublished, the 220-page manuscript was a melding of Griffith's psychological research and Zuppke's twenty-nine years of observational experience.[7]

In the 1920s, the strong demand for physical education administrators, teachers and coaches created a national market for students with a degree in athletic coaching. This demand was reflected in the increasing percentage of football players majoring in education and physical education. Nine members of Zuppke's 1929 championship team majored in the athletic coaching curriculum. In 1929, the Carnegie Report alleged that the Illinois Athletic Coaching program was an example of professionalism. In a broad sense, the entire university hired professional teachers to prepare students for professional careers. Collegiate administrators embraced professional education for the technical and social training of the urban middle class. The phenomenal popularity of the athletic coaching program was paralleled in the College of Commerce, where business student enrollment increased from 215 in 1913 to 2,063 in 1921. As school and college curricula expanded, there was also a general increase in course offerings and enrollments in the performing arts of art, drama and music.[8]

The demand for coaches and physical education teachers created a market for sporting goods. From his high school coaching experience, Zuppke learned that the prevention of injuries was an important factor for successful competition in contact sports. His continuing interest in football equipment also had publicity and financial benefits. He supplemented his salary with endorsements. In April 1925, the Rawlings Company, a national sporting goods manufacturer, introduced the "New Zuppke Line" of football pants, shoulder pads and helmets. The catalog advertised Zuppke, Heisman and Notre Dame pants. The Zuppke pants featured the "famous Zuppke groin pads" and knee pads endorsed by "the great Red Grange." The patented construction of the pads in the pants had been used by Illinois teams for four years. By 1928, Rawlings advertised Zuppke pants, shoulder pads, helmets and footballs along with the coach's letter extolling their use by his national championship team. From 1929 to 1937, these Rawlings advertisements appeared in the Illinois football programs. The Bailey and Himes sporting goods store in Champaign featured Rawlings-Zuppke designed equipment.[9]

The growth of secondary education not only provided an expanding market for graduates of the Illinois coaching school and for the Zuppke line of Rawlings sports equipment, but it also resulted in a pool of thousands of young football players who looked for opportunities to play collegiate football. In 1921, Athletic Publicity Director John Griffith and former quarterback George "Potsy" Clark began publication of *The Athletic Journal* in Champaign. The *Journal* published seasonal articles on collegiate sports and advertisements for equipment, literature and summer schools. Zuppke was listed as a contributing editor for football. His only contribution was joint authorship of a September 1926 article on defensive football. Griffith continued to edit the *Journal* in Chicago after his appointment as the first Big Ten commissioner in the summer of 1922. In a 1928 squabble between the Amateur Athletic Union and the NCAA, Gus Kirby, an AAU official, stated that Griffth believed in commercializing everything, had no quarrel with professional baseball and professional football, and was organizing the sporting goods manufacturers.[10]

Highly regarded by other coaches, Zuppke was active in the formation of their professional organization. Organized in 1921, the American Football Coaches Association met each December during the NCAA meetings to consider rules changes and mutual concerns. Zuppke represented Illinois at the 1924, 1927 and 1928 NCAA meetings. Major Charles D. Daly of West Point was the first president of the coaches association. At the 1923 meeting in Atlanta, Georgia Tech's John Heisman was elected president and Zuppke was chosen as first vice president. At the December 29, 1924, NCAA meeting in New York, he read Coleman Griffith's paper on psychology in athletics and added a few remarks and observations of his own. The coaches elected him as president of the association to succeed Heisman. His account of his election had him presiding when the Army and Wisconsin coaches nominated Fielding Yost of Michigan as a candidate "from the north" to replace Heisman. When a motion was made to close nominations, Zuppke announced his candidacy. When no one nominated him, he nominated himself and delivered a stirring oration that asked coaches to vote for "a little guy, like me, whom you can push around." The legend was that he was elected by a 500 to 1 vote, in which he voted for the coach who nominated Yost. As president, he appointed Knute Rockne to the coaches' Rules Committee and presided at the 1925 meeting in New York. Zuppke was a member of the Rules and Coaching Ethics committees. In 1925–26, he was a member of the Walter Camp Memorial Committee. While the President's Office was largely honorary, he was popular among his fellow coaches and became a life member of the association.[11]

Zuppke's rivalries with Yost of Michigan and Rockne of Notre Dame were reflected in stories about pranks, gags and tricks. Rockne praised his splendid job as toastmaster at the coaches' 1927 banquet and declared that he was "the life of the party." Appointed as Ohio State's coach in 1913, John Wilce, also a Milwaukee West High School graduate, was a friend of Zuppke. His closest friend among college coaches was Howard Jones, who coached at Iowa from 1916 to 1922 and Southern California from 1925 to 1940. They served on the same committees and roomed together at conventions. On one dark winter night, the pair were jailed in Evanston on suspicion of burglary. Braven Dyer of the *Los Angeles Times* mentioned Zuppke's storytelling in an all-night party at a Hollywood supper club the night before the 1935 Illinois' game with Southern California. Before kickoff, Zuppke acknowledged that he "drank a leetle too much of that visky." He then masterminded his team to a 19–0 win over Jones, a teetotaler who "had gone to bed at a sensible hour." Zuppke was 3–2 against Jones at Iowa and 1–3 against him at Southern California in 1935–36 and 1939–40. Jones died before Zuppke's final 1941 season.[12]

Coach Zuppke enjoyed intensive football publicity and contacts with undergraduate students. Sigma Delta Chi, the college journalism fraternity, held an annual Gridiron Banquet, which featured lampoons of faculty members and administrative staff. He was a popular target. In 1922, caricaturing his oratorical idiosyncrasies delighted the audience. In 1923, he was the fifth recipient of the fraternity's Brown Derby, which was awarded to the "most regular" faculty member. At the same banquet, he also received the May Queen's scepter as one who didn't smoke cigars and was a teetotaler.[13]

10

Building Memorial Stadium

The years following the end of World War I and the influenza epidemic of 1919 led not only to a political "normalcy" but also to an optimism and support for undertaking new projects at public universities. Zuppke's career coincided with increased public demands for entertainment by the performing arts and competitive sports. The rapid growth of universities hastened the development of the performing arts on campuses. One of the most festive and popular forms of mass entertainment the autumnal football games at the athletic field or stadium. Attendance at games grew from a few bystanders on the sidelines to thousands of alumni and fans seated in huge stadiums. Football weekend entertainment also included pep rallies, bonfires, marching bands, cheering sections, bands singing the fight songs and the alma mater, parades, homecoming house decorations, halftime ceremonies and victory celebrations. Football games also provided opportunities for the state university to bond with alumni, the community and the state through celebratory homecomings, Dad's Days, Boy Scout Days and postseason Rotary Club and alumni banquets.

In the 1920s, public demands for larger arenas supported stadium building, which, in turn, contributed to the commercial viability of college football. The 1929 authors of the Carnegie Report identified the demand as the pressure from alumni and the prospect of profits to be reaped from vast crowds attending the games. Ohio State opened its stadium in 1922. Illinois followed in 1923. Purdue and Minnesota opened stadia in 1924, Northwestern in 1926, Michigan in 1927 and Iowa in 1929. Before the Great War of 1914–18, the Illinois Alumni Association had sought support for a memorial for the university's first regent, John M. Gregory. After the war, a memorial for students who had died during the conflict gained support. At the same time, the postwar popularity of football demonstrated the need for a stadium to replace the 22,000 seat "lumberyard" on Illinois Field. With its wooden bleachers and spectators in nearby trees, it was no longer adequate. In 1920, nearly 28,000 attended away games in Ann Arbor and Chicago and 20,000 attended the Ohio State game in Urbana. Three thousand of the latter crowd were fans from Ohio, which included 100 members of the visitor's marching band. In a July 1921 appeal, Zuppke supplemented the sentimental reasons that justified the stadium with the need to raise the visiting team's share of receipts to the levels provided by Ohio, Michigan, Minnesota and Iowa. Ohio State supporters had gone over the top by pledging $970,000 in a campaign for a new $1.3 million stadium. A highly visible structure for widely publicized public events would also be an impressive demonstration of support for the state university's building program.[1]

Zuppke's coaching success led to his role as a moving force and most ardent supporter in the campaign for the construction of the Memorial Stadium. On December 1, 1920, he called for a new horseshoe stadium that would seat 60,000. On December 9, 1,353 out of 4,005 students voted for a new stadium. A war memorial was favored for a combined project. Budgetary difficulties resulting from rising enrollments led Illinois to seek private funds for a large stadium and war memorial. On December 14, the Board of Trustees authorized the Athletic Association to solicit subscriptions. The campaign was timed to coincide with a legislative visit and the university's campaign for a $10,500,000 budget. After a December vacation in Florida, Zuppke visited stadiums to study structural plans. On January 22 and February 2, 1921, as Stadium Executive Committee Chairman he urged senior men and committee women to educate the students and faculty about the stadium plans and the importance of loyalty. Fannie joined him for the women's meeting. Zuppke also chaired the Stadium Drive's budget and ways and means committees. In January he enlisted the advice, aid and support of builders, businessmen and state officers in Decatur, Springfield and Bloomington. George Huff hired alumnus Samson Raphaelson for three months to organize a student pledge drive and handle publicity. On January 25, students set up a stadium campaign office at the Illinois Union. In a March appeal for the support of Peoria alumni, Zuppke declared that the stadium would be financed by alumni and friends and urged graduates to inform the public about the needs of the University, which belonged to the people of Illinois. At a mass meeting in the Auditorium and parade on March 21, Zuppke talked about the War Memorial to 6,000 students. On March 31, he urged 600 county committee student solicitors to campaign for a stadium that would represent Illinois' sportsmanship and culture. The stadium would represent "Illiniwek," or the complete man. The final campus campaign drive began on April 5 with a *Daily Illini* editorial proclaiming that athletic success depended on the "financial and moral backing of the student body." The 6,000 copies of a promotional magazine were distributed to students and faculty. Posters proclaimed that

"You don't pay a cent until January 1, 1922." Smaller print cautioned against overgiving and advised students to estimate their resources and consult their parents. On the 9th, an all-campus picnic coincided with the end of an eight-week spring football practice. The Zuppkes were chaperones at the rally, picnic, party and dance in Washington Park. Sponsored by the Illinois Union and Women's League, 3,000 students consumed box lunches and joined in a balloon scramble. The Athletic Association distributed posters, bulletin boards and a solicitor's handbook, which provided lessons in salesmanship. Luncheons and dinners for workers instilled enthusiasm. On the 14th, Zuppke spoke to a senior mass meeting on their role as "teachers of School Spirit and Builders of Tradition." With Raphaelson's guidance 2,500 students served on committees, and their participation and news releases led to statewide newspaper publicity.[2]

On April 24, 1921, a parade and a full-page advertisement summoned the student body for a mass meeting on Monday, April 25. The meeting was staged by Elmer Ekblaw and Business professor Frederic Russell. With the noisy support of the Illinois band, glee and mandolin clubs, the Rantoul air field's "Flying Circus" and ROTC artillery, eleven speakers made their appeals to 7,000 students in the Auditorium and the Gym Annex. Russell directed the Auditorium meeting, which included appeals by President Kinley, three deans, George Huff, Zuppke and Speech professor Charles H. Woolbert. At the Gym Annex, Kinley, Huff, Zuppke and Raphaelson took care of the enthusiasm. Kinley and George Huff spoke of their vision for Illini spirit and the students' need to start the campaign that the alumni would finish. In the closing speech, Zuppke's sentences "zigzagged" across the halls ... like lightning.... With careful preparation and ... priming ... of the students, his appeal produced student pledges ... far beyond ... what was expected. After the pledging, student solicitors switched from arousing enthusiasm to getting subscriptions, which added to totals shown on a posted thermometer, campus displays and publicity releases. In a memoir, Raphaelson stated that "it was brutal ... they were bullied into it, so that each one of them signed a pledge and we raised the money all right. I shudder when I think of it. I've never done anything like it, before or since." When the student drive closed on May 1, $665,560 had been pledged. Michigan's Fielding Yost had been on hand to observe the student campaign. Zuppke remembered how proud he was when coach Tad Jones of Yale told him that nothing had ever impressed him so much as the demonstration of loyalty by the students of Illinois in the big mass meeting that launched the drive for the Memorial Stadium.[3]

President David Kinley had justified his support of football as being better than the alternative of student involvement in class wars and theater riots. Keyed to an emotional peak at the mass meeting on Monday, the students launched their own celebration on Tuesday the 26th. Proclaiming a Tramp, Poverty or Roughneck day, the "imbibers of stadium wine" dressed as tramps and launched their own celebration. The "Thundering Thugs" and "Calico-eds" soon had the campus "reeling in the most joyous toot that was ever home-brewed from happiness." To celebrate the passing of old Illinois Field and the purchase of a real stadium, they left classrooms to engage in rowdyism, paint-ing, tracking mud in the Library and swiping apparel from lockers in the Women's Building. Kinley turned to Zuppke. The coach sent athletes into the classrooms to announce that morning classes were dismissed and requested male students to attend another mass meeting in the Auditorium at eleven o'clock. Kinley announced the suspension of classes until noon. Zuppke then suggested that a proper response would be their return to afternoon classes, which they did. The *Daily Illini* concluded that when the lid is off, "Zup and Prexy can put it back on."[4]

Zuppke's 1921 speeches drew upon the stadium campaign for thrills, but another major purpose was to support the university's request for a $10,500,000 state appropriation. His argument for the appropriation cited Illinois' wealth and the higher budget at the University of Michigan. Under the astute management of Raphaelson, the $100,000 stadium publicity cam-paign went into high gear. The Athletic Association used Alumni Association records and hired an office manager, clerks and stenographers. The staff pro-duced a model for the state fair. Movies and recordings were sent to Illini Clubs throughout the country. A $40,000 souvenir stadium book was dis-tributed to facilitate the collection of the pledges. As president of the Alumni Association, George Huff led the campaign for alumni support and organ-ized thirty-nine new Illini Slubs. Under his leadership, the university had established eighty-one Illini Clubs in Illinois and fifty-one clubs in other states. Zuppke "warmed up" Illini Clubs at Watseka and other towns. At the request of Huff and Zuppke, Alumni Association president Chester invited Illini Club presidents to attend a March 5 Relay Carnival. He urged them to write Zuppke and tell him that you will be there to support the great proj-ect of a new Memorial Stadium and Recreational Field. From April 28 to May 4, Zuppke and Huff spoke at alumni meetings in Cleveland, Columbus, Philadelphia, New York and Washington. At the capitol, they met with Sen-ator William B. McKinley and the entire Illinois House delegation. The leg-islators spoke in favor of the University appropriations bill pending in Springfield and endorsed the stadium plan. Between meetings, Huff and Zup-pke traveled to New Jersey and Connecticut to inspect the Princeton stadium and Yale Bowl. On May 10, Huff and Zuppke and the University band per-formed before a large crowd at an alumni banquet in Decatur. On May 26, 250 Schenectady alumni responded with support after hearing Zuppke's fiery talk and Huff's story of athletic successes. The speakers then moved on to the Detroit Illini Club. In June, they appealed for pledges from three alumni groups in Illinois. In August, they took their "oratorical fireworks" to Milwaukee, Minneapolis, Seattle, Tacoma, Portland, San Francisco, Santa Monica, Salt Lake City, Denver, Omaha and Moline-Rock Island. Accompanied by their wives, they formed a quartet to sing the "Build the Stadium" song in Minneapolis.

> Standing in our stadium are all Illini true,
> Singing to our fighting men: "We built this just for you!"
> So fight for Alma Mater, Boys, as warriors proudly do,
> Bringing home a victory for Orange and for Blue.

The travelers proceeded to Seattle by way of Banff and Vancouver. The party returned to Champaign on September 2, in time for Zuppke to prepare for the fall football season.[5]

From 1921 to 1927, the Stadium Fund Drive was the university's first public attempt to secure private financial support for a major project. Zuppke put "his heart, soul, mind and body" into stadium fund-raising. On December 22, 1921, he joined Huff in speaking at the Chicago Illini Club's football banquet. Huff reported that $1,642,000 had been pledged for the stadium campaign. "Robert the Devil" talked about philosophy, psychology, architecture, religion, politics, literature, relativity, science, agriculture, law, music and football. The whirlwind orator concluded his remarks in "a blaze of pyrotechnics that would make W.J. B(ryan) seem like a stuttering schoolboy." He served on a donor committee with Huff, Avery Brundage and Robert Carr, which secured the trustees approval of Holabird and Roche of Chicago as architects for the stadium. On November 13, he explained to the Alumni Association directors why the Chicago firm was chosen as the architects rather than the university's Architecture Department. In February 1922, the Board of Athletic Control appointed Zuppke to the Stadium Drive Executive Committee. He subscribed $1,000 for the stadium fund and served on the Building, Memorials and Continuing Subscriptions committees. On February 8, 1922, the Board of Trustees acknowledged pledges of $1,776,535 and receipts of $219,265 and designated the Athletic Association as its agent for the construction of the stadium. In March, April and May, Zuppke consulted with architects and attended trustees meetings where the stadium location was approved. Ground was broken on September 11, 1922. On October 16, the first of 30,000 barrels of concrete was poured. As the two-million-dollar stadium rose on the prairie, Chicago was building a four-and-half-million-dollar Soldier Field on its lakefront. The Illinois War Memorial Stadium was more than twice the size of the University of Chicago's Mitchell Field. The concrete poured for the stadium was complemented by a network of concrete highways under construction throughout Illinois. A main trunk road would connect Chicago and Urbana. The hard roads would enable many motorists to drive to and from a game in the stadium in a single day. Coincidentally, a leader in the hard roads movement was Danville lawyer Arthur Hall, Zuppke's predecessor as football coach. In November, Zuppke and Huff spoke to new "Flying Squadron" solicitors. At a 1922 mass meeting, he declared that the Illini war dead would tell the living to build a "temple of sportsmanship" where men would fight for honor.[6]

In June 1923, the *Alumni News* credited the influence of support for the stadium for bringing about legislative appropriations in full as requested. The university's 1923–25 budget included $500,000 for a new gymnasium and equipment. It housed athletic offices, basketball and minor sports. The construction program also convinced Champaign to put subways under the Illinois Central Railroad tracks. As the stadium neared completion in September 1923, only $875,370 had been collected and 5,000 slow-pay Illini were delinquent. The Athletic Association borrowed $400,000 to complete the stadium. An 8–0 championship season with a game in the stadium brought collections up to $1,167,097. The highly successful 1924 to 1926 football seasons, enabled the Athletic Association to reduce the debt. From 1926 to 1929, stadium subscribers received ticket preference. Each pledger received seat location preferences for four or five games over the 1927–33 period. Guarantors of the stadium loan received complimentary passes. By 1927, the $1,652,532 received represented 76.4 percent of the initial subscriptions. In 1929, the stadium debt was reduced to $413,107. By 1931, 77.7 percent of the pledges were collected. All but $25,365 of the borrowed money had been repaid. Uncollected pledges amounted to $482,000.[7]

A gift of the alumni and people of Illinois, the stadium was the key factor in the "golden" era of Illinois football. From 1923 to 1930, football began producing substantial profits on the field, in the grandstands and in the accounting office (table 10.1).

10.1. Attendance and Financial Figures
(figures in thousands)

Year	Won/Loss/Tie	Home Attendance	Total Attendance	Income	Expense	Profit
1919	6–1–0	5.3	$73.9		$42.1	$31.8
1920	5–2–0	50.1	125.5	162.6	71.1	91.5
1921	3–4–0	58.3	114.0	102.0	58.7	43.3
1922	2–5–0	57.9	160.3			
1923	8–0–0	118.0	202.1	187.5	29.3	158.2
1924	6–1–1	146.6	231.8	256.2	54.5	201.7

1925	5–3–0	192.1	357.4	376.4	71.2	305.1
1926	6–2–0	162.9	257.9	299.8	72.1	227.1
1927	7–0–1	150.0	288.6	346.2	51.3	294.8
1928	7–1–0	149.5	301.5	356.3	52.0	304.2
1929	6–1–1	197.8	374.8	401.2	61.3	339.8
1930	3–5–0	145.4	320.4	352.9	59.8	293.2

The success of the Stadium Drive prompted the Alumni Association staff to point out that 7,500 alumni had subscribed $750,000, which would go into the Athletic Association's coffers and prevent the Alumni Association from seeking a permanent endowment fund. Dean Thomas A. Clark and Alumni Association secretary Frank Scott noted that ninety percent of the contributors were alumni. As this "alumni gift" would yield a larger income than the current expenses of the Athletic Association would need, they declared that it would be "fair and sound" to donate a substantial percentage of that income to alumni interests. A committee was appointed to study the disposition of Athletic Association receipts. On April 13, 1923, they reported that George Huff was not ready to share receipts. From 1924 to 1926, there was continued agitation for profit sharing. Huff provided "material aid" and Zuppke spoke to clubs, but the profits were invested in athletic facilities for students rather than payments to the Alumni Association. Reports on Illini Clubs and Big Ten Clubs indicated that the dominating interest was in athletics, especially football. Efforts to persuade Stadium subscribers to become Alumni Association members were not successful.[8]

The massive stadium rising on the southwest corner of the campus attracted the attention of the faculty and the president. On December 26, 1922, President Kinley appointed fourteen faculty men to a Commission on Athletics and Physical Education. In March 1923, the Commission recommended separate physical education departments for men and women and Senate appointment of the five members of the Athletic Association Board of Directors. It also recommended that the Association prepare an annual budget and that its accounts should be audited by the university comptroller. In a comment that revealed their avoidance of the administrative and financial factors in college athletics, the faculty stated that intercollegiate athletics are a proper stimulus and reward for success in intramural athletics and that there should be no expansion of intercollegiate athletics. Before the Commission report was published, Kinley explained the administration's position in a letter to Huff. "We are content that you may handle Athletic Association business as a personal matter," but your successor will not have this complete confidence. Noting that the completion of the stadium meant that Athletic Association receipts would be far greater than ever before, he suggested a plan for financial management with budgets, income estimates, and funds put aside

Memorial Stadium, the stage for Zuppke's performing artistry, 1946. Courtesy University of Illinois Archives.

for upkeep, improvement and development of the stadium, and a policy for handling receipts in excess of the needs of Athletic Association work. He assured Huff that the policy should be "so elastic as to be modifiable at your wish."[9]

Each year, Kinley, a parsimonious Scottish economist, and Huff, an athletics director and university lobbyist, stretched their elastic agreement. The football profit supported eight minor sports with about $40,000, facilities repair and maintenance, and intramural and student recreational and entertainment sports with about $10,000. As profits mounted, Huff's "athletics for all students" program produced capital improvements to reduce Athletic Association surpluses. In the 1923 to 1927 period, the money went toward the retirement of the stadium debt. In 1929, he reported that a large part of the football profit had been used for the development of facilities for intramural athletics. In 1930, $300,000 went for an ice skating rink. The Association built sixty tennis courts. In 1931, profits paid for a south end zone stand at the stadium.[10]

In addition to the direct benefits to the Athletic Association and the university, the stadium had a major impact on the local economy. Land purchases, construction contracts, landscaping, and the business generated by large crowds attending football games had a significant effect on the growth of Champaign and Urbana. The English Brothers construction company in Champaign had built fourteen university buildings before receiving the general construction contract for the stadium. The $1,221,743 general contract equaled the amount of all their previous university projects. By 1922, the stadium builders had employed 3,600 workers.[11]

The new stadium accommodated larger crowds and provided an attractive stage for the spectacular performances of the football band. The entertainment rituals associated with football, such as parades, rallies, bonfires, songs and cheers, were borrowed from the rivalries associated with political campaigns, religious meetings, baseball games and the student riots common in nineteenth-century colleges. Zuppke's success in winning football championships was paralleled by the rising popularity of high school and college football and student marching bands and cheering sections. The university's band was a major attraction on football weekends. When Austin Harding was appointed director in 1906, the band began marching and singing. Harding and his staff developed music, innovative pageantry and timely stunts for Homecoming and Dad's Day ceremonies. By 1922, the Illinois band had 280 marching musicians. In 1923, they moved from the Block I formation to spelling Illini. Twenty-one student committees were involved in planning Homecoming events. As large stadia became available for college football, the band increased its pageantry, secured travel funds and boarded trains for a 1925 game at Franklin Field in Philadelphia, a 1930 game in New York's Yankee Stadium and a 1933 game in Cleveland's Municipal Stadium. The band's late and dramatic entrance at Franklin Field set the stage for an inspired victory over Pennsylvania. When Harding retired in 1948, Zup wrote that he had been a most ardent admirer of Austin Harding and his glorious band all these years.[12]

College athletic teams followed the professional baseball clubs in adopting team names. As students at the state university, Illinois chose to call themselves the Indians in honor of the tribes for which the state was named. In 1874, the student newspaper became the *Illini*. By 1908, the term was applied to the athletic teams. An account of a 1912 game referred to the fighting comeback of the Illini. In 1914, the lettermen's organization took the name of "Tribe of the Illini." By 1921, "Fighting Illini" came into general usage in newspaper accounts and administrative publicity. In 1923, the Council of Administration adopted a resolution discouraging the use of the word Illini for private profit as it had come to be regarded as a term applicable to the university. In preparing a halftime program for an October 30, 1926, return match with

Pennsylvania, Ray Dvorak, assistant band director, arranged special halftime music. The Quakers sent a costume for a William Penn figure and Dvorak asked Lester Leutwiler, a former Urbana Boy Scout, to dress as an Indian to represent the Illini. Dvorak also consulted Zuppke, who drew on his 1916 to 1921 work with the Boy Scouts in suggesting Chief Illiniwek as a name for the symbolic celebrant of Illinois' Indian heritage. The Chief's halftime dance was done as a band member. He was not a cheerleading mascot. The performance and the name were accepted by the spectators and became a halftime ritual for all subsequent Illinois home games. In 1928, bandsmen composed the "Pride of the Illini" and the "March of the Illini" for the Chief's entry and dance at halftime. The second Chief sought to extend the performance to include a horse for parades and halftime celebrations. When the horse tore up the turf in 1931, Zuppke terminated the horse's stadium appearances.[13]

11

Commercialism and Red Grange

The popularity of college football attracted spectators to the stadium, and the games became a profitable and commercial extracurricular activity. The prosperity of intercollegiate football contributed to the professionalization of athletic coaching. It yielded an annual income and profits, which supported the construction of athletic facilities for the spectators, the hiring of additional coaches, professional courses for sports educators, recreational facilities for students, funding for minor sports, intramural athletic programs, and new student activities. It also benefited local business enterprises.

At Illinois, the new stadium provided a stage for the coach and a star player, and brought national publicity. Arriving at Illinois after the 1905–12 period of scheduling and rules changes, the "Dutch Master" had continued the successes he achieved at Muskegon and Oak Park high schools. His thirty conference victories exceeded those of Chicago's Amos Stagg, Michigan's Fielding Yost and Minnesota's Henry Williams. Between 1913 and 1919, the Fighting Illini won or shared four Big Ten championships. The 1914 and 1919 teams won recognition as national champions.

In 1922, graduations and the Taylorville betting affair had dampened Illinois' football prospects. In May, at the state interscholastic track meet, Zuppke impressed a Wheaton High School sprinter with his warm and friendly manner. He advised Harold Grange that he would have "a good chance of making our football team." In 1920, 1921 and 1922, Grange had won four events at the interscholastic track meets in Urbana. In the summer, the Zuppkes traveled to Lake City in the Colorado mountains with the Huffs. They went on to Los Angeles for an August 3 meeting of the Southern California alumni club. Back in Champaign, Zuppke skipped the opening game to scout conference champion Iowa's upset of Yale in New Haven. Coached by assistant Justa Lindgren, the Illini lost a 10–7 game to Butler. Before the Homecoming game with Iowa, Zuppke pleaded for sympathy for his green and dazed team. They lost to conference co-champions Iowa 8–7 at their Homecoming and Michigan by 24–0 in Ann Arbor. The Illini gained a 6–3 win over Northwestern on Dad's Day and a 3–0 win over Wisconsin in Madison. They finished the season with close losses to Chicago and Ohio State. In the last four games, a strong line gave up only eighteen points. Despite a 2–4 Big Ten record, Zuppke praised guard Jim McMillen, who was a very active 200-pound wrestler and blocking guard. McMillen would be one of two Illini to win All-American honors in 1923. At the football banquet, team captain Dave Wilson presented a letter of appreciation to the coach for his sincerity of purpose, skill, indomitable spirit, and devotion to duty. They credited him with teaching them the spirit of never quiting. The returning players promised to bring back the conference championship in 1923. Zuppke urged the team to avoid being known as the fumbling Illini.[1]

After the 1922 season ended, a controversy about the ineligibility of a Wisconsin player and a Wisconsin countercharge about four Illinois players continued. In December, school officials agreed to play in 1923 and then suspended the rivalry until 1931. The gridiron misfortunes of 1922 did not deter Zuppke from speaking engagements. Amid rumors that he might return to coach at Wisconsin, he watched the Cornell-Pennsylvania game on Thanksgiving, addressed high school banquets, scheduled a game with Nebraska, spoke to the New York Illini Club on December 27, and attended meetings of college and high school students in Ames, Iowa, on January 16, 1923. In March, he spoke at a Boys' Work conference. In April, Huff responded to a South Dakota State professor's questions about Zuppke's salary. He couldn't conceive of "how the scandalmongers so persistently make misstatements about the coach's salary." He declared that the salary was less than half of that of the president, and that the coach received no percentage of gate receipts or salary from alumni. He also denied that Zuppke cursed and struck players or used dope to get the team to the "proper fighting pitch." On April 21, Zuppke joined Minnesota alumni in Minneapolis in an appeal for a two-million-dollar stadium for the Twin Cities. He also reminded prospective donors that college athletics was not a sideshow, nor the university a circus. In May, he urged the audience at a twilight concert to pay their stadium pledges. In the spring, he began annual trips with the Illinois baseball team on its pre-season southern tour. He was a very democratic and genial "life of the party" on the trips and while watching track meets. One player remarked that while he was a regular comedian in the spring, you ought to see him in football season when he was after the boys.[2]

In the fall, the returning players were joined by members of a strong 1922 freshman team. In the spring practices, Zuppke drilled the team on fundamentals and concentrated on building a strong defensive line. Two promising backs had transferred to Northwestern and Michigan, but among the new players was Harold E. Grange from Wheaton. Zuppke declared that the prospects were better than in 1921 and 1922, when the teams won only three conference games and lost eight. Seventy candidates reported for practice, which started at three in the afternoon and ended at five forty-five, so that the players could have hot meals in their fraternity houses. Of the eighty who tried out for the varsity, fifty-three made the team. The prospect of the new stadium and a strong eight-game schedule created a demand for tickets. The season opened on October 6 with a 24–7 win over Missouri Valley champion Nebraska. Although not listed on varsity football charts, sophomore Harold "Red" Grange scored three touchdowns. He added two more touchdowns in a 21–7 win over Butler and one in a 9–6 win at Iowa. On October 27, when Illinois played Northwestern before 33,000 at the Cubs' baseball park in Chicago, Grange scored three touchdowns. On November 3, Illinois hosted the Chicago Maroons in the first game at the new stadium. Governor Len Small, Senators Medill McCormick and William B. McKinley, Chicago president E.D. Burton, baseball commissioner Kenesaw M. Landis and other dignitaries were among the 61,319 spectators. Trustee Robert Carr invited the entire Industrial Club of Chicago to join him as guests on a special train. The Industrial Club responded with a resolution requesting legislative support for the university's budget. In the mud-splashed crowd were 7,500 Chicago rooters. Huddled in the rain beneath umbrellas, boxes and newspapers, a few complained about plowing through a sea of mud to reach the stadium. Grange's third-quarter touchdown supplied the margin in a 7–0 win. Chicago radio station KYW broadcasted the game, and hundreds of appreciative letters were received from owners of wireless crystal sets. A week later, 21,400 saw Illinois defeat unbeaten Wisconsin 10–0 in the first Dad's Day game in the stadium. A 5–0 season was concluded at Ohio Stadium, when Grange ran for a 32-yard touchdown. Zuppke defined interference as a service and asked the team to render service. The Illinois defense had given up one touchdown in five Big Ten games.[3]

The post-season banquets were celebrations of the championship. The Champaign Rotary Club's football banquet on November 26 featured President Kinley's defense of college athletics. He maintained that a great increase in receipts from the successful season in the new stadium represented healthy growth and did not involve "corruption." Huff defended large stadiums for the people of the state. Dean Kendric Babcock listed great moments. Kinley's was the passage of the appropriation bill. Huff's was seeing the Homecoming crowd in the stadium. Zuppke's was the end of the Ohio game, which gave Illinois an 8–0 record. Mike Tobin was toastmaster at the November 8 banquet in Chicago. As the final speaker, Zuppke covered "the whole range of human endeavor from Adam to dropping Wisconsin from the 1924 schedule." Alumni were kept in an uproar with his cyclonic sallies. The Illini Club program paid tribute to the team's tremendous spirit of aggressiveness inspired by our Zup. The closing string of five consecutive games without giving up a point was recognized by Walter Eckersall in a *Chicago Tribune* article: "Few of the Zuppke elevens can be said to have been weak defensively." He also praised the coach for building offensive plays around the talents of his players.[4]

The celebrations of the championship season overshadowed major changes in Illinois football. The commercial possibilities of the intercollegiate game were revealed by the contrast between the 4,154 tickets that were sold for a game with a strong Nebraska team at Illinois Field, and the first game in the new stadium. For the Chicago game, 52,000 tickets were sold to the public, 2,879 complimentary tickets were distributed, including 960 to the press. In the third game in the stadium against Mississippi A&M, free tickets were provided for 9,600 prospective Illini from high schools.[5]

The 1924 season began with a close 9–6 win over Nebraska and a 40–0 rout of Butler. The stadium was dedicated at the October 18, 1924, homecoming game, when Illinois hosted Michigan, which had not lost a game since 1921. Zuppke employed psychology in his careful preparation of the players for the game. He gave a rousing and painfully loud talk at the Friday evening rally in the Armory. Halfback Harold "Red" Grange scored four touchdowns in the first twelve minutes to lead the team to a 39–14 victory. He credited three of his end runs for touchdowns to Zuppke's strategy of having him cut back after he was outside the defensive end. Walter Eckersall commended Zuppke for evolving the plays for Grange and developing the open field blocking that led to Grange's running for 402 yards and passing for 64 yards. His five touchdowns and 473 yards gained became Illinois' single-game record.

Many of the 66,639 spectators came on twenty-one special trains, which lined the railroad sidings. The sale of 58,145 tickets produced a profit of $74,127. After decisive wins over DePauw and Iowa, Illinois met Chicago on November 8. Stagg's heavier team played a ground-gaining possession offense in building a 21–7 lead. In the second half, Grange led an Illinois rally that produced a 21–21 tie. A month after the Michigan game, the Illini lost a 21–7 game at Minnesota's stadium dedication. A win over Ohio State enabled them to finish the season tied with Iowa for second place. Chicago's Maroons were champions with three wins and three ties.[6]

Grange's four touchdowns against Michigan in the stadium dedication game became implanted in the minds of the sporting public. The rest of the story was the continued development of the commercial marketing of football in the stadium. The program depended on gate receipts. The difficult

Harold "Red" Grange, Zuppke and Earl Britton, 1925. Courtesy *The News-Gazette.*

game at Nebraska brought in half of the gate at Lincoln. The Michigan game was preceded and followed by easy home wins over Butler and Depauw. These games drew 21,903 spectators, but only 3,871 tickets were sold. Students admitted on coupons accounted for 10,959. Mike Tobin issued press passes for 590 sportswriters. Football players received 284 passes. At the Depauw game, fifty-eight gatemen and ushers welcomed 5,577 high school students. Three Big Ten home games provided most of the football income.

Table 11.1 Attendance of the Three Big Ten Home Games

Game	Attendance	Local Fans	Visitors	Students	President Guests	Press
Michigan	66,639	48,075	10,072	6,760	746	793
Iowa	31,330	22,460	1,028	6,855	43	536
Ohio State	27,378	16,887	2,524	6,824	87	587

A capacity crowd at Chicago and another stadium dedication in Minnesota provided Illinois shares amounting to $78,527.[7]

While the Athletic Association organized the marketing of commercial football, Zuppke's players had a different perspective. Dwight Follett, a fullback on the 1924 team, recalled that every fall he remembered the sound of crashing lines at old Illinois Field; the battle cry "Get in there, you bloke!"; the creak of the tackling dummy; the smell of leather, wintergreen oil, and wool jerseys; the burn of benzine on taped ankles; the warmth of a hot shower; and the memories of a vital little man in an enormous lambskin-lined coat. He remembered most the Friday evenings at the country club before an open fire with Zuppke trying to relight a half-inch cigar that had gone out while he was telling stories about the giants and boobs of other days. He continued, "I can see you walking back and forth, head down, hands behind your back. I can almost hear you tell about the game tomorrow and feel the surge of excitement that sends a shiver down my back and leaves my legs weak."[8]

A successful season brought heavy demands for public speaking. At the November 24 Champaign football banquet, George Huff announced that the coach had signed a new contract. The press reported rumors that Zuppke refused offers from Princeton, Columbia and Wisconsin. Zuppke declared that Grange was greater than Jack Dempsey and Babe Ruth because he played "for the glory of his school, and not for big money." At the December 5 coaches meeting in Chicago, he announced that Illinois would play Knute Rockne's Notre Dame team on October 10, 1925. While Butler later replaced the Irish on the schedule, both Zuppke and Rockne received the publicity. On December 6, Zuppke spoke at the Chicago football dinner. Between December 24, 1924, and May 6, 1925, he addressed thirty organizations. In New York for the NCAA meetings, he spoke at the Players Club, the Physical Education Association and the Football Coaches Banquet. January travel involved trips to Monticello and Freeport, Illinois. In February, he searched for linemen at spring football practice and spoke at the Chicago Commonwealth Club, at the Rockford University Club and to groups in four other Illinois cities. In March, he spoke to four organizations in St. Louis, two in Buffalo and Mattoon, and one at Syracuse University. In April, his itinerary included Pittsburgh, Grand Rapids, Elkhart and two meetings in Illinois. On May 2, the coach addressed a meeting at Onarga Military Academy and, on May 6, a young engineers meeting in Chicago. Mike Tobin distributed enthusiastic press commentary on Zuppke's speeches in East St. Louis, Pekin, Pittsburgh, Rockford, and Springfield.[9]

The years 1925 was "the year of the big mud" at Illinois. It rained at the home games with Nebraska, Michigan and Chicago. While the Illini won four of their other five games, Red Grange and his smaller and faster teammates were able to score only thirteen points in the three mud games. The Illini lost a 14–0 opening game to a Nebraska team coached by Zuppke's former assistant Ernest Bearg. Large parties of state legislators and journalists watched the 3–0 loss to Michigan and the 13–6 win over Chicago. Grange gained national fame on October 31, 1925, when he led an Illinois team with three losses to a 24–2 victory at Pennsylvania, which was the leading team in the East. In all, 62,000 fans watched Zuppke's "perfect football machine" dominate a team that had not lost a game in two years. The intersectional victory brought national acclaim and supported Zuppke's claims for the superiority of midwestern football. It also brought reports that Grange would turn professional. After a season-ending 14–9 win at Ohio State, Grange signed a professional contract with his agent, C.C. Pyle, and the Chicago Bears. George Halas, an end on Zuppke's 1917 team, was a co-owner and coach of the Bears. Grange had finished his eligibility to play college football, but Zuppke attempted to persuade him to complete his course work and then accept other more permanent offers. Grange had accumulated about 87 of the 130 hours needed for graduation. Without the demands of football practices and games, he could have completed his academic work in another year or two. The examples of a half-dozen Illini who were playing professional football with the Bears and Pyle's offer of instant wealth persuaded him to seize the opportunity to join the Bears.[10]

The Memorial Stadium had provided the setting for Zuppke's productions and Grange's exploits. While Grange's second and third years on the Illinois varsity had not produced championships, spectators thronged to the new stadium. Intercollegiate football in the new venue entertained thousands of visitors and strengthened ties between the university, its alumni and taxpayers On game days, excursion trains lined the Illinois Central sidings a quarter of a mile west of the stadium. Hard roads also brought thousands of additional spectators to watch the football games. In 1925, football income was $305,283. In his three years at Illinois, Grange had played in Champaign, Iowa City, Evanston, Columbus, Lincoln, Chicago, Minneapolis, and Philadelphia. As a professional, he joined George Halas's touring company. Playing for spectators across the nation, the "Galloping Ghost" made $370,000 in New York and received extensive press coverage. Most of his earnings were deposited in the Illinois Savings and Trust Company in Champaign. The *Literary Digest* described his defection as a shameful example of gridiron demoralization and blamed the president and faculty for not advising him. A friend of David Kinley reported that Red was putting the University of Illinois on the map and that he was glad of it. Kinley disapproved of the newspaper agitation about Grange and said that they should mind their own business.[11]

When the season ended, Zuppke spoke at football banquets in Champaign, Chicago and Detroit. Grange returned for the Champaign banquet and was "bawled out" by Zuppke for turning professional. Zuppke was more concerned about losing additional players to the professional game. Despite his unhappiness, Grange regarded his former coach with the greatest respect. After the banquets, Zup and Fannie headed for Southern California. On January 15, 1926, he held the Los Angeles Illini Club audience spellbound for forty-five minutes. He chatted with Grange at the dinner and then joined a thousand Illini, who were among the 62,000 fans who watched Grange and the Chicago Bears defeat the Los Angeles Tigers. Red made $50,000 in Los Angeles, and critics of the commercialization of college football cited the Bears' nationwide exhibition tour as an example. Grange's early departure for a professional career challenged the Big Ten's amateurism standard. On December 16, 1926, Commissioner Griffith sought to discourage defections with a memorandum to athletics directors on the failure of C.C. Pyle's American League and the losses sustained by the National Football League. Despite criticism from *Literary Digest*, *New Republic* and *Colliers*, Grange's decision did no harm to the university and the Illinois football program. In April 1933, Red returned to Champaign in a glittering Stutz roadster for a vaudeville engagement. Zuppke introduced him to a thousand students at a smoker as the greatest football player. Red credited Zup for his success. Boston sportswriter Bill Cunningham likened Zuppke to an architect and Grange as his artistic masterpiece. Grange did not return to complete a degree, but was a loyal supporter of the university and successful in his chosen professions. His success in college and professional football led to motion picture contracts in 1926–29, a career in radio and television sportscasting from 1934 to 1964, and an insurance business from 1941 to 1952. He also served on the university's Board of Trustees from 1950 to 1955.[12]

12

Renewed Glory

In Grange's last two years at Illinois, Zuppke's team finished in second and fourth place in the Big Ten. The coach faced the challenge of developing a new championship team. The year of the big mud had convinced the Athletic Association to purchase a rubberized fabric raincoat to protect the Memorial Stadium field. In the spring of 1926, he returned to Illinois and accompanied the track team to the Drake Relays before spring practice. In all, 123 candidates tried out for the varsity and 305 for the freshman team, from whom 58 and 127 were selected for fall practice. In the summer, the Zuppkes went to Pullman, Washington, where Bob taught a four-week football course at Washington State. After a week in Seattle, they took a three-week tour of Alaska before visiting Bob's parents in Long Beach.[1]

Without Grange, the Illini had a second 2–2 Big Ten season. They defeated Iowa 13–6, and Chicago 7–0, and lost to Michigan 13–0, and Ohio State 7–6. They won their three regional games with Coe, Butler and Wabash and a second intersectional match with Pennsylvania. An official at the Penn game praised Zuppke's "real smart" team, which took advantage of every opportunity and never called a wrong play. Their defensive alignments stifled the Quakers' offense, and Forest "Frosty" Peters dropkicked a field goal. From Billings, Montana, Peters found housing at the Champaign Fire Department. The press hailed him as the "fireman" to replace Grange, the departed Wheaton "iceman." His kicks also supplied the winning margin in the Iowa game. Forced to kick from midfield against Michigan, he missed three times. At the Illini Club smoker before the Chicago game, Zuppke made "his customary survey of mankind from cavemen to tea-hounds" and praised Russ Daugherity as "our greatest football player." The half back responded the next day, when he ran for the only touchdown.[2]

Win or lose, the alumni celebrated the team's performances at the post–season banquets. Knute Rockne appeared at the Champaign banquet. After Zuppke's introductory remarks about his bald head, the Notre Dame coach gave his pep talk on purpose, enthusiasm and perseverance. The December 4 Chicago Illini Club event featured tributes to George Huff, who was recovering from surgery while in Europe. Zuppke's oration closed the proceedings. Unable to keep up with the speech, the *Alumni News* obtained notes from his office after Zup had left for California. Among the ten items were "The aim of our university should be the unfolding of personality." and "Most of our university courses teach the theory of life, whereas some of our extracurricular activities introduce the human element and thus realize the practice of life." He concluded by cautioning that athletic activity, like life, was not an unmixed blessing.[3]

Extensive publicity during the Grange years continued to attract talented football players to enroll at Illinois and enhanced Zuppke's reputation. Red Grange recalled that "every kid in Illinois wanted to play for Coach Zuppke if he thought he could make it." The September 30, 1926, *Big Ten Weekly* described Zuppke as a striking individualist, rare iconoclast, great kidder, remarkable student of psychology and best backfield coach in the business. A February 12, 1927, *Liberty* article listed him as one of the Big Three in college football coaching. After discussing Michigan's Fielding Yost and Notre Dame's Knute Rockne, Hugh Fullerton described Zuppke as the keenest and most analytical type of coach and added that "the talkative, merry, witty little Dutchman" was supreme in football. Noting the twenty-five million paid attendance at college games, Fullerton quoted Zuppke's statement that football made the United States college conscious. Zuppke "rides them hard — calling them nicknames, scolding, chattering, ridiculing — but he gets the lesson over to them." He fraternizes with his players, lets them be as familiar as they please, and jokes with them constantly, but familiarity does not ruin respect with this "little fellow." Such national publicity helped recruitment. Zuppke denied that Notre Dame and Rockne built up college football and attributed its popularity to automobile transportation, that is good roads and Henry Ford. The growing interest in football also prompted increased criticism of the commercial exploitation of players who lacked academic ability and the exalted status of coaches. In 1927, President David Kinley condemned hiring players, giving monetary inducements to high school students to go to particular institutions because of their prospective athletic prowess and employing and paying coaches with the idea of getting winning teams, irrespective of the methods employed.[4]

After three rebuilding years, Zuppke's teams won conference championships in 1927 and 1928. On September 15, 1927, he opened his fall practice with eighty-four candidates. Fox, International and Kinograph newsmen took motion pictures. Worldwide, Pacific and Atlantic, and Underwood men took still photographs. After two hot days, the coach held a two-and-a-half-hour scrimmage. Following time for registration, the practice continued until seven in the evening. The weary team was then bused to a turkey dinner as a reward for their efforts. A week later, Zuppke followed President Kinley and George Huff in speaking at the annual "Freshman Welcome." Kinley spoke about the Ephebic Pledge taken by Athenian youth as they began gymnastic, military and literary training for citizenship. Huff discussed good sportsmanship, courtesy and respect. He warned against too much emphasis on athletics. The student newspaper reported that Zuppke concluded the session by saying exactly the opposite. He placed physical education first and said that he didn't care whether we won or lost, as long as we won.[5]

Zuppke's 1927 team was light, but speedy, and had a strong defensive line. They began the season with a 19–0 win over visiting Bradley. In a steady rain, he used many reserves and intricate and deceptive plays, often without a huddle. Taking advantage of rules changes, he used shifts and a back in motion. The next two games were a 58–0 defeat of Butler and a sobering 12–12 tie with Iowa State. Moving to the Big Ten schedule, he used frequent substitutions. On October 22, Illinois edged Northwestern 7–6. A week later, Illinois defeated Michigan before a capacity Homecoming crowd of 63,000, including 1,123 admissions on press passes. The Illini closed the season with a 14–9 win at Iowa, a 40–0 trouncing of Chicago and an 8–0 victory in Ohio Stadium. At the five home games, 150,000 happy spectators purchased 22,506 boxes of weiners, 221 boxes of cigarettes, fifty-seven boxes of cigars and 1,122 boxes of candy bars, including the last ninety-two boxes of "Red Grange" bars, which were consumed by 2,500 Boy Scouts at the Bradley game. The concessions sales produced $5,155 for student activities.[6]

To celebrate the sixth championship season, the university held a November 21 football convocation in its new gymnasium. President Kinley congratulated the team on its success. George Huff attributed their achievements to every man doing his best. Zuppke reminded the university's 12,000 students that they were in a small nest compared with the world, even though they included plenty of "hard-boiled eggs." He advised them to keep moving, thus to fight against time. He explained that the team's success was due to harmony, exactness, speed, punctuality and enthusiasm. After a distribution of awards and the reading of congratulatory telegrams, the team "roared off in a big Pierce-Arrow coach" to the Rotary banquet at the Champaign Country Club. Huff told the players that their football careers were just incidents in their lives and that success would come in other fields. After Justa Lindgren passed out sweaters, Captain Bob Reitsch thanked Assistant Coach Milt Olander. President Kinley defended his support of football and said that any evils in the sport were due to the behavior of the general public and the alumni. He concluded by saying that he loved Zup in spite of his vagaries.

Branch Rickey then talked about Michigan and baseball. Zuppke closed the proceedings with remarks about Mike Tobin, Frosty Peters, Butch Nowack, President Kinley, Arthur Schopenhauer and Friedrich Nietzsche. His accolades for his publicity man, a talented but sulking quarterback, next year's captain, the diminutive president and two German philosophers were as varied as his coaching game plans. In excellent humor, he confided that he was obstreperous, but added that his beloved old electric car ran slowly and gave him time to think. His comments about the team were more friendly than usual and included some especially kind words for the coaching staff. After praising track coach Harry Gill and George Huff, he ended with "Our defense is our home. Cooperation, harmony, lack of envy, strong hearts — that is our combination."[7]

On December 3, the oratorical scene shifted from Champaign to the Chicago Illini Club's football banquet. At the banquet, Illinois captain Bob Reitsch had received the Rissman national championship trophy. In explaining the factors that led to their success, Reitsch listed a coach who knew his business and had an offensive and defensive system. "We knew the rest was up to us. When Zup told us that he had confidence in us, it made us proud and resolved to merit his belief. Zup never drove us too hard and he took good care that we wouldn't go stale." Knute Rockne of Notre Dame got in some good cracks at Zuppke's expense, but praised him for the difficult schedules he played. After several football stories, Rockne concluded with observations on Zuppke's reading habits. He mentioned the little Dutchman's "pocket editions of the psychology classics" that he carried around with him and read with all the "fiery enthusiasm" he used in "whooping the team up and down the field." George Huff praised Rockne as one of the two greatest football coaches in the world and recommended him to Kinley as a potential vice president. He predicted that the Carnegie Foundation report on college athletics would cause a sensation and hoped that it would be specific about rules violations and give actual instances. Zuppke admitted that Rockne was a better storyteller, but said that he had to depend only on coaching for his living. He said that "Lindy and I, we old piles of bones, we used our heads, and sat on the bench, while Olander and others took the team up and down the field." His speech meandered to such sensitive topics as "the covering up for Northwestern and the no covering up for Michigan." He made staccato references to the co–eds, the swing-pushers, the anti–curricular rather than the extracurricular, "the price is always punishment" and "the greatest responsive team I ever coached." President Kinley said that he was there to protect Zup, but that Robert appeared to be able to take care of himself. He then spoke on the alleged evils of college football. He dealt with the accusations of over–excitement, excessive interest, distortion of values, commercialization, drinking, betting, coaches' salaries, and attempts to equate ethical and economic values. In considering the coaches' salaries, he referred to the peculiar factors in the work of the coach that justified a higher salary than that received by teachers of other subjects. In any event, he insisted that institutional control of finances was essential.[8]

Zuppke's banter with Rockne was an expression of a strong personal relationship with the Notre Dame coach. Zup signed himself as "cordially yours, without vitriol" and "hoping that your bald dome will continue to glitter even more than the golden dome of Notre Dame." Rock responded with "your ideas were always interesting if not good." Both coaches wrote newspaper articles, exchanged information on teams, and broadcasted football games. After the 1925 Pennsylvania game, Rock congratulated Zup for "the fine way you showed up eastern football," which tended to make up for "the way that we fell down on the job" in the Army game. When Notre Dame began planning for a new stadium, they exchanged views on architects and construction. Rockne attended the Illinois interscholastic relays in his search for football talent. In 1929, Zup felt that Rock's new formations "would do justice for you." Rock hoped that Illinois would win another championship, despite the handicap of high expectations in the press. After Zup's season ended on November 23, he used Rockne's tickets to attend the Army-Notre Dame game in New York. Rockne had been confined with a circulatory illness, missed the annual coaches' meeting in New York, and was unable to deliver "several snappies" that he had been saving. The 7–0 victory of the Fighting Irish completed a 9–0 season. Appearing at a Notre Dame banquet, Zup had "one of the greatest evenings of my life," which included a mass at three o'clock in the morning with seven Notre Dame men.[9]

By 1927, the national football powers in other regions had replaced the Ivy League and Chicago in press ratings. According to Commerce professor Frank Dickinson's system, the Illini were 21.5 compared to Pittsburgh's 21.42, Minnesota's 20.88, Notre Dame's 20.83 and Yale's 20.0. At the close of the season, newspapers listed the top nine college teams during the 1923–27 period. In games won and lost, Illinois was seventh behind Notre Dame, Southern Methodist, Alabama, Washington, Stanford and Michigan, and ahead of Washington and Jefferson and Army. In points scored, they were eighth. In points allowed, they were third. Sportswriters used comparative scores as the primary means of rating teams.[10]

Zuppke's post–season speeches continued through the winter. On December 28, he addressed the Rochester, New York, Advertising Club, whose 225 members sat and "snortled with glee" as Zup put across in thirty-five minutes what the ordinary speaker would have taken from ten days to two weeks to say. The reporter described Zup as "one of the most interesting, colorful, forceful (and most incoherent) speakers to whom it has ever been our pleasure to listen." On January 24, 1928, Zuppke was in Pittsburgh for the university's football banquet. After a luncheon with his hosts and Illini guests, he told stories until 3:30 P.M. In the evening, his humorous stories were a big hit at the banquet. On the 26th, he made appearances in Peoria for a talk to Bradley students in the afternoon and an address at the Peoria Illini Club banquet in the evening, where he scored "several touchdowns with his highly interesting and humoristic address." On February 2, he gave the main address to 246 guests at the annual banquet of the St. Louis Illini Club. The toastmaster introduced Zuppke as a great artist, psychologist, and opportunist and then tossed aside the cowbell used to time speakers. Zuppke proclaimed that he was to provide the rough element in the program and "rattled hurriedly over Socrates, Xantippe, Plato, Schopenhauer, Pavlowa, or what have you." "And as for Pavlowa," he roared, "what of her? Nobody ever tried to knock her down." He was comparing a dance by Anna Pavlowa to a touchdown run by Red Grange. For Zuppke, the only difference was that Grange expressed his artistic rhythm on a gridiron and her art was that of the stage. The coach also referred to tackle Butch Nowack and how he tried to shoot the mule, to Nowack's coal mine "tipple number 1 team playing against tipple number 2," and to Sir Oliver Lodge, the deep blue sea, the blue birds against the olive background, and the colt full of oats. "Why," he thundered, "even old Erasmus was complaining about over–emphasis." By this time, the crowd hardly knew whether "to laugh or cry." His oddly assorted philosophy, psychology, philology and anthropology brought yells of delight from the hilarious Illini. He gave his famous simile, "Football is to physical culture as a bullfight is to agriculture." He closed with "Hope springs eternal. If hope is with you, you are champions for life." Warmed by his efforts, Zup spent the rest of the night talking philosophy with a post–banquet gathering of alumni on the west side. On February 23, he spoke on alumni criticism and football letters at the Decatur Illini Club stag dinner.[11]

After summer travel to California, Oklahoma, Nebraska and Pennsylvania, Zuppke returned on September 15, 1928, to open fall practice on the twenty-third with a lecture on the philosophy of football. With the aid of his six assistant coaches, he selected twenty-six players from the eighty-six varsity candidates. The Illini won seven games, losing only a 3–0 game at Michigan. The home game with Northwestern drew 59,871 spectators, including 8,168 holders of student coupon books, 5,354 Northwestern fans and 3,702 recipients of complimentary tickets. The strong defense gave up only ten points in five conference games. The 4–1 record brought Zuppke's seventh, and final, Big Ten championship.[12]

One of college football's blessings for the university's Athletic Association was folding money. Five home games and trips to Ann Arbor and Indianapolis resulted in a football income of $309,020 that nearly equaled the 1925 record (table 12.1).

Table 12.1. Illinois Football Income

Game	Score	Attendance	Illinois Income
Bradley	33–6	21,477	$970
Coe	31–0	8,562	1,220
Indiana	13–7	26,683	22,330
Northwestern	6–0	59,871	69,732
Michigan	0–3	83,109	100,719
Butler	14–0	10,000	8,990
Chicago	40–0	48,714	70,023
Ohio State	8–0	35,712	35,086
	145–16	294,128	$309,070[13]

The financial achievements of the Illinois football program and its publicizers were impressive. Despite their location in a small market community, they were competitive with the programs of Big Ten universities in or near large metropolitan areas. A 1931 survey provided comparative data on annual football profits for the 1927–29 period.

Michigan	$403,400
Minnesota	348,500
Illinois	313,000
Ohio State	290,400
Chicago	262,300
Northwestern	not available
Wisconsin	186,200
Iowa	142,400
Indiana	71,500
Purdue	44,900

After the 1928 football season, Zuppke entertained the audience at the Champaign Rotary Club banquet and shared the glory with line coach Justa Lindgren. Lindgren was also honored by the Aurora Illini Club, where a chemistry professor identified Lindy as the man who made Mr. Zuppke famous. At the Chicago banquet, President Kinley praised Huff, Zuppke and Lindgren. Ohio State coach John Wilce lauded the Illini coach as the greatest coach in the world. Zup praised his fellow Milwaukeean as a coach among coaches. He also emphasized the importance of publicity in projecting football success to the world. He added that his eastern travels were to have his "unfertilized ideas fertilized." At the December 17 Springfield Civic Club banquet, Zup delighted 600 men with his combination of philosophy, aphorisms, and his praise for Grange.[14]

The 1928 Illini won championships in football and four other sports. However, George Huff said the outstanding event of the year was the students' adoption of the Illini Code of Sportsmanship, which stated that "A True Illini Sportsman"

1. Will consider all athletic opponents as guests and treat them with all the courtesy due friends and guests.
2. Will accept all decisions of officials without question.
3. Will never hiss or boo a player or official.
4. Will never utter abusive or irritating remarks from the sideline.
5. Will applaud opponents who make good plays or show good sportsmanship.
6. Will never attempt to rattle an opposing player, such as the pitcher in a baseball game or a player attempting to make a free throw in a basketball game.
7. Will seek to win by fair and lawful means, according to the rules of the game.
8. Will love the game for its own sake and not for what winning may bring him.
9. Will "do unto others as he would have them do unto him."
10. Will "win without boasting and lose without excuses."

Huff had rejected an NCAA athletic creed and was unimpressed by the eastern universities domination of the NCAA because they were longer on talk than they were on accomplishment. He also dismissed a Big Ten Code of Honor. Strong administrative and alumni support for Huff at Illinois, Stagg at Chicago and Yost at Michigan indicated the extent to which athletics directors had eclipsed faculty representatives in managing college athletics.[15]

13

Academic Criticism

From its emergence in the 1890s, there had been academic criticisms of big-time football. Harvard president Charles W. Eliot, Cornell professor Burt Wilder, Wisconsin professor Frederick J. Turner and Chicago president Robert M. Hutchins called for the abolition or drastic de-emphasis of intercollegiate football. The crisis years of 1905–10 led to reforms in rules and scheduling limitations, but few colleges chose to abolish a popular and profitable sport. In December 1922, the NCAA Football Rules Committee listed five problems resulting from the public demand for intercollegiate football. They were professionalism, gambling, proselytizing, eligibility and commercialism. The committee concluded that the enormous receipts produced by larger stadiums tended to make the modern, intensely spectacular game a great business proposition: "One to be conducted for the money that is in it." At the 1923 NCAA meeting, Charles Savage from Oberlin College accused universities of becoming great intercollegiate machines with expensive coaching staffs. He held that football had become a "mighty beast of the jungle" and "a real white elephant" that required corrective action. In its 1923 and 1925 annual reports, the Carnegie Foundation for the Advancement of Teaching issued its negative conclusions about athletic sports in colleges and universities. [1]

While Red Grange toured with the Chicago Bears, academic criticism of intercollegiate football gathered momentum. In January 1926, the Carnegie Foundation authorized a more extensive investigation of American college sports. In April, an American Association of University Professors committee published a report in the *AAUP Bulletin*, which called for immediate reforms. Members from sixteen universities and colleges, including two Illinois faculty members, charged that football caused a distortion of values and that the financial rewards available at once to the successful player who turns professional are such as to unsettle ideas and ideals. The AAUP report also proposed faculty status and pay for coaches. New England reformers went further in proposing four-game seasons, one-year eligibility, captains to replace coaches and an end to intersectional contests. University administrators denied that abuses on their campuses were as bad as alleged by the AAUP committee. They also doubted the wisdom of a direct attack on college football.[2]

The preparation of the Carnegie study ignited extensive media coverage. In May, Carnegie Foundation president Henry S. Pritchett condemned commercialism and mass rivalry in college sports. The *New York Times* hailed the investigation as a keen and realistic diagnosis of the college athletic evil. Both Pritchett and the *Times* added condemnations of democratic slogans and the rising tide of admitting students with mediocre natural ability. As record numbers of spectators attended games, *Forum* ran a series of articles on deflating or abolishing collegiate football. Albert Dashiell attacked the "national religion of football." Morton Price called for the elimination of professional coaches. Upton Sinclair launched an attack on the alumni and townspeople in the "plutocratic world" who funded commercialized college athletics as "organized class privilege." He suggested the elimination of gate receipts, reducing the pay of overesteemed coaches and mass athletic contests.[3]

Other responses presented cautionary viewpoints. The *New York Times* editorialized that the idea that young men may be made to hero-worship scholarship by blocking their tendency to hero-worship athletic prowess involved a non sequitur of the kind that led to the prohibitionist Volstead Act. Cautioning against democratizing universities, Yale president James R. Angell lamented that "the great public that ultimately supports education has a good deal more appreciation of athletics, and especially of football and all that it symbolizes, than it has of distinguished Greek scholars." He also used the prohibition analogy in citing the thirst for the collegiate experience that was almost as urgent with eager youth as was the craving for alcohol with arid middle age. Abraham Flexner, a professional educational reformer, found no justification for the "athletic orgy" and denounced colleges and universities that were "mad on the subject of competitive and intercollegiate athletics" and too timid to tell their alumni that excessive interest in intercollegiate athletics was proof of the cultural mediocrity of the college student.[4]

As pressure mounted to de-emphasize football, Big Ten commissioner John Griffith sent a May 25, 1925, memorandum on amateurism to 10,000 high school principals and coaches. In September 1926, he published a conference athletics directors' agreement on equal competition and illegitimate recruiting for use in an educational campaign among alumni. The illegitimate recruiting agreement banned loans and scholarships, unless made by a faculty committee whose duty was to support needy and worthy students. It also banned coaches from corresponding with or interviewing prospective high school athletes and forbade soliciting alumni or student assistance in recruiting, such as urging fraternity men to rush prospective athletes. The athletic directors were to discourage alumni from sending athletes to a game or the university and understood that coaches would not attend interscholastic athletic meets to contact athletes. High school principals were requested to report any violations of the agreement or the amateur rule to the commissioner. While field workers gathered data, the Carnegie Foundation provided Griffith with typical extracts on proselytizing and subsidizing athletics. Griffith added that there were reports of cases in the Big Ten, mentioned that names of institutions might be given in the Carnegie report, and urged athletics directors to join the campaign.[5]

The Carnegie investigation leaks had an effect at Illinois and in the Big Ten. Nearly half of President Kinley's 1927 "Thoughts About Education" concerned the athletic program. He maintained that football was not conducted in order to make a profit and that the size of the enterprise did not make it bad. Speaking to the Midwest Student Conference, Zuppke defended college sports as interesting, stimulating and provocative. In response to the Carnegie investigation, the Big Ten office compiled information on scholarships, loans and employment provided for athletes. Illinois awarded twenty-three scholarships, loaned $2,900 to thirteen individuals and had thirty-one athletes employed on campus. Illinois and Northwestern led the conference in scholarships awarded to athletes. Most of the Illinois scholarships were established by law and awarded by state legislators without recommendations by the athletics department. Half of Northwestern's scholarships were made from the university's endowment fund and eight were awarded by alumni and business groups. Wendell S. Wilson was the only Illinois varsity football player to receive a scholarship. Two players received loans. The employed athletes included seventeen gatemen at athletic events and none were on the football team. While Illinois led the conference in the number of employed athletes, it was ninth in the amount loaned. The leaders in compensated employment were Northwestern, Indiana, Ohio State, Wisconsin, Iowa, Chicago and Michigan. No athletes at Michigan and Minnesota were reported as receiving scholarships, and none at Ohio State received loans.[6]

On January 28, 1927, the Big Ten conference called a Chicago meeting of a Special Committee of Sixty, including athletics directors, coaches, trustees, faculty representatives, administrators and alumni assembled to "crystallize sentiment on certain matters." The committee studied conference data and adopted positions defining legitimate scholarship awards, the roles of athletics directors, coaches, alumni and students in recruiting athletes, and rules for the employment of student athletes. Stagg and Yost were both coaches and athletics directors at their universities and were suspected of opposing any reforms. When a four-game schedule was proposed, Zuppke asked "who was going to pay their salaries and who was going to pay for intramural activities." He said that college presidents "didn't expect us to schedule ourselves out of business." His "corny speech" was effective and there was no curtailment of schedules. After the vote, he recalled that Stagg "put his arm around my shoulders and together we walked out of the room. I knew then that he had a lot of warmth about him." Some of Stagg's warmth may have been because of his respect for Zuppke's success in the annual games between Illinois and Chicago. Since 1914, Stagg's Maroons had won only two of the thirteen contests. On April 9, 1927, the Big Ten Alumni Committee followed the lead of the Committee of Sixty and proposed seven rules relating to recruiting and preserving the amateur status of athletes.[7]

The 1929 publication of Carnegie Bulletin 23 on "American College Athletics" was a direct challenge to athletic directors and football coaches. Although Illinois was the only public university in the Big Ten in a list of twenty-one American colleges and universities that did not use subsidies in recruiting athletes, it could not evade the broad charge of the commercialization of college football and the allegation that athletics were an over-rated by-product of the educational process. The Carnegie report noted the huge stadium at Illinois, which signified the commercialization of athletics. It also cast doubt on the validity of David Kinley's defense of Zuppke's salary as a case of supply and demand. Illinois also fitted the description of a state university engaged in "mass production in education" with open admissions. Tax-supported state universities could not restrict educational opportunities with the high tuitions and quotas employed by private institutions.[8]

Zuppke questioned the Carnegie critics' ability to attack a sport they did not understand and claimed that football was an educational experience for both players and spectators. In his view, the millions who attended college games testified to football's popularity as entertainment. This popular enthusiasm also provided a means of communicating with a mass audience about sportsmanship and institutions of higher education. Athletes capitalizing on their athletic prowess by becoming professionals also made higher education attractive to the public. Some athletes did not follow or finish the higher-education path. When Oak Park's Bart Macomber led Illinois to a 14–9 upset of Minnesota in 1916, he left school for the Orpheum vaudeville circuit. After a 14–9 victory over Ohio State on November 21, 1925, Harold "Red" Grange left for a contract with the professional Chicago Bears. A Seattle report described the touring halfback as "collegiate to the soles of his gold-bringing feet." Zuppke had failed to dissuade Grange from a professional career and reflected public opinion when he confessed that "we do not know when amateurism becomes professionalism." With Huff, he obtained George Halas's support for a National Football League rule that collegians would not be signed as professionals until their classes had graduated.[9]

Public reaction to the Carnegie Foundation's exposure of college football in "American College Athletics" reflected the varied interests of the respondents. Some academics and writers in journals of opinion hailed the criticism of college football and defended the amateur ideal. University administrators objected to the critics' neglect of the promotional and community benefits of football. Most sports columnists and local sportswriters were not impressed by the case for amateur purity and opposed reformation. Under pressure from the Carnegie study, the Big Ten handed Iowa a nine-month suspension in May 1929 for compensating student athletes.[10]

Amateurism, or sport for sport's sake, remained the underlying credo of college athletics. The trends toward high salaries paid to professional coaches and the hiring of more assistant coaches contrasted with the enforced amateurism of the players. The academic faculty envied the compensation and recognition accorded to successful coaches, who were well paid for their seasonal productions. The development of large universities, which involved the hiring of visiting lecturers, artists in residence, graduate assistants and researchers, further blurred distinctions between academic and staff professionalism and student amateurism. Gross inequalities in faculty compensation reflected the competitive academic marketplace, as well as the demands represented by legislative appropriations and the priorities of the university trustees. Administrators especially favored profitable university enterprises that captured public attention.

The problems of amateurism and financial aid for students engaged in college sports arose from the popularity of athletic competition in a society dominated by the ethos of market demand. After World War I, academic leadership became business minded and the academic curriculum had become inextricably tied to the nation's economic structure. The public demand for entertainment, corporate demand for accountants and engineers, government demand for lawyers and scientists, and popular demands for medical practitioners and performing artists shaped academic curricula, especially in state universities. Colleges of Agriculture, Engineering, Commerce and Physical Education developed rapidly in the same decades as intercollegiate athletics. The alumni of each college lobbied the state legislature through their professional associations. In public universities, the problems were compounded by institutional competition and legislative mandates for minimal admission standards.[11]

The authors of the Carnegie Bulletin and other critics singled out intersectional games as examples of the commercialization of amateur sports. Such games were sought for their financial return and the institutional publicity desired by administrators. In 1919–20, Northwestern, Indiana, Ohio State and Michigan played intersectional games. In 1921, Stagg had scheduled games with Princeton in a breach of a Big Ten agreement not to play intersectional games. From 1919 to 1931, Chicago, Indiana, Michigan and Ohio State played the most intersectional games. Purdue, Illinois and Northwestern played the fewest. Both Notre Dame and Army recruited football talent and scheduled games on a national basis. In 1923, they moved their profitable series to New York. Navy had dropped Army from its schedule for flaunting eligibility rules. In 1927, Notre Dame's football profit reached $529,400, some of which was used for faculty salaries, academic facilities and residence halls. Big Ten schools did not favor the barnstorming schedules adopted by Notre Dame. By the late 1920s, it became apparent that intersectional games brought valuable national publicity for the university and strengthened relationships with increasing numbers of alumni who lived in distant cities. On April 11, 1928, Kinley, Huff and Zuppke met with the Army graduate manager and coach "Biff" Jones and scheduled the Military Academy's first western game with a Big Ten team for Champaign in 1929, with a return match at New York's Polo Grounds in 1930.[12]

At Illinois, faculty criticisms of football were infrequent. A 1912 eligibility booklet, a 1915 faculty senate report and a 1923 committee report on athletics and public welfare related primarily to faculty control and compliance with conference rules. In 1930, incoming president Harry W. Chase appointed a Committee on the General Educational Organization and Administration of the University. In January 1931, this Committee of Nine invited faculty suggestions. Most responses dealt with the growing bureaucracy and budgetary problems. Of 103 letters with suggestions, three respondents favored reducing the evils of football, abolishing the Athletic Association and putting the coaches on the university payroll. Political science professor Clarence Berdahl believed that the major evil was in linking athletic participation with scholarship. As examples, he cited some faculty who favored athletes and granting academic rank to coaches. Engineering professor Cloyde Smith maintained that varsity players were professionals, who played for the possibility of cashing in on their reputations after graduation. He alleged that intercollegiate sports spectacles were part of a money-logged amusement industry and urged that bona fide undergraduates in good academic standing should compete regardless of past affiliations. He also contended that the Athletic Coaching School was a scholastic subsidy and that its curriculum was not on a par with science and engineering and lowered "already too low scholastic standards."[13]

Smith's letter was referred to a subcommittee on physical welfare that included both George Huff and mathematician Olive Hazlitt, who had signed the 1926 AAUP condemnation of college football. The subcommittee approved the 1923 report and the publication of the Athletic Association's financial statements. They concluded that athletic coaching courses corresponded very closely with comparable courses in other colleges and submitted grade distribution tables for agriculture, art, education and engineering curricula to refute the intellectual subsidy charge. The report of the faculty subcommittee on the relation of alumni to the university also addressed football. For them, it was a student activity, not an agency to advertise or make money. They added that the opportunity to foster a valuable and lasting feeling of loyalty was lost when students and instructors found that the Athletic Association had taken possession of their game, and that heavy subscribers to the stadium fund and members of the public willing to pay high prices were treated as having equal and even superior rights to theirs. The years 1931 was not a propitious time to confront taxpaying alumni and the public about the loyalty of students and instructors. The final committee report included recommendations for fiscal accountability and action to create a School of Physical Education.[14]

Coleman Griffith provided a more balanced view of college football as a performing art that publicized the university. Citing the Carnegie Report authors for a "sad and woeful lack of proper perspective," he noted that the immense size of the annual football public justified football as an end. He dismissed "thoughtless and ill-advised" attempts to eliminate the game. On the other hand, he disputed Zuppke's arguments that football could be justified as instinctive, character building and contributing to sportsmanship. As the gane was a function of the modern university, it should be studied as an "expression of the play spirit."[15]

The criticisms sparked by Carnegie Bulletin 23 continued in the 1930s. In 1931, Carnegie Bulletin 26 on "Current Developments in American College Sport" proclaimed the deflation of American football. It noted the negative impact of the economic decline on college football programs, cited reform efforts and discerned a loss of undergraduate enthusiasm for college sports. The AAUP repeated its attacks. In 1938, University of Chicago president Robert Hutchins proposed ten-cent admissions to eliminate commercialism in intercollegiate sports. In 1939, he persuaded Chicago's trustees to discontinue intercollegiate football. While Hutchins was able to ignore "the needs and taste of the public," administrators in public universities could not. The unique story of football's demise at Chicago had no parallel among land-grant universities. As Chicago's football fortunes declined from 1925 to 1939, a similar decline occured at Illinois as it failed to meet competition in the market for talented players. Large enrollments provided a pool of young men at Illinois, but the popularity of football created a seller's market. High school players looked for the best offer from a winning program, preferably located near their home city.[16]

Despite the lack of financial resources during the economic depression, football continued to grow in popularity. Autumnal alumni nostalgia, glamorous young athletic heroes, free publicity in newspaper sports pages, radio broadcasts, newsreels, motion pictures, building contracts for sports facilities, marching bands and cheerleaders, free tickets for state legislators and administrators and competition among universities all contributed to making college football an All-American sport. Its popularity as a means of community entertainment and identification had a strong appeal to both students and alumni as well as a statewide impact. As a present achievement, athletic success attracted more public attention than the potentialities of academic excellence.

14

Recruitment, Fraternities and Boosters

The Carnegie Bulletin identified the recruitment of athletes as a major problem in intercollegiate athletics. It listed coaches, alumni and fraternities as groups involved in personal recruiting. The Carnegie survey showed that fifty-one percent of the recruitment was done by athletics staff members, thirty-one percent by alumni and eight percent by administrative officers. Print media and students probably accounted for the remaining ten percent. Alumni referrals to athletics departments were a major method of identifying football talent. The letter winners in the Tribe of Illini were urged to take an active part in advocating and formulating athletic policies and recruiting. Coaches' speeches, alumni dinners, and free tickets and transportation were recruiting tools. The Big Ten's Rule XIX governed recruiting and subsidizing athletes. This somewhat unrealistic credo stated that coaches should not initiate correspondence, distribute literature or seek interviews to recruit athletes and that they should also discourage recruiting by alumni and students. It was somewhat vitiated by the conference commitment to home rule and the lack of a staff to investigate charges of rules violations, which allowed each university to police itself. Football coaches publicly condemned proselytizing and undue persuasion in recruiting, but their success and tenure was dependent on the quality of the players, or material, that entered their programs. The competition for prime talent often took precedence over compliance with conference rules.[1]

Eight of the Big Ten universities were public institutions that drew heavily upon their home states for both students and athletes. Illinois recruited in-state high school players in direct competition with Northwestern and Chicago. The conference's two private universities were located in the Chicago area, which was a leading supplier of football talent. Their location in the largest metropolitan area in the Midwest made them major competitors with the state university. In the twentieth century, the Chicago area supplied 20 percent of the Big Ten's football players, followed by Ohio and the Cleveland-Pittsburgh area with 10 percent each. Chicago, Ohio State and Illinois led the conference in the percentage of players from their home state. The primary Illinois talent pool was within the state. Of the 367 members of the 1914 to 1941 football teams, eighty-four percent were from 48 of Illinois' 102 counties, and sixteen percent were from 19 other states. Of the Illinois players, 30 percent were from Chicago and Cook County. Champaign County was second with 12 percent. Another 8 percent came from Aurora, Elgin and Rockford in Kane and Winnebago counties. The other half came from forty-two counties in northern and central Illinois. The only exception was Franklin County in the southern Illinois coal-mining region, which supplied 3 percent of the players.[2]

The Carnegie Foundation criticized the policy of tax-supported state colleges that admitted any high school graduate. All graduates of Illinois high schools accredited by the university's High School Visitor were certified for admission. Other students could be admitted by passing entrance examinations. Football players met these requirements. A substantial proportion of all university freshmen did not return after their first year. This attrition dropped gradually from 49 percent in 1920 to 24 percent in 1935. As football players were not eligible for intercollegiate competition until their sophomore year, most of those who made the varsity team also graduated. The percentages were 76 percent in 1914, 82 percent in 1919, 89 percent in 1924, 94 percent in 1933, 93 percent in 1938 and 82 percent in 1940. In the 1914 to 1940 period, 50 percent of the football players majored in education or physical education, 17 percent in business or commerce, 12 percent in engineering, 11 percent in liberal arts and sciences and 8 percent in agriculture. Established in 1918, the College of Education at Illinois required three units of English, one of algebra, one of plane geometry and ten electives. Students in athletic coaching and physical education were also required to pass physical and medical examinations.[3]

Academic critics challenged the relevance of intercollegiate football to higher education. In 1928, the Carnegie Foundation's twenty-second annual report cited poor performance of 1925 athletes at Columbia University. There were significant differences between the student bodies at private and public universities. At Illinois, a 1921–25 comparative study of four varsity athletic teams, four groups of students and general university grade averages showed that the athletes' averages were higher than the campus averages. Football trailed track, basketball and baseball, but was only a small fraction below the general university averages. The time required for practices and performances of undergraduates in games tended to affect course selection, special examinations, delays and grade point averages. At Illinois, the graduation percentages did not show a significant difference between athletes and other students.[4]

Coach Zuppke was a vocal opponent of proselytizing and often refused to contact prospective football players. His system relied on freshman coaches to sort out the promising players and then his positioning them, drilling them and selecting his starting eleven and their substitutes. He chose not to be involved in recruitment and enticement. He relied upon alumni referrals, coaching school contacts, interscholastic track meets, fraternity rushing, and employment offers to provide a large pool of prospects, from which the coaches selected the varsity players. He opposed payments to athletes and alleged that it would lead to the schools with the biggest bank balances cornering the market. It would make the game "a school of bad manners, vulgarity, subterfuge, evasion and brutality." Avoiding personal recruitment of players, he responded to the Carnegie Foundation condemnation of proselytizing by noting that nobody complained when the churches did it. He usually referred inquirers to the Admissions Office or the Registrar for admission requirements, to fraternities for housing, and to the Athletic Association for information on employment and financial aid. He pointed out that Illinois had no athletic scholarships or free rides. About 80 percent of the athletes at Illinois worked their way through school. Out-of-state boys needed additional funds even if they were successful in obtaining employment. He objected to a President's Office proposal to use legislative scholarships to attract players, as it would cause Illinois to be known as a proselytizing school. He thought that a political scholarship would bring bad publicity. He opposed alumni control of athletics and referred alumni and prospective students seeking financial aid to George Huff, who had a staff member who kept a list of athletes applying for jobs. After Huff's death in 1936, Bill Pfister, Athletic Association personnel director, placed student athletes. The Big Ten prohibited job offers until the student applied for admission and his high school credits had been accepted. With the cooperation of local business men, Pfister found employment for about half of the 350 applicants.[5]

The popularity of winning football appealed to many alumni as much as it did to administrators and students. In 1920, athletics director George Huff was president of the 3,267-member Alumni Association. The Illini Clubs supported university budget requests, took a keen interest in the success of the football team, and held football banquets. In the same year, the *Daily Illini* attacked Michigan for a policy of deliberately recruiting high school athletes. On June 2, 1923, and March 14, 1924, the Big Ten athletic directors sought to determine if alumni or other groups provided athletic scholarships or paid for student athletes to visit universities. A survey indicated that there were many charges that athletes were being hired, but little evidence of illegitimate recruiting. Huff urged alumni to talk to students about the advantages and entrance requirements at Illinois and follow the recruiting guidelines. Alumni, especially coaches and former players, often wrote to the coach for appointments to meet prospective student athletes.[6]

Inspired by the wave of concern about college sports, the Carnegie investigators found ample evidence of fraternity involvement in college football. They lacked direct experience in college football and an understanding of the complex role of fraternities in large state universities. After coaches and alumni, they listed fraternities as the third means of recruiting football players. They also cited interscholastic athletic meets on university campuses as occasions for fraternity "rushing" of prospective football players. In 1925, without a strong fraternity system, Chicago appointed an all-university rushing committee to attract high school athletes.[7]

During Zuppke's coaching career, fraternities were an essential part of the Illinois football program. They recruited talented high school athletes, hosted campus visitors, provided room and board for students, offered employment for athletes lacking financial resources, and provided social activities and academic assistance for members. The Athletic Association contacted fraternities for housing during visits by prospective players. Fraternities provided alumni-supported housing, social events, and academic assistance for students. They also provided room and board for needy students in exchange for service and maintenance work. Housing, academic assistance and room and board were important benefits for football players. Fraternity alumni were the most active group in urging athletes to attend the state university. Chapter newsletters reported the athletic records of pledges, news of the active members who made the football team, and players who lettered or were elected as captains. They also urged alumni to return to the campus for Homecoming and Dad's Day games and carried items on alumni in the coaching profession or playing professional football. Fall issues contained photographs of Zuppke and the team and descriptions of Homecoming house decorations.[8]

Fraternities and boarding houses were the two housing options for male students at Illinois. No dormitories existed. Nearly all the players on Illinois varsity football teams were fraternity members. They were not concentrated in one or two fraternities, but scattered among about sixty-one fraternity houses. Though there was a wide distribution of players, the most popular fraternities for football players were Delta Tau Delta, Phi Gamma Delta, Sigma Nu, Tau Kappa Epsilon, Beta Theta Pi, Alpha Sigma Phi, Phi Delta Theta, Sigma Pi, Zeta Psi and Chi Beta. Fraternity linkages with football alumni, faculty and administrators were evident. Delta Tau Delta's alumni editor was sports publicity director Mike Tobin. Phi Gamma Delta's administrative and faculty connections were with presidents David Kinley and Arthur Daniels, physical plant director James M. White, faculty representative George Goodenough, the Athletic Asociation's James P. Kratz, alumnus Charles Lovejoy and coach Ray Eliot. Sigma Nu's advisors included the Athletic Association's Frederick Russell and coach Doug Mills. Tau Kappa Epsilon was the fraternity of George Halas, Laurie Walquist and assistant coach Milt Olander. Athletic Association business manager Charles Bowen was a Beta Theta Pi. Student aid for athletes was the responsibility of William Pfister of Sigma Pi. Red Grange was recruited by George Dawson, a boyhood friend and Wheaton High School football player. Dawson took Grange to the Zeta Psi house, where Grange lived from September 1922 to November 1925. George Huff's Kappa Sigma was fifteenth on the list of players' choices.[9]

The fraternity system provided peer group academic counseling. The university's annual publication of fraternity grade point averages stimulated competition. Fraternity averages were lower than those of non–fraternity men. There was no correlation between academic performance and the fraternity membership of football players. Alpha Kappa Lambda, Beta Theta Pi and Phi Gamma Delta were among the top five in academic standing, whereas Tau Kappa Epsilon and Alpha Sigma Phi were ranked between thirty-first and forty-third.[10]

Zuppke was not an active fraternity member at Wisconsin and did not tolerate fraternity politics in his football teams. During his early years at Illinois, he attended fraternity house dinners to arouse interest in the football program. In the 1930s, he was the featured speaker at the Kappa Sigma banquets after Homecoming games. Homecoming victories in 1933–35 and 1939 offset losses in 1931–32 and 1937–38. In June 1933, the "adopted brother" joined the Illinois chapter of Kappa Sigma, which included George Huff, Carl Lundgren, Burt Hurd and the Carr brothers among its members. The October issues of the Kappa Sigma alumni newsletter carried photographs of Zuppke directing football practices. In 1938, he offered to take the wives of four Kappa Sigs alumni to his home for dinner during the business meeting.[11]

The severe economic depression from 1930 to 1938 forced many fraternities to limit employment opportunities or close their doors. The eighty-four fraternities listed in the 1929 *Illio* were reduced to sixty in the 1939 yearbook. Consequently, a major contributor to the recruitment and housing of athletes was weakened in a decade when the football program was also handicapped by a location in an area remote from athletic talent. Limited student scholarships and financial-aid programs were rationed by university administrators.[12]

In addition to the support of alumni, lettermen and fraternities, community support for the athletic program came from private booster organizations. Boosterism was a "basic American trait." Land speculators, settlers, businessmen and community leaders all promoted the locations and merits of their properties and institutions. Coleman Griffith thought that their conceptions of ethics were to "put the town on the map." Their interests were stronger than those of the readers of the sports pages and those who made small wagers and argued in the barber shop. Boosters perceived a financial or professional advantage in their support of a successful athletic program and were willing to organize and contribute to its support. In state universities, they were usually the first group to create and support foundations to receive private gifts. They were especially interested in the promotion of intercollegiate athletics and public entertainment. These external constituents were also useful in cultivating support for higher education. Public universities had continuing needs for money, students and support in the form of appropriations and gifts. Noting the increased enthusiasm for spectator sports, university presidents recognized that football boosters could help solve problems stemming from increased enrollments, new curricula and larger physical plants.

With the directors and coaches in the athletic profession, they encouraged contributions and sacrifices for the glory and publicity that college football provided for their universities. Multimillionaires, such as Avery Brundage and Robert Carr, were among the leading champions of amateur sports. They saw a common bond between those who achieved financial and athletic success through diligent practice and hard work. Usually located in or near the campus town, boosters often had personal interests in the success of university athletic teams. With business, civic or service orientations, they provided part-time employment, awards and recognitions. Other informal booster groups enabled local business and professional men to support university sports.[13]

At Illinois, the first boosters were local merchants. Beginning in 1919, the Champaign Rotary Club sponsored an annual football banquet. In 1923, Zuppke was presiding at Rotary meetings. In 1933, twenty-eight members of the Urbana Chamber of Commerce received complimentary tickets to the Drake game, along with 10,000 Boy Scouts and schoolchildren. The Champaign and Urbana Chambers of Commerce created University of Illinois Athletic Relations Committees. The membership included two loan association officers, a hotel manager, a grocer, a restaurant proprietor, two automotive services supervisors and a theater manager. The committees sponsored a dinner for the freshman varsity team. Commerce professor Fred Russell from the Athletic Board of Directors was toastmaster and freshman coach Wendell Wilson distributed the letters. An Urbana booster, who loaned money to rooming house proprietors, stated that the purpose of the committee was to ensure that there was greater attendance at football games and "greater benefits to the business firms of the Twin Cities." Groups of boosters often collaborated to support college football. Championships and winning records increased their enthusiasm and support. A string of losing seasons produced Monday-morning quarterbacks and, eventually, the howling of the wolves.[14]

15

Riding the Crest to the Crash

Bob Zuppke rode the crest of a nationwide interest in football. Coaches were obliged to win games, receive regular recognition based on ratings and championships, inspire the team during practices and games, raise funds for the athletics program, deal with media representatives, attract crowds to home games, speak to alumni groups, recruit talented players, and assist in the placement of graduates in career positions. All these activities necessitated a distinctive public image and an ability to generate favorable publicity. Zuppke's talent as an extempore inspirational speaker was an invaluable asset in his long coaching career. His German accent and the use of humorous stories and nicknames amused audiences and held their attention.

Another obligation of the coach was to respond to public criticism of football. Zuppke's general response was often included in popular magazine articles extolling the benefits of the game. He also attacked critics in his speeches. On January 17, 1930, he spoke to the Chicago Executives Club on "Playing the Game." Rebutting the Carnegie Commission's criticisms of football, he regaled the audience with humorous stories, prohibition jokes, comments on student behavior, classical allusions, and affirmations of the benefits of the game. There were forty-nine interruptions for laughter and applause. After the Chicago speech, he returned to Milwaukee where he spoke at three schools and an Illinois alumni dinner. Before the 1930 football season, he predicted that the public would still be interested in college football despite the "sisters of Carnegie" and proclaimed that alumni were the backbone of interest in the game. He contended that intercollegiate athletics seldom yielded a substantial profit and that football retained its appeal to the instinct for virility." In March 1931, he told school administrators at the University of Pennsylvania that football provided better models for youth. He added that the reformer was all right until he became the persecutor.[1]

From Zuppke's time in New York and his coast-to-coast travel with the Oak Park team, he delighted in business and recreational travel. He drove

Fannie's electric car on campus, bought a Ford in 1928 and later covered a lot of territory in his big Buick. In 1925, he took his sketchbook to Alaska. By 1926, when his parents had retired and moved from Milwaukee to California, he obtained a two-month leave to care for his mother. While there, he addressed an August 26 meeting of the Redondo Beach Rotary Club. In the summer of 1927, Bob and Fannie toured Europe. In 1928, they were guests of honor at the August 21 beach frolic and dinner with the Southern California Illini Club. In July 1931, he joined alumnus Charles Moynihan for a painting and hunting trip in the western Colorado mountains. In the summers, Bob and Fannie vacationed in Muskegon and Canada.[2]

Most of Bob's business travel incorporated football events. In 1929, he taught at football schools at San Diego State College and Utah State College. In 1930, he taught a coaching school in Southern California. On January 1, 1931, he coached the Middle West All-Stars in the Dixie Classic game in Dallas, Texas. After the game, the Zuppkes vacationed at the Seville-Biltmore in Havana. Bob helped Jim Kendrigan, a Wisconsin friend, who was in the import business and taught physical education at the University of Havana. In diagramming football plays for students by the drawing of *X*s and *O*s, Bob was suspected of planning a revolutionary bombing attack. In late January, Zuppke and New York University coach Chick Meehan were photographed at the Roney Plaza Hotel pool in Miami. In June, he taught at a coaching clinic at Wittenberg College in Ohio.[3]

Returning to Champaign, he claimed that football had made the nation college conscious and that he taught sportsmanship to classes of 70,000 on autumn afternoons. He regarded the Saturday spectacles as not only entertainment but as an opportunity to demonstrate sport ethics and institutional loyalty to many people at a time. Football games in the stadium brought trustees, faculty, administrators, students, alumni and townspeople together on five autumn afternoons. Pageantry and patriotism were closely associated with college football. The university's Football Marching Band's performances before, during and after games were part of the entertainment package. The presentation of the colors and the national anthem preceded games. At a 1925 Fourth of July program in Moline, Zuppke had declared that life was "an adventure in behavior and a struggle for self-respect and advocated military preparedness and personal responsibility. The Carnegie Bulletin had maintained that true loyalty to a university must lead to institutional pride, activity, and control. It did not address the issue of community or state loyalty.[4]

In 1929, both the university and the football program had enjoyed sunny days. With 14,000 students, Illinois was the second largest land-grant university. It also had the second largest physical plant for athletics. Fraternities and football were major activities in campus life. The defending Big Ten champions finished in second place with a 3–1–1 record. They set a home attendance record of 197,842 that would last until 1946. The Michigan, Northwestern and Army games were broadcasted throughout the Midwest by WGN in Chicago. University stations carried games in Champaign and Iowa City. There were only two bad marks on the team's record. The first was a 7–7 tie with Iowa. Coached by Burt Ingwersen, an All-American tackle on Zuppke's 1920 team, Iowa had been suspended from the Big Ten for giving irregular financial aid to two players. The Hawkeyes played an inspired game in the driving rain at the homecoming dedication of their new stadium. The second mark was a 7–0 loss to Northwestern, the first in seventeen years. The loss of two members of the starting backfield due to injuries contributed to the team's problems in Evanston. On October 26, a 14–0 win evened the score with Michigan at five and five for the ten games played between 1919 and 1929. Relying on intricate and deceptive plays, the Illini closed out the season with decisive wins over Army, 17–7, Chicago, 40–0, and Ohio State, 8–0. Rockne congratulated Zup for the "way your team came through with increasing power every Saturday."[5]

The highlight of the season was the November 9 game with Army. Secretary of War James W. Good, Governor Louis L. Emmerson, assorted generals, Grantland Rice, Paul Gallico and nearly 70,000 fans came to Champaign for the spectacle of the first appearance of a Military Academy team and Army fans on a midwestern campus. Gallico reported that for thrill and color, the western bands and cheering sections were in a class by themselves. A Milwaukee cousin described Bob's appearance in a "dark overcoat and light grey hat pulled down over his eyes, hands in his pockets, pacing up and down, and now and then stopping to give a few curt orders." The spouse of the Illini commander was complimented for her charming friendliness and genial hospitality.[6]

The final year of Illinois' football dominance attracted a total attendance of 321,357, which produced a record $339,880 profit. Student interest in the sport increased as income from coupon book sales rose from $43,271 in 1927 to $57,355 in 1929. In his first seventeen seasons, Zuppke's teams had won ninety games, lost twenty-nine and tied eight. They led the Big Ten with seven championship seasons and had a winning record against eight conference teams and were tied with Michigan. While they were noted for their trick razzle-dazzle plays, such as the flea-flicker and the flying trapeze, it was their consistent defense that brought success. The coach's skill in designing effective defenses was the key to his ability to upset favored teams. In 127 games, the defense had given up an average of 5.3 points per game. Only Minnesota in 1917 and Michigan in 1922 had been able to score more than twenty points against the Illinois defense. Line coach Lindgren quoted Zuppke's maxim, "Our defense is a citadel from which we sally forth to attack."[7]

At the annual football banquet at the Champaign Country Club on November 29, 1929, Zuppke was introduced as "the cleanup man." The *Alumni News* commented on his style: "Just when you think you have Zup all tagged and keyed and earmarked, away he goes through the fence and into another pasture." "We would like to know how many football coaches now in active practice can discuss Count Keyserling, President Van Hise, Westbrook Pegler, the Dekes and the sunny south and land on their feet." His charm "seems to be in his disconnectedness." "Take a tip from Zup and be abrupt, contradictory, fill your talk with spinners, fake punts, and what have you. Keep the audience guessing. Say the ideal education is three years in high school, three years in jail and three years in college." Ask them "what is a second set of backs, anyhow?" The three big things of life? "Eat, love and fight." At the Chicago Illini Club dinner on December 15, "Zup the Dutch Master" leaped "from the short-circuited English of the street to the super compounds of the scientist and philosopher." He hurled "his voice all over the place and suddenly sat down as if in the middle of a sentence." For the Duquesne football banquet in Pittsburgh on December 17, he presented his views on subjects from Abelard to Zythepsaries.[8]

Zuppke's success in 1929 led to concerns about his salary. The Carnegie investigators had criticized the high salaries of coaches and challenged President Kinley's statement that salaries were governed by the laws of supply and demand. In 1927, Zup had received an offer from a California university and there were rumors of another offer. In December 1930, he quelled rumors by stating "Illinois means too much for me ever to think of leaving." After nineteen years at Illinois, the fifty-two-year old Zuppke said that he would stay.[9]

Illinois presidents were especially sensitive about publicity and public criticism. The state university's size and favored position resulting from the 1911 mill tax made it a target for the criticism of rivals and the press. To counter media criticism, the university's football games provided a venue for favorable publicity. American politicians delighted in public appearances at sporting events. As ex officio members of the university's Board of Trustees, governors attended football games and pep rallies. Administrators were aware of the value of favors in maintaining good relations with those who funded university operations, shaped public opinion and decided legal questions. When the stadium was built, George Huff suggested to David Kinley that the university should give each member of the legislature four tickets to every game. By 1937, the President's Office was delivering 2,000 "free" tickets to the president's and governor's parties, state officers, supreme court justices, state department heads, ex-governors, members of the General Assembly, heads of state industrial and labor organizations, newspapermen and other guests.[10]

With a longtime coach and political support, Illinois football prospered. Continued success depended on the availability of the best athletes. The prosperity of the late 1920s brought increased competition for talented football players in the Chicago area. The Carnegie Bulletin had singled out Illinois and Chicago as universities that did not subsidize athletes. This would become a factor in their declining fortunes in the 1930s. As Chicago tightened its control of Amos Stagg's recruitment opportunities and apparatus and Illinois continued to rely upon the occasional support of alumni clubs, Northwestern launched an aggressive program featuring recruiters and student loans. After a winless season in 1921, Northwestern's trustees had hired Glenn Thistlethwaite, Zuppke's successor at Oak Park, as their first full-time football coach. In 1922, President Walter D. Scott led the cheers in an upset of Minnesota. In 1925, Northwestern hired Kenneth "Tug" Wilson, a 1920 Illinois athlete and former assistant to George Huff, as their athletic director. Wilson found that alumni were providing jobs and tuition money for athletes and persuaded Commissioner Griffith to permit the university to replace private support with university loans so they could start with a clean slate. Northwestern moved to Dyche Stadium in 1926 and tied Michigan for the Big Ten championship. Wilson also arranged monthly meetings with the "N" Men's Club and alumni groups in the Chicago area. In 1927, he drew on his Illinois background in establishing a summer coaching school. Zuppke, Warner and Rockne were among the coaches who taught at his clinic. The coaching school in Evanston attracted talented athletes for the Wildcats football team. With its hometown advantage, Northwestern outperformed Illinois in recruiting football talent in Chicago and its suburbs. In 1928, it led 30 to 20. By 1930, the Wildcats had a 36 to 13 advantage.[11]

The public demand for entertainment at institutions of higher education had led to the building of stadia for publicized athletic contests, which led to football profits, which led to the Carnegie Foundation's criticisms of commercialism. In 1928, the Ohio State University trustees reported that, with the building of their stadium, the very considerable enlargement of facilities devoted to athletics required making a distinct contribution to the educational processes to avoid charges of attaching a disproportionate importance to amateur athletics. At Illinois, the completion of the concrete south bleachers increased Memorial Stadium's seating capacity to 73,000. The economic depression led to increased concern about athletic budgets. The quasi-independent status of the Athletic Association provided some protection from control, criticism and interference by trustees, faculty and alumni. George Huff's athletic career, Alumni Association service and lobbying for the university strengthened his position as an ex officio member of the Athletic Association directors. Substantial profits in the postwar decade prompted the trustees and faculty to question the propriety of its financial independence. Trustee Merle Trees sought to increase the trustees' role by adding a member of their board to the Athletic Association Board, but administrators were leery of allowing the participation of trustees or alumni in the control of intercollegiate sports.[12]

The main administrative intervention came from the Comptroller's Office. Following a 1923 recommendation of the faculty Commission on Athletics and Physical Welfare, the comptroller began auditing athletic ticket sales. In 1925, Comptroller Lloyd Morey reported that Athletic Association business management was improving, but there was a general laxity in approving vouchers. In 1927, auditors were concerned about the salary advances to Huff and Zuppke and the purchase of training supplies from Bullock Brothers without competitive prices. After surveying the handling of athletics income in other conference universities, Morey recommended that university regulations should govern purchases and issued a critical report on Association purchasing. In a report to conference business managers, he explained that the Association was a separate corporation. While he was responsible only for auditing ticket sales and accounts, he favored the handling of intercollegiate athletics funds through regular university channels.[13]

The stock market crash in October 1929 coincided with a decline in Illinois' football fortunes. Before leaving for a summer vacation in 1930, Zuppke observed that it would be a case of starting all over again in the fall, but that there was no use telling the world that Illini material was scarce, as nobody would believe him. Losing twelve lettermen, Illinois faced a difficult schedule with a green team. The defense provided a 7–0 win over Iowa State and a 27–0 win over Bradley. The Big Ten season began with an October 18, 1930, Homecoming game with Northwestern. In all, 35,572 tickets were sold in Urbana for the game. The defense gave up a touchdown in the first half before the offense gave up two in the second half, which led to a 32–0 defeat. On the following Monday, incoming President Harry W. Chase jested that his resignation was in the hands of the trustees. The Illini then lost close road games to Michigan and Army and a home game to Purdue. They closed out the season with a 28–0 win over Chicago and a 12–9 loss to Ohio State. In the final home game, local ticket sales were 5,384. In their first eighth place finish since 1921, they gave up more points to Northwestern, Michigan and Purdue than they had allowed in 1927, 1928 and 1929.[14]

Zuppke's annual banquet orations reflected the losing season. At Champaign on November 24, he observed that he had spent a rather miserable autumn. After complimenting the boys for giving all they had, he objected to their giving away touchdowns. In Chicago, the team presented a testimonial scroll to the coach for his work through thick and thin. He appreciated the gift but said that he didn't want too many of them around the house. "You boys probably don't like me very well right now, but you'll like me better later. I *have* to be hard — someone *has* to be." Before departing to coach a Midwest team in a charity game in Texas, Zuppke denied interest in coaching offers and affirmed his intention to stay at Illinois.[15]

The highlight of the 1930 season had been the Illinois appearance in New York. The team left on Thursday for a Friday practice at Yankee Stadium and Zuppke's evening NBC radio talk. The 160-piece Illinois band arrived on Saturday morning, November 8. From the Grand Central Station, they were preceded by a Fox Movietone truck as they paraded down Fifth Avenue to their hotel while playing the "March of the Illini." Playing "Illinois Loyalty," they led the Military Academy's 1,600 Corps of Cadets into the stadium. A 44-page souvenir program and the band's orange spats added to the gaiety. After the game, the band played a half-hour concert for the NBC radio network. The band's performances were hailed by the five New York daily newspapers, one of which noted that the football team "was also present." Playing in Yankee Stadium before 70,000 spectators, Zuppke's team was outweighed eleven pounds per man by an Army team that had a 6–0 record and included two former Illinois players. The Military Academy recruited many players who had played at other colleges. The Illini defense took advantage of a muddy field and excellent punting to hold on for a scoreless first half. They made only one first down in the game and lost 13–0. Army hosted an evening dinner and theater party for the Illinois team. In a period of economic gloom, the game afforded excellent publicity for the University of Illinois. It also produced $116,112, or thirty-eight percent of the year's football receipts.[16]

While attendance at games declined, radio broadcasts played a major role in bringing the color and excitement of college football to the public. By 1930, radio coverage brought Illini football to expanding midwestern markets. Powerful WGN in Chicago carried games with Michigan and Northwestern. Before the Army game in New York, WOR in New York, WMAQ in Chicago and WLW in Cincinnati carried Zuppke's pre-game talk. Yost and Stagg had similar pre-game radio appearances. Cleveland's WTAM and Cincinnati's WLW broadcasted the Ohio State game. For the local community, the university's WILL carried all home games. By 1934, Big Ten teams in or near major cities were selling broadcasting rights. With a small-town location, Illinois was not competitive in attracting sponsored advertising. Short football highlights footage in motion picture theaters also publicized Big Ten football.[17]

As a professor in the College of Education, Zuppke defended collegiate football at professional meetings. On February 26, 1931, he supported interscholastic and intercollegiate athletics at a Detroit meeting of the Superintendents Division of the National Educational Association. He recited the criticisms of college football. The list included dangers to the health of the players, tough-minded coaches, students following teams, campus hysteria, spectatorism, proselytizing, overemphasis and victory motivation at the expense of recreation. He claimed that competitive athletics promoted health, strength, endurance, teamwork, virile literature and the emotional life of the community. Defeats were a part of the "inevitable alternations of life." Collegiate and school teams became a social force around which the student body or community manifested its loyalty. He urged school authorities to give students as many extracurricular opportunities to excel as possible. Concluding with the statement that learning was the great central scheme of university life, he added "football simply makes more noise."[18]

At a March 20 educators' meeting in Philadelphia, he again responded to criticisms with the statement that "football is charged with being commercialized and professionalized, but we are doing no more than the churches, universities as a whole and other institutions are doing when they have too much spending money." This classic "everybody else is doing it" defense was an essential part of college football's response to criticisms of overemphasis and charges of rules violations.[19]

16

Football Economics in the Depression

In 1930–33, rising unemployment, bank closures, stock market losses and declining tax revenues marked the beginning of a national economic depression, with severe consequences for state universities and intercollegiate sports. The number of wealthy alumni declined and many families could not afford the costs of higher education. At Illinois, the economic depression also coincided with losing football games. For every football victory, there was a defeat. Defeated teams still received a percentage of the gate receipts at each game. The Illinois Athletic Association continued to benefit from road games in leading sports entertainment markets at New York, Los Angeles, Chicago, Ann Arbor, Cleveland and Columbus. The Association's profits did not benefit local businesses, which depended on football crowds in Champaign-Urbana. In 1931, advertising rates for football programs were cut from $200 to $100. Though income declined and expenses were curtailed, Zuppke's teams continued to show a profit in the 1930s (table 16.1).

Table 16.1. Profits of Zuppke's Teams in the 1930s

Year	Won/Loss/Tie	Home Attendance	Total Attendance	Income	Expense	Profit
1931	2–6–1	125.4	233.4	148.7	47.2	101.4
1932	5–4–0	110.6	175.1	65.5	31.5	34.0
1933	5–3–0	74.1	163.7	104.3	26.5	77.8
1934	7–1–0	99.3	223.6	159.2	30.6	128.6
1935	3–5–0	114.1	243.1	162.5	43.5	119.0
1936	4–3–1	121.0	210.1	124.7	37.2	87.5
1937	3–3–2	136.1	237.1	180.4	44.1	136.4
1938	3–5–0	121.1	202.0	145.5	43.2	102.2
1939	3–4–1	85.5	231.2	160.9	52.8	108.1
1940	1–7–0	140.6	268.6	190.0	50.9	139.1
1941	2–6–0	78.1	240.5	175.8	47.1	128.7

Zuppke argued that football was only a part of life and spent his last twelve years at Illinois coaching players who were not heavily recruited and lost more often than they won. There were no championships and four ninth-place finishes. They had winning seasons in 1932–34, but were not successful in recruiting the talented players required for a championship. Inspired by their coach, the Illini continued to fight and produced several upsets of favored opponents. His reluctance to meet the challenges of aggressive and increased recruiting competition and waning administrative support would contribute to his retirement in 1941.

The disappointing 1930 season was followed by a disastrous 1931 record. The Illini lost all six Big Ten games. Playing before dwindling crowds, they defeated St. Louis and Bradley, but lost close games with Purdue and Wisconsin. The top three — Northwestern, Ohio State and Michigan — outscored the Illini 107–6. The 40–0 loss to Ohio State was the worst defeat a Zuppke team had suffered and was the first time that Ohio State had consecutive wins over the Illini since 1917. Chicago won its first game with Illinois since 1922. The *Alumni News*' "Weekly Football Edition" described the game as one where "one misfortune after another overtook the embattled Illini," and their general morale went from bad to worse. "They fumbled, they forgot signals, and the line...was unable to protect the backfield operations. Time after time the pass thrower would be so badly rushed that the ball had to be practically thrown away." A post-season charity game with Indiana to raise money for the unemployed resulted in a scoreless tie. Called at halftime, the game was awarded to the Hoosiers, who made more first downs. In the *Chicago Tribune*, a sympathetic Arch Ward noted that Illinois had played the toughest conference schedule.[1]

At the post-season banquet in Champaign, Zup ripped into his players' faults, but he so tempered his criticisms with witticisms and at times with "downright sympathy and understanding" that reporters thought this was the best speech he had ever made. He said players must learn to fight and to take criticism. He closed with an attack on sportswriters for unjust criticisms and hasty conclusions. Questioned about reasons why his small team did not win, he suggested too much social life, no training table and strict eligibility rules. President Kinley received several letters from disappointed alumni complaining about the football team's winless Big Ten season.[2]

The depression had a direct impact on the attendance and the profitability of college football The two home victories had produced $160, whereas six losses brought in $114,052. For the last home game with Chicago, local ticket sales dropped to 2,285. The profit supported six minor sports and intramurals. In 1932, tickets were reduced to $2.20 and the Illinois Central Railroad offered five-dollar round-trip tickets from Chicago to Champaign for the home games with Northwestern, Indiana and Ohio State. Local ticket sales for five home games averaged 5,410. Student attendance was stable, but eight-dollar coupon books did not provide the additional revenue that came with big games. In 1939, the average ticket sale was 9,012. The loss of paying customers was offset by free or low-cost admissions for special groups, especially school children and Boy Scouts. In 1935–36, Civilian Conservation Corps men attended. In the 1937–41 period, Reserve Officer Training Corps, American Legion members, war veterans and men in military service were admitted. Filling the stadium with potential supporters of postwar intercollegiate football was a wise investment in the future.[3]

The nationwide financial crisis brought cutbacks at the university. When football income fell short of estimates in 1931, a Senate committee recommended that the Athletic Association's budget be reviewed by the University Council, sent to the Board of Trustees for approval, and printed in the Trustees' Proceedings. In a 1932 "Method for Intercollegiate Athletics Business," Comptroller Morey proposed an alumni, faculty and student board to replace the Athletic Association. Under his plan, the comptroller would handle budgets, tickets and purchases as it did for all other university departments and prepare financial reports. In January 1933, the Board of Trustees decided that the Association's income estimates were too optimistic and relied on a single road game. The Board requested considerably increased economies and a budget reduction of twenty to twenty-five percent. The trustees' call for drastic action to reduce the Athletic Association budget was avoided by a tentative budget subject to revision. Morey had mentioned a 7 percent reduction in salaries in 1932 and suggested that an additional 10 percent would save $7,500. He doubted that the 1933 Army game in Cleveland would produce as much income as the 1930 Army game in New York and believed that Association salaries were too high. Huff's $10,400 a year was reduced to $9,900 in 1932, but was still higher than the usual $9,000 for deans and directors. Zuppke's $9,200 was lower than the $10,000 paid to the Wisconsin coach, whereas other conference universities paid football coaches less than $8,000. Morey was unable to obtain information on coaches salaries at Northwestern and Michigan.[4]

The football program was a small part of the university's financial problems. Legislators regarded higher education as an expensive investment in the future. Its critics maintained that the university was often too expensive and wasteful. It seldom reported profits or dividends. At state universities, the appropriation bills competed with demands to remedy social and economic problems, promote American industrial and commercial recovery, support charitable and penal institutions, and regulate public service agencies. President Kinley's successor, Harry W. Chase, sought to liberalize student regulations and reform administrative structures. His Committee of Nine recommended that health and physical education work should be moved from the College of Education to a new School of Physical Education. Approved by the Board of Trustees on June 11, 1932, the new school joined instruction and research in physical education with the Athletic Association through a common director, George Huff. Initial successes were soon overshadowed by budget cutting and financial aid problems. In 1932, Huff announced that declining football income had deprived swimming, water polo, fencing, gymnastics, golf and tennis of financial support.[5]

Budgetary problems did not dampen Coach Zuppke's popularity and oratory. He had recovered from the effects of the losing season when he delivered the closing speech at the St. Louis Illini Club's annual banquet on April 16, 1932. He had won five of his seven Big Ten championships before moving to Champaign, and suggested that the recent lack of football success may have been Urbana's revenge for his calling that community the "city of the unburied dead." He opened with the comment that Americans were "still full of oats," whereas "German universities are soused with tradition and 4 percent beer." He criticized "sophomoric youngsters of empty grandiloquence who are too wise to come out for football, who can't even march in the band, and who...qualify for nothing better than the flower-smelling championship." Although football provided financial support for other sports, he complained that the football staff was seldom consulted about their management. If the reformers kept on, it would be commercialism for players even to take a train. Regarding recruitment, he said that while it might "be true that we shouldn't proselytize, but the churches certainly do it." He cautioned that disgruntled scrubs can be the ruin of almost any coach. He denied another speaker's statement that he was a Demosthenes and claimed to be a horrible example of the product of a public speaking department. Acknowledging critics of his extempore speaking, who charged that he didn't know what he was talking about, he opined that he was no different from most other people who made speeches.[6]

Zuppke's 1932 team regained respectability with a 5–4 record and was 2–3 in Big Ten competition. After doubleheader wins over Coe College and Miami University, the Bradley game drew the largest attendance of the year. The 35,482 spectators included 23,498 schoolchildren, 5,000 Boy Scouts and 2,198 adult escorts. In the Big Ten, the Illini were not able to cope with powerful Michigan and Northwestern squads, but a stout defense yielded only forty-three points in the other seven games. On December 10, 1932, in the midst of a national financial crisis, the Chicago Illini resumed their annual football banquet. Toastmaster Otto Seiler of the undefeated 1910 team introduced President Harry Chase, who suggested that he and Zuppke might be on the lunatic fringe as, like bootleggers and professors, they both met lots of fine people. Zuppke supplied his usual hammer and tongs oratory with his "torrent of thoughts, ideas, both raw and cooked, impressions, sudden questions, and condemnations." He said that in 1907, he was the only coach who could spell psychology and quoted the absent George Huff as saying "I believe everything you say, Zup, but I wouldn't say it."[7]

As banks closed and President Franklin D. Roosevelt's New Deal sought to restore confidence in the economy, college football offered interesting entertainment and diversion to the public. On February 4, 1933, Zuppke returned from a southern vacation to speak to the Indianapolis Illini. Introduced by Potsy Clark, coach of the National Football League Portsmouth Spartans, Zup produced his one-line jokes and quips. He observed that the Carnegie Foundation had no business holding up athletic Europe as a pattern for us to follow. Amid the laughter, he protested that he was "just trying to give you an idea of how it affects one to be around a university." Ninety other alumni groups saw the *Illini Trail* movie with its climactic scene of a Zuppke pep talk to the football team. The Illinois Glee Club, a vocal team, accompanied the film on a summer tour from Florida to Quebec. Zuppke taught a summer coaching school in southern California.[8]

The depression led to public criticism of university programs, which prompted officials to monitor the Athletic Association. In 1933, Grayville lawyer Claude Ellis and Freeport journalist O.S. Hitchner attacked wasteful spending at the University. Their flyers claimed that the Athletic Association money made from the general public belonged to the people and was shamefully wasted on the $10,000 salaries of Zuppke and Huff, both non-essential to education. The university's response was that the Association's policy was to use surplus funds to provide additional recreation facilities for students. Ellis contended that the students were not studying and that the Association "must be the only moneymaker up there." Hitchner also attacked the Association's independent financial status and its gift of a $355,000 ice rink to the university.[9]

When the economic and football depressions set in, the main impact on Illinois football was a marked increase in players who came from outside the Chicago area and a decline in out-of-state players. The football candidates in the transitional 1927–33 period reflected a shift in Zuppke's material. Seventy-eight percent were from Illinois and twenty-two percent from twenty-three other states. Twenty percent of the Illinois men were from Chicago and eighteen percent from the Chicago suburbs. Thirteen percent were from Champaign County and forty-nine percent were from other counties. Ohio and Missouri were the primary sources of out-of-state football talent. The lack of national publicity and economic conditions contributed to the diminishing number of out-of-state players. Before 1930, Chicago and Cook County had provided forty-one percent of the players for Illinois. Afterward, they contributed twenty-two percent. Before 1930, nineteen percent were from other states. Afterward, out-of-state men were fourteen percent. Recruiting in the Chicago area no longer involved competition with Stagg at Chicago, but faced increasingly vigorous competition from Northwestern, Notre Dame, Michigan, Iowa, Indiana, Purdue and Wisconsin. Zuppke observed that few players of any class came to Illinois after 1929 because of the "concentrated drive" of Northwestern, Purdue and other universities. He reported that 167 football players left Illinois for out-of-state teams in 1932.[10]

Recruiting problems led to eligibility problems. Each year, college football coaches developed their game plans according to the availability of talented players. In 1933, Zuppke delegated eligibility responsibilities to Assistant Coach Milt Olander, who reported on the scholastic standing and health of eleven players. A tackle was tutored and passed special examinations in Rhetoric I and History. He made the best out of what appeared to be a hopeless situation and lettered the next three years. Five others also took special examinations early in the fall semester and became eligible. Of the eleven players, four won letters in 1933 and five never won a letter at Illinois. Assistant coaches also found employment for players. Olander found a truck-driving job for a prospect from southern Illinois. He reported to Zuppke that Bob Reitsch was coming from Chicago to go over a list of freshman prospects and classify them for jobs.[11]

The coaches' concerns about eligibility were shared by a group of faculty advisers to athletes. In 1935, faculty and staff from the departments of Accountancy, Chemistry, Economics, Education, English, Geography, Geology, History, Hygiene, Journalism, Physiology, Psychology and Sociology received thirty complimentary athletics coupon books for their services in advising athletes.[12]

Zuppke believed that his veteran 1933 squad lacked weight and stamina, but that they would play good football. He did not think that they would win more games, but thought they were strong enough to avoid being routed. On September 26, he drove to Cleveland with Mike Tobin and Chilly Bowen to finalize plans for the Army game and speak at a Chamber of Commerce luncheon about the game. Zuppke fielded his usual light team that relied on a passing attack. A strong defense yielded only fourteen points in five Big Ten games. The team was again competitive with a 3–2 Big Ten record. At the October 14 Homecoming, the Illini employed the flea-flicker play in a 14–0 defeat of Wisconsin. The two losses to Michigan and Ohio State were 7–6 decisions. A 160-piece football band accompanied the team to road games at St. Louis against Washington University and at Cleveland against Army. Many of the spectators who saw the Illini lose a 6–0 game to Army in the new 70,000 seat municipal stadium were Illinois alumni or supporters.[13]

After the season, the *Chicago Tribune's* Stewart Owen likened praise for the generalship of Zuppke's quarterback to praising a great artist's hand because it wielded the brush that produced a great painting. Zup's forty-minute talk at the post-season banquet kept the audience in a continual uproar with "literary pivoting," "lightning changes of pace" and "sudden sallies of blasting humor and sarcasm." At the December 16 Chicago Illini banquet, ex-president Kinley and acting president Arthur Daniels complimented him for going through difficult seasons and standing by us in spite of all offers. End Fred Frink described the week before the Michigan game as the greatest coaching week in history. The theme of Zuppke's thirty minutes of "swash-buckling mythology" was "Can you take it?" He declared that the economic depression was the best thing that ever happened to the University. The popular slogan of the boom days, "What is there in it for me?" was replaced by "Can you take it?" Reflecting on the close losses to Michigan, Ohio State and Army, he told his audience that he never worried about winning or losing, but was concerned that the team stayed in the game. He said that the message he wrote in autograph books was "Do not let hope elude you, or it will be the greatest fumble in your life." His digressions included tales of his Germanic origins and taking his Oak Park baseball team to see Annette Keller-man's curves.[14]

The nationwide publicity after the 1925–29 football successes and his speaking style contributed to a continuing demand for Zuppke's public appearances. Between successful 1933 and 1934 seasons, he received fifty-two invitations to speak and accepted half of them. Thirty-one requests came from Illinois. Ten other states were represented. An updated version of the *Illini Trail* movie often replaced his personal appearance. Alumni sponsors of football banquets reported that "we have some splendid college material up here and some of us are anxious for you and Illinois to reap the benefits." An automobile dealer offered to tune up his Buick. Zuppke collected $150 plus expenses for inspirational talks, such as a March 1934 appearance at the American Society of Bakery Engineers meeting in Chicago. In the middle of his post-season speaking engagements, he went to Miami, Florida, to help coach Tom McCann, a former student, prepare the Hurricanes for a New Year's Day game against Manhattan College. Zuppke led the team to the two-yard line on the practice field and gave them the play that they were to use in defeating Manhattan 7–0. The upset of the favored New York team at the Palm Festival led to the annual Orange Bowl. In declining a Milwaukee invitation in the spring of 1934, he explained that he had "spring football, classwork, and talks to make in this vicinity. Our football has suffered in the past because

I continuously accepted invitations to speak instead of concentrating upon coaching at home."[15]

While the demand for Zuppke as a speaker and coach continued, declining economic conditions stimulated public criticism of the high salaries. The depression forced the university to make across-the-board cuts in faculty and administrative salaries. Zuppke's five-digit salary corresponded with the seven-digit salaries paid to leading coaches in the early twenty-first century. In 1932, over his protest, his salary had been cut to $8,500 before it was restored to $10,000 in 1935. His salary exceeded that of the deans of Engineering and Liberal Arts and Sciences and, after Huff's death, that of the Athletics Director. Financially successful, Zuppke was skeptical of government efforts to provide protection, security and pecuniary independence for the masses. In a 1935 syndicated story, he defended a self-disciplined minority who trained themselves to guide and lead. While sports were on the "fringe of the educational world," he said that they exemplified the virtues of self–reliance, morale, spirit and intelligence and led to teamwork, cooperation and honor.[16]

17

"Taking It" in Champaign

"Taking it" in victory or defeat was not the stuff of legends and lore. Coaches of losing football teams were condemned for their failure to win games. The emergence of highly publicized big-time football between the two world wars brought increased pressures to produce winning teams. Public criticism prompted administrators and athletics directors to replace losing coaches quickly. Athletes and the public celebrated and remembered victories and tried to forget defeats. Sportswriters seldom dwelt upon the fact that for every victory, there was also a loss. Nor did they concede that competition built character and that defeat could provide a learning experience for life in the real world. Zup praised the athletes' enthusiasm for competing with "the wild Bills from over the hills," but warned that meeting demands for public entertainment was less important than playing up to the team's capacities.

Zuppke's reputation and oratorical skills sustained him as he took it on the football field. From 1930 to 1941, Big Ten football was dominated by Minnesota, Michigan, Northwestern and Ohio State. Illinois was 1–11 against Ohio State, 3–9 against Northwestern, and 5–8 against Michigan. The Illini were fortunate in scheduling only one game with Minnesota, which had six undefeated seasons in this period. In his final seven years from 1935 to 1941, the decline in Illinois' football fortunes accelerated. His teams won 34 percent of their games, but only 28 percent of their Big Ten contests. Zup served on the Rules Committee from 1933 to 1941 and was abreast of changes in collegiate football, but the problems at Illinois were local. The severe economic depression brought a rapid drop in the average attendance at games in the small rural city of Champaign from 39,568 in 1929 to 18,535 in 1933. In 1935–38, the average attendance in the huge Champaign stadium was 24,694. It did not reach 35,160 until 1940. Local business leaders were unhappy about the declining attendance and began to exert pressure on university officials to replace Zuppke.[1]

The closing of the Illinois Athletic Coaching program in 1932 limited national contacts and publicity, but the primary causes of the lean years in the 1930s were marketing football in the economic depression and Zuppke's passive approach to the recruitment of players. A depressed economy limited his contacts with prospective football talent through fraternity rushing and interscholastic track meets. His success had been based on recruiting football players from the large freshman classes enrolling at the University of Illinois. He responded to letters about excellent high school football prospects, state track champions, outstanding basketball players, brilliant students and financially able prospects. A typical Zuppke reply to a recruiter was, "We certainly all want him to come here. This is his school and his state and he ought to be loyal to it. Please remind him of the California trip. Of course, you understand that we cannot go down there and carry him up here bodily, but we expect him to become one of us in the near future." To another inquiry, he responded, "We do not pay our athletes in any form, but if these boys are really interested ... I know they will be able to work their way through school just as others have done." "If they are sincere in seeking an education and like football ... this is an honest place to come to." In the highly competitive recruiting of the 1930s, his approach did not impress high school stars.[2]

In 1934, Zuppke predicted that courage, alertness, and smartness must compensate for his squad's weight disadvantage. The team gave him his last Big Ten winning season. A 7–1 record included wins over traditional conference rivals Ohio State, Michigan, Chicago and Northwestern and non-conference wins over Army, Washington University and Bradley. The Ohio State and Michigan victories were one-point wins that avenged one-point losses in 1933. The Ohio State win was secured by the execution of Zuppke's "flying trapeze" play, which involved three lateral passes followed by a diagonal forward pass. On October 13, Red Grange returned to the campus for the opening Big Ten game against Ohio State on the tenth anniversary of his famous game against Michigan. The Shell Oil Company flew Grange to the pre-game festivities and the Columbia Broadcasting System aired the Homecoming ceremonies. Zuppke presented a scroll to Red at halftime. Grange responded by declaring that Zup was "the greatest coach in the world." When rain grounded Illinois quarterback Jack Beynon's passing offense against Army and Michigan, the defense won the games. Their only defeat was a 7–3 loss to Wisconsin at a homecoming game in Madison. The winning score came when the Badger center blocked a punt and ran the ball in for a touchdown.[3]

Buoyed by a successful year, Zup praised the team that had developed so well despite its physical limitations. The banquet followed the Chicago game, where Illinois had contained star halfback Jay Berwanger and scored on a deflected pass for a 6–0 win. For the alumni, Zuppke said that it was very difficult for him to praise anybody, but that Yost was one of the greatest coaches, in spite of some things he had said about him, and thatClark Shaughnessy's Chicago team were a bunch of gentlemen. At the November 26, 1934, Champaign football banquet, Indiana coach Alvin "Bo" McMillin praised Zuppke as a fine man who had taught discipline, which was a great builder of character. Introduced as a "peripatetic philosopher," Zuppke gave one of his characteristic exhortations. He stressed that the idea was more important than the rhetoric and expressed his disdain for logic and order in oratory. He enjoyed following a long series of academic talks at an educational meeting with his unconventional remarks on literature and life.[4]

In contrast with his fiery demeanor on the practice field and vigorous speaking at football banquets, Zuppke usually did not pace the sidelines during games and was a quiet individual at most social occasions. Speechmaking was tiring, and he did not enjoy midwestern winters. The Big Ten faculty representatives' ban on competition with Army provided an opportunity to schedule another major opponent in 1935 and 1936. In September 1933, he wrote to Howard Jones and proposed intersectional contests with Southern California. Bob and Fannie left Champaign a few days after the 1934 football banquet for five weeks in California, where he made forty speeches and four radio broadcasts. Although his official business was making arrangements for the 1935 Southern California game in Los Angeles, he enjoyed meetings with the movie stars and Grantland Rice. In a December 6 radio interview, while scouting Southern California, he criticized football rating systems and the naming of All-American teams. He justified the Big Ten ban on post-season games and favored a six-game schedule, citing the coach's responsibility for the health and condition of players on the field. He said that a longer schedule made players merely entertainers for the alumni and the general public. On one day, he spoke at breakfast and luncheon meetings, before speaking to Southern California, Notre Dame, Pittsburgh and Carnegie Tech alumni groups. He also attended a Pacific Coast Conference game between California and Washington and the Rose Bowl game between Alabama and Stanford. A week after he returned to Champaign, the Zuppkes drove to Arizona for a three-week vacation to improve Fannie's health. They stayed at Jack Stewart's Wigwam Inn in Phoenix, where his paintings were exhibited in the Zuppke Lounge. Stewart remembered that Zup ate three raw onions and drank two bottles of beer for breakfast.[5]

Though Zuppke was a philosopher and exhorter in public, co-captain Chuck Bennis described him as a "loner" on the practice field. The coach was a keen observer, who seldom complimented his players. Most players realized that his constant criticism was an indication that he was interested in their development. Bennis had been recruited by Dr. Forrest Van Hook, who

Zuppke with lineman Chuck Bennis (left) and quarterback Jack Beynon (right), who were members of his last winning team, 1934. Courtesy University of Illinois Archives.

had been a star on the 1908 team. Van Hook invited Bennis to play on a town team, persuaded him to attend Illinois and insisted that the freshman recruit be given an opportunity to scrimmage against the varsity. As a co-captain, Bennis joined Zuppke on speaking engagements. After graduation, Zuppke took him to see George Halas about an offer to play professional football. When Bennis declined, Zup said that he did the right thing and that if "I knew you were that smart, I would have played you in the backfield." In 1936, Zup drove Bennis to Toledo, Ohio, for a coaching interview at Waite High School. When the president of the Board of Education withdrew an offer because Bennis was a Catholic, Zup became angry. A year later, he hired Bennis and Doug Mills as freshman coaches at Illinois.[6]

As Zuppke prepared for the 1935 season, he was aware that many of his coaching contemporaries were giving way to newer men. In 1931, Rockne was killed in an airplane crash. Zup and Rock told amusing stories about each other and remained friends. Upon the death of the Notre Dame coach, Zup described him as interesting, colorful, generous, loyal and human. In 1933,

Stagg was dismissed at Chicago. In 1934, Francis Schmidt took over from Sam Williman at Ohio State. In 1935, Lynn Waldorf replaced Dick Hanley at Northwestern. Zup's success in 1934 was also tempered by the sudden death of Huff's assistant director and baseball coach Carl Lundgren, who had won five conference championships in fifteen years, and the retirement of track coach Harry Gill, who had twenty-nine highly successful seasons.[7]

Zuppke's challenge was to replace the 1934 backfield. On September 10, he greeted seventy-eight candidates for the team. Two weeks later, Illinois lost a 6–0 game with Ohio University. Don Peden, who had played on Zup's 1920 and 1921 teams, was the Ohio coach. A week later, the Illini defeated Washington University, 28–0. The highlight of the season was the intersectional game with the Southern California Trojans. Zup's friend Howard Jones had moved from Iowa to Southern California. On the long train trip to the West Coast, Illinois practiced in Arizona. The Trojans outweighed the Illini twenty-one pounds per man. Zuppke uncovered his "flea circus" and the backs passed for 109 yards and a 19–0 win. For its halftime show, the Southern California band formed an outline of Illinois and a silhouette of Zuppke. After the game, the team attended a dinner dance. Radio stationWGN broadcasted the game in the Midwest, and Illinois received $40,678 for their California triumph. The team was gone for a week and a half. On their triumphal return, they were greeted by crowds along the railroad track in several Illinois towns. In all, 6,000 welcomed them at the Illinois Central Station in Champaign. A second welcome packed Wright Street on campus, and the *Alumni News* editorialized that the athletic depression had ended. Two weeks later, the situation was reversed, when Iowa defeated Illinois 19–0 in Champaign. Led by African-American fullback Ozzie Simmons, the Hawkeyes rushed for 233 yards. On November 2, Northwestern celebrated its homecoming with a 10–3 win over Illinois. The Illini claimed their only conference win at their November 9 Homecoming with a 3–0 win over Michigan. A heavy rain preceded the game and the Illinois defense held the Wolverine ground attack to ten yards. On November 16, in another mud game, Illinois lost to Ohio State, 6–0. The Illini closed out their 1–4 Big Ten season with a 7–6 loss to Chicago. The defense had held Southern California scoreless, and after its encounter with Iowa's Simmons, they gave up only twenty-three points in four games. The faltering offense lost four Big Ten games.[8]

At the Champaign post-season banquet, Zuppke acknowledged that a series of injuries, fumbles and poor kicking contributed to their losing record in 1935. At the Chicago dinner, George Huff praised Zuppke as one of the great coaches in America: "A great coach, not a great recruiter." Commissioner John Griffith hailed Illinois as an example for the world in the conduct of, and its attitude toward, athletics. As the closer, Zuppke "fairly out–Zupped himself" with fourteen quotes, including "A twist here and a turn there and we'd have won those games." "All the boys came through. We have students, not shoppers for cheap jobs. No weakness but fumbling." "I couldn't get mad at these boys. Sometimes I put on a big act for their benefit but my heart wasn't in it. Maybe you think I'm getting soft?" "If the time ever comes when an Illinois team does not give all it has, then I hope you will criticize to beat the devil."[9]

While Zuppke was not an active recruiter, Illinois used traditional recruiting methods. Founded in 1932, the Student Alumni Association circulated the *Illini Trail* film and entertained high school guests at the interscholastic track meets. These efforts led to a pool of interested prospects each spring. In 1937, eighty-four men came out for football, including forty-three sophomore prospects. By October, the team was down to fifty-four, with nineteen sophomores. The major attrition was twenty-eight among fifty-nine Chicago and downstate hopefuls. Twenty-three of the twenty-five prospective players who came from the Chicago suburbs, Champaign-Urbana and other states made the team. By 1937, the number of sophomore candidates declined to thirty-eight. Illinois high schools supplied seventy-five of the eighty-seven players on the spring roster. The fifty-two who were invited back for fall practice included seven of the twelve out-of-state players.[10]

While taking it on the football field, Zuppke's financial situation was secure. His substantial income exceeded his modest living expenses. In 1930, he retained Burt Hurd of Champaign as his broker. In 1930–31, he received about $40 a month from a Texas oil well lease. Through the depression, war and postwar periods, Hurd handled most of his investments. From 1929 to 1941, he received additional income from work as a technical advisor and co-author of "Ned Brant at Carter College" a sports comic strip, which was distributed by the *Des Moines Register and Tribune* syndicate. Featuring the football exploits of Ned Brant, the strip's caption credited "Bob Zuppke — Famous Football Coach." Zup sent notes on plays and shifts to the artist. In July 1933, he received commissions of $84 for Ned Brant's publication in ten newspapers from Boston to Winnipeg. In 1934, the Albert Richard clothing company of Milwaukee published Zuppke's 32-page booklet, "10 Things a Boy Should Know How to Do!" The headings were play, dress, read, eat, obey, study, sleep, think, give and work. He received $250 for speaking "to the stuffed shirts at their banquets," but was often not paid for speaking at high school dinners. In 1937, he wrote a 179-word introduction for *American Boy Short Stories*, a collection of fourteen short fiction articles. He observed that in the twentieth century we had become a nation interested in athletics.[11]

Newspaper contracts were Zuppke's primary source of income in addition to his salary. From 1930 to 1934, he contracted with John Dille's National Newspaper Service of Chicago to provide feature articles for sports pages. He supplied a series of "Follow the Ball" articles for the North American Newspaper Alliance, in which he extolled the virtues of football as providing good examples for youth and the public. Among his tips, he recommended the use of scouting reports to drill quarterbacks in varying plays to confuse defenses. In September and October 1931, the *Champaign-Urbana News-Gazette* published eight of his news service features before switching to his pre-game predictions during the Big Ten season. In 1933, with the assistance of Mike Tobin, he produced twenty columns during the twelve-week football season. From September to November 1934, he predicted the likely results of games in general language and sent the material to Mike Tobin for Monday, Wednesday and Saturday football articles for the National Newspaper Service. He predicted Big Ten games with 84 percent accuracy. He was less successful in predicting the outcomes of Notre Dame games, but averaged about 80 percent. Southern California coach Howard Jones mentioned that he had received $2,000 in 1933 from sports publicist Christy Walsh. After 1934, Zup's football articles were distributed by the Christy Walsh sports syndicate to a national newspaper market. Walsh had assigned sportswriters to follow Babe Ruth, Knute Rockne, Pop Warner and other sports notables. They collaborated with the authors to produce syndicated copy for subscribing newspapers. Zuppke was a member of the Christy Walsh All-American Football Board composed of coaches whose stories were sold to newspapers. At the end of the season, the board of four coaches selected an All-American team.[12]

As salaries were reduced, the faculty showed little sympathy for the higher compensation for coaches. On December 9, 1933, the Big Ten faculty representatives issued opinions that coaches should not lend their names to manufacturers of athletic equipment unless they had a bona fide interest in the equipment and that it was improper for coaches to coach all-star games. On May 19, 1934, they issued an opinion that it was improper for coaches to publish articles with comments on teams and current games. The opinions expressed sentiments and did not have the force of rules. Zuppke's name remained on Rawlings football equipment. In 1938, he received $1,666 from the Rawlings sporting goods company for the use of his name in equipment advertising. He collected royalty payments until 1940. Zup published articles on teams and current games, but he did not coach post-season games between 1934 and 1942.[13]

After twenty years at the university, Zuppke was a long-term staff member. When Engineering dean Arthur C. Willard was chosen as president on March 13, 1934, Zup responded, "He's all right. He came here the same year I did." While coaches did not have academic tenure, Zuppke's seven championships and notable upsets provided job security. With a keen eye for athletic performance on the practice field, he also watched football players who were members of university basketball and baseball teams and participated in track meets.[14]

Ouside of coaching duties, the Zuppkes maintained family ties during winter and summer visits to his brothers in Minneapolis, his parents in Los Angeles and Fannie's family in Muskegon. Brother Paul came to Urbana for the 1916 Colgate game. Brother Herman, with his orange and blue tie, frequently attended Illinois games. In July 1923, the Zuppkes vacationed at the Grand Canyon and visited Bob's parents in Long Beach, California. On December 15, 1926, Hermine Zuppke died in Long Beach after a long illness. In 1930, Franz Zuppke died in Minnesota. In 1934, Bob and Fannie drove to Muskegon for a two-week vacation. In the fall, Brother Paul's son, Bob Zuppke, came from Minneapolis to try out for the Illinois football team. Bob visited and corresponded with Edna Erwin, Fannie's sister in Muskegon, and his nieces and nephews in California and Minnesota.[15]

Bob and Fannie enjoyed smal-town life in central Illinois. Arriving in 1913, they moved to the Gregory Apartments in Urbana, where football players would drop in for visits. Zuppke played chess with President James' secretary. They often visited Henry and Harriet Ward in Urbana. Ward was a distinguished member of the zoology faculty. At games, Mrs. Zuppke sat in a box seat behind the Illinois bench and joined the coach in post-game visits to the infirmary. From 1916 to 1923, they were chaperones at many campus dances. Zup once declared that the leading contact games in college were football, wrestling and dancing.

In 1926, they moved to the new and larger Parkview Apartments in Champaign. Located at 305 West University Avenue, the flat overlooked West Side Park and had thirty-three windows and an art studio for Bob. George Huff lived on the other side of the park. The coach and athletic director often walked the sixteen blocks to their offices in the new gymnasium. Zup did not care to drive on campus, so Fannie drove him to work in her electric car. Their home life was centered on reading and social events. They enjoyed music, theater and dancing. They attended synphony concerts. At the 1929 Army game, the 1927 captain greeted her and a starting guard gave her his glasses to hold to guarantee a win. She was a member of the Daughters of the American Revolution, St. Paul's Episcopal Church in Muskegon and the Women's Auxiliary of the Emmanuel Memorial Episcopal Church in Champaign. She also belonged to Gamma Phi Beta and art and card clubs. She hosted luncheon and bridge clubs and served on a United Charities committee. At home, they played chess and bridge. He smoked cigars on occasion and borrowed cigarettes, but was not a habitual drinker or smoker. He paid little attention to clothing and relied on Fannie's judgment. They did not have many social relationships with the academic faculty. In May 1931, after Bob spoke at a Rotary meeting in DeKalb, the Zuppkes visited the Reitsch families in Rockford for golf with former players and a talk to newspapermen. They returned to Rockford for a Christmas visit.[16]

In the summer of 1935, Fannie's health began to fail. By 1936, she was critically ill. On April 5, Bob drove her to Mercy Hospital in Muskegon. In June and July, he made two daily trips to the hospital to be at her bedside. They celebrated their thirtieth anniversary at the hospital on June 27. Bob donated blood on July 29, but she did not recover from a second operation. Her death on July 31 deprived Zuppke of "the only pal I ever had." In 1940, radio commentator Bill Stern, "the Colgate shave cream man," told the love story of Bob and Fannie on his national network sports show. Fannie was Bob's loyal and devoted wife, who was always at his side. She kept a scrapbook containing accounts of Illinois wins and explained that she remembered only the victories. Fulfilling a promise to Fannie, Bob placed a Gorham glass window depicting "The Transfiguration" in Champaign's Emmanuel Memorial Episcopal Church. Upon returning from her funeral, Bob directed that her room should be left exactly as it was before her death. Red Grange regarded her as a counterbalance to Zup's tempestuous energy and believed that he was never the same Zup after her death.[17]

After Fannie's death, housekeeper Leona Ray kept his immaculate apartment in Champaign, where order and cleanliness prevailed in all but one room. In Zup's room, in impressive disorder, were piled paintings and sketches, scrap-books, artists kits, photographs, football plays and unrelated bits of clothing, which typified his casual approach to the intricacies of living. His housekeeper checked him out when he left the apartment and accompanied him on trips to Michigan and Arizona. He avoided fashionable clothes and delighted in high-powered automobiles. His eating habits were irregular in time and content. He preferred vegetables and a special boiled red cabbage with an apple. While painting, he snacked on melons, celery, carrots, olives and pickles. Visitors described Zuppke as an omnivorous reader and noted that his sun parlor was piled high with books and magazines. Chicago reporter Jack Ryan characterized his demeanor as shrewd, thoughtful and instinctive, and observed that he seldom stepped out of character. His German accent was retained long beyond the day he mastered precise enunciation. Players noted that he turned on his accent when he desired to make a point. In 1941, Ryan recognized that "age may have blasted a gulf" between Zuppke and the undergraduates, but the sincere warmth of the players' admiration for Zup bridged the gap.[18]

18

The Howling of the Wolves

As performing entertainers had press critics, sports figures received criticism from "wolves" in the press and in the published comments of alumni, businessmen and politicians. In 1936, Zuppke shifted several experienced players to new positions and counted on sophomores to provide a heavier, but inexperienced, team. The Illini opened with wins over DePaul and Washington University and lost the final non-conference game to Southern California. A tie at Iowa and wins at Michigan and Chicago offset home field losses to Northwestern and Ohio State. In their three losses, the weakened offense scored only eight points. With a 2–2–1 conference record, Illinois finished in sixth place. At a mass meeting before the Ohio State game, Zuppke's comments were blunt. "We have the players the other universities didn't want." "All boys in football suits are not players." "There are not many of you here tonight. Of course not! The team is not winning." Before the final game in Chicago, a reporter for the *Daily Maroon* interviewed Illinois captain Elvin Sayre, who said that he was dead tired and wanted some rest. The reporter elaborated on Sayre's remarks to include an endorsement of professionalization, which was due to the lack of control over wealthy alumni, and a condemnation of spring and fall practice sessions, which required eighteen hours a week.[1]

The year 1936 was Zuppke's last winning season. For three decades, the University of Illinois Athletic Association board was an informal group that had acted on the requests of George Huff and ratified his actions. Beset with health problems since 1926, he retained widespread respect in the Midwest and the university community. Praised for his honesty, morality and abiding by the rules, Huff's death on October 1, 1936, left a huge vacancy in the leadership of the Athletic Association. It also ended twenty-three years of close collaboration with Zuppke, who said, "I will surely miss him. It was a great loss to me." The illnesses and the deaths of his beloved Fannie and the redoubtable George Huff within two months isolated Zup, limited his coaching activities, and opened the way for more administrative and faculty criticism.[2]

On February 27, 1937, the university Board of Trustees appointed 37-year-old Wendell S. Wilson as Athletics Director. After the death of Assistant Director Carl Lundgren in 1934, Huff had designated the personable Wilson as a possible successor. "Weenie" Wilson was a member of the 1925–26 football teams and had been on the coaching staff since 1926. He was Huff's third choice for his successor and had been appointed as acting director on September 30, 1936. Older football alumni had preferred George "Potsy" Clark for the position. Wilson also became a member of the Athletic Association Board. The other four members of the Board were James P. Kratz, a farmer from Monticello; William E. C. Clifford, a Champaign businessman and politician; Frederic Russell, an advertising professor who had trained solicitors for the Stadium Drive; and Frank Richart, an engineering professor. Kratz, Richart and Wilson were alumni, but only Wilson had played football. In 1933, Russell promoted Wilson as a coach whose work with freshman teams would produce fine varsity squads. In December 1936, Richart became a Big Ten faculty representative. On March 28, 1937, Russell asked Zuppke to support Wilson at a welcome dinner for Wilson and Physical Education director Seward Staley. The event was sponsored by the Athletic Association and the Champaign and Urbana Associations of Commerce. Zup's guarded endorsement was, "You Illini have been with us when we were up, and you have stayed with us when we were down — that's the spirit it takes to give a banquet for a couple of fellows who haven't yet gained a yard for Illinois." Wilson pledged to do all he legitimately could do to attract high-grade young men to the University. On August 7, emeritus president David Kinley referred to this time as "our period of football depression." He observed that in many universities this would have brought demands to fire the coach and attributed Illinois' status of mental balance and sane viewpoint to the high standards of George Huff. At the same time, the Athletic Association Board of Directors was discussing the possibility that a new coach would silence the football wolves.[3]

While the Athletic Board was seeking a return to winning football, Zuppke invoked loyalty to the state university and supported no financial incentives for recruitment. In 1937, he told prospective players that Illinois was a great school where you will get a great education. Other speakers at the Champaign and Chicago banquets were emphatic in declaring that Illinois alumni had not been zealous enough in talking to high-grade high school students in their communities. In the January *Alumni* News. Wilson cited Big Ten Resolution XIX on recruiting and Rule VI on financial aid and listed fourteen things that Illini Clubs or alumni groups could do. Professors Russell and

Richart endorsed the use of alumni in securing athletes. Zuppke missed George Huff and asked for the loyal support of Wilson as a young man who had energy, foresight, organizing ability, and a broad knowledge of athletics. Beginning in 1938, an All-State High School team was invited to the annual football banquet.[4]

Since 1922, the preservation of virility in a coeducational institution had been a cause of increasing concern among the older generation. Their concern was related to the growth of social life centered in fraternities and sororities as the percentage of women undergraduates grew from 22 percent in 1913 to 28 percent in 1937. In a March 3 Founders Day radio talk, Zuppke said that athletics were important as the only truly masculine note in a university environment and that learning and culture would fade unless they were sandpapered by the grinding forces embodied in the true meaning of the word virility. An all-around institution must nurture this indispensable requisite of human fitness. The playing fields *outside* were just as important as the books and ink *inside*.[5]

The depressed economy posed financial problems for the whole university. Assisted by the Alumni Association, the administration created the University of Illinois Foundation in 1935. In 1937, the Foundation launched the Illinois Plan of Coordination to raise funds for an Illini student union and other projects. Russell directed the campaign from December 1936 through February 1937. Wilson spoke to alumni groups in the East and Midwest to enlist their support. In a letter for a fund-raising brochure, Zuppke recalled that during the stadium campaign, he and Huff made a promise that when the stadium was paid for they would help the alumni build a student union. Citing the lack of a campus facility for a social life, he appealed for contributions for a student center. On March 3, he supported the Plan of Coordination in a Founders Day radio talk. On April 27, he spoke at a community meeting on the benefits that the planned student union would bring to Champaign County. On May 5, as many as 2,500 Chicago alumni heard him follow President Willard's appeal for money with a plea for building loyalty among students at the university. Three weeks later in a radio broadcast to promote a Foundation mass mailing requesting contributions for a student union, Champaign County chairman Jack Watson interviewed Zuppke, who discussed the football team's strengths and weaknesses.[6]

Zuppke's oratory and football's appeal aided the alumni campaign, but 1937 was not a good year for fund-raising. A Foundation loan and a federal grant paid for the construction of the $1,500,000 student union. The $250,000 in alumni support for equipment and furnishings was still being solicited in 1942. Hints that some of the Foundation funds might be used to recruit student athletes bore little fruit. Zuppke started spring football practice on February 8, 1937. There was a decline in the number of students who tried to make the football team and a weakening of the freshman squads, which had supplied winning teams. In September 1937, the Foundation proposed solutions for the financial problems caused by a system that allowed every voter in the state to assert the right to send his children to a state-supported school at public expense. The solutions were raising tuition, adopting higher admission standards and increasing university appropriations. As none of these alternatives were feasible at a state university in an economic depression, the Foundation's newspaper concentrated on appeals to loyalty and increased coverage of the football team.[7]

The football program was not well positioned to generate new income. With the gradual stabilization of the economy, gate receipts remained a factor, but the electronic media now reached a wider market. The university regarded broadcasting as an advertising opportunity, rather than a source of income. In 1933, listeners to its WILL station reported good reception of the broadcasts of the Michigan and Chicago games. In 1936, it yielded only $1,650 and commercial stations were demanding exclusive rights. In June, Detroit poet Edgar A. Guest interviewed Zup on his football success for an inspirational "It Can Be Done" NBC radio program. The network claimed a listening audience of eight to ten million. By 1938, college football would become the most popular Saturday radio program in the nation, but statewide, radio broadcasting in Illinois did not have the impact that it did in Michigan and Ohio. As the commercial value of broadcasting became apparent to the Athletic Association, changes occurred. By 1940, broadcasting rights fees were nearly $4,000.[8]

In a depressed economy, appeals for loyalty to the state university were less effective in recruiting than providing financial aid to athletes. The declining fortunes of the Illini did not prompt Zuppke to emulate Chicago's Clark Shaughnessy's financial support of needy athletes. Responding to mounting criticism about recruiting violations in August 1937, John Griffith's Big Ten office surveyed the conference athletic directors for information on recruiting freshman athletes. The results indicated that the most active coaches were at Purdue, Michigan and Indiana. Alumni and Athletics offices were the most active recruiters. The numbers of athletes surveyed at Ohio State, Iowa, Chicago, Minnesota and Wisconsin were significantly smaller than the numbers at other universities.[9]

Zuppke thought that his very green 1937 team would be stronger, but it would lack the numbers required for success in the Big Ten. He hoped for improvement in the line and the kicking game. A 20–6 win over Ohio University was followed by scoreless ties with DePaul and Notre Dame. The Notre Dame game attracted 40,000 spectators and was regarded as an upset.

The Fighting Irish had a statistical advantage over the Fighting Illini, but the determined defense of Zuppke's team stopped all scoring drives. In their first meeting, the Irish and the Illini split the $91,576 gate receipts. Losses to Indiana and Michigan preceded a 19–0 defeat at Ohio State. In Columbus, Francis Schmidt's razzle-dazzle offense baffled the Illini. At halftime, the Ohio State band paid tribute to the veteran Illinois coach with a "Yea Zuppke" formation. A 5–4–2 Illinois defense secured the first conference win with a 6–0 upset of Northwestern. The second was a 21–0 win over Chicago, which was played before 13,627 in subfreezing snowy weather on November 20.[10]

The Athletic Association Board recognized that terminating the coach's twenty-five years at Illinois required careful planning and the cultivation of his friends and supporters. The first event was the celebration of a Zuppke Homecoming on October 31, 1937. On Friday evening, the weekend began with a testimonial tribute to him on a Gridiron Smoker program aired by WHN in New York. The narration closed with a statement of the coach's influence on football through the summer courses that he taught. Since 1919, more than 400 graduates of the football course were teaching his ideas to their teams. John Depler, a center on the championship 1919 team, recorded a radio tribute in Rock Island. He praised Zuppke's coaching ability, technical knowledge, color and drive. He described Zup as a keen student of human nature and psychology, who never permitted his reputation to depend on games won and lost. In mentioning the coach's sense of humor, he recalled making three bad center snaps, which prompted the 140-pound coach to attempt to shake the 200-pound lineman. As Zup shook himself, both the coach and the entire squad broke out laughing. Red Grange and Fielding Yost also spoke at the pep rally before the Homecoming game. Illinois outgained Michigan, but the Wolverines won the 7–6 game with a point after touchdown.[11]

Wendell Wilson arranged a colorful halftime tribute to Zuppke. Governor Henry Horner and other dignitaries honored the coach as the band played "For He's a Jolly Good Fellow" and the Block I cheering section formed a "Zup" picture. Zuppke received an illuminated parchment testimonial and 366 congratulatory letters from former players, alumni, coaches and friends in twenty-nine states. Though negative views were absent, the volume was impressive, and their content was more impressive. Most of the players regarded football as the most important college influence in their careers. He taught most of his "blokes" how to be fighting Illini in victory or in defeat. Alumni pleaded with him to continue coaching. The director of the Catholic Newman Foundation praised his fine ethical ideals and urged him to continue his fine ministry among Illinois athletes. The net effect of the public tributes and the testimonials of former players was to rekindle Zuppke's determination to continue and demonstrate the extent of his support among alumni and former players.[12]

The second tribute to the coach was a biography. A Chicago publisher suggested an account of Illinois football and the life and work of Bob Zuppke. In four weeks, Red Grange and his associate, George Dunscomb, produced *Zuppke of Illinois*, a 200-page commemorative publication. With forewords by Grantland Rice and Grange, the book's lively style was embellished with Zuppke stories. Its theme emphasized the players' views of their coach. It featured quotations and sayings of the picturesque and pictorial coach. Among the illustrations was a photograph of Zuppke and Grange identified as Polybius and Scipio Aemilianus. For a chapter on alumni, Zuppke conceded that "we may have been too quiet about the advantages Illinois has to offer and that high school athletes may have mistaken our conservatism for indifference toward them." He supported the Foundation's Illini Plan of Coordination to locate good high school students and secure funds for a student union. He said that it was definitely *not* a plan to get athletes. The book was put on sale for two dollars at the October 9 Notre Dame game.[13]

The third tribute came after the season had ended. The Champaign Rotary Club honored Rotarian Bob Zuppke at its November 22 annual banquet. Over two hundred members and guests included thirty "Zuppmen of the past." They heard 1921 fullback Jack Crangle recall that the only way to get into the good graces of Zup was to kill somebody. Remarks by Justa Lindgren, President Willard, and Mike Tobin led up to Zuppke's talk on "Earning a Living." Burt Ingwersen and Justa Lindgren told Zuppke stories. Lindgren said Zuppke worked hard, used his material to the best advantage, was an expert in diagnosing opponent's plays and was honest with his men. President Willard declared that Zuppke was his personal friend. Mike Tobin offered a vest pocket biography of the coach. He said that Zup's best year was 1918, when the S.A.T.C. team was marched off to the football field each morning after breakfast. He mentioned Zup's use of the onside kick in 1919, his volcanic haranguing of his men and his refusal to admit that any of his teams would have lost had they played up to their capabilities. The coach gave a totally serious talk with an apology for talking too harshly during the season and for insisting that it was for the good of the players. He advised them to disregard flattery and learn from your own self. He concluded with "I don't want to be called the greatest coach. I just want to be your friend."[14]

A fourth tribute occurred at a December 2 Zuppke Banquet at the Palmer House in Chicago. In all, 1,400 guests of the Chicago Illini Club met in the Grand Ballroom to hear Governor Henry Horner preside over a long series of testimonials by athletics directors, state legislators, newspapermen, coaches, university staff and officials. Zuppke was the chief sage and entertainer. He pàid tribute to Williams, Stagg, Wilce, Yost and Rockne, and recalled that George Huff had "built up the Illinois philosophy of good sportsmanship and sanity in athletics" and "made it possible for me to be tolerated by you." Harry Stuhldreher presented Zup with a Wisconsin sweater and letter. Zuppke and Branch Rickey spoke a second time for a national NBC radio broadcast. Before Presidents Kinley and Willard, university trustees and deans, Big Ten commissioner John Griffith praised him as a stabilizing influence in the conference. Governor Horner and Chicago Major Ed Kelly joined in the revelry and Zup returned to Champaign with another collection of scrolls and testimonial letters.[15]

Beneath the good feelings in the 1937 twenty-fifth anniversary tributes to Zuppke were the conflicting motivations of the athletic director and the coach. These were evident at a November 12 meeting of the Cleveland University Club on the evening before the Ohio State game. Before his first official visit to Ohio Stadium, Athletics Director Wendell Wilson declared that Columbus was "the football capital of the world." Unhappy about the 1928 firing of football coach and fellow Milwaukeean John Wilce, Zuppke said that Columbus was a "center for second-guessers."[16]

As the depression deepened, there was increased pressure to relax strict regulations on amateurism and "adopt a more practical and materialistic standard" for college athletics. The critical indictments in the Carnegie Report were negated by increased public interest in competitive intercollegiate football. Alumni and fraternities intensified their efforts to persuade talented athletes to attend their alma maters. Big Ten commissioner Griffith received reports of intense competition between Pittsburgh, Florida, Tennessee, and Michigan for the services of Charles Maag of Sandusky, Ohio, before he chose to attend Ohio State. Griffith also investigated a report that Northwestern had outbid Iowa for Don Clawson of Kankakee, Illinois. George Halas sent six plays in June, but the Illini lacked offensive speed to execute them. On September 16, 1938, three sophomore prospects from the St. Louis area left Zuppke's squad, reportedly to go somewhere they could "get something for our football playing." A halfback and a guard transferred to the Washington University freshman team. The wire service reports quoted a tackle as saying Illinois was too pure. Wilson said that it was well that they left and did not stay to stir up discontent among the other players.[17]

Starting his twenty-sixth season as coach in 1938, Zuppke faced the usual difficult schedule that included successive games with Notre Dame, Northwestern, Michigan and Ohio State. All these football powers had aggressive state and national recruiting systems. As in 1935, Illinois lost the opening game to Don Peden's Ohio University Bobcats. In attendance were 13,461 high school guests in forty-cent seats in the south stands, 9,691 Boy Scouts and advisors and 5,980 university students. The Illini outgained the visitors 205 yards to 59, but costly fumbles thwarted the offense. After the game, Bob called for "skull practice tomorrow at three," On American Legion Day, 2,102 Legionnaires and 864 Army Air Corps men from Chanute Field watched as Zup used forty-three players in a 44–7 win over DePaul. On October 8, 7,260 students cheered as Illinois upset Indiana, 12–2, and "smashed its way" into the Big Ten title picture. In another epidemic of fumbles, the cheering faded as Notre Dame outplayed the Fighting Illini 14–6. On October 28, the Northwestern Wildcats shut out Illinois 13–0 before 26,850 Homecoming fans, 1,103 members of the president's party and 543 reporters in the press box. A trip to Ann Arbor brought a 14–0 defeat for Zuppke's team. Injuries plagued the Illini, whose five sophomore linemen could not stop Tom Harmon and Forest Evashevski. The Illini finished the season with a 32–14 Dad's Day loss to Ohio State before 18,000 in Champaign, and a 34–0 win at Chicago for a seventh-place finish in the Big Ten.[18]

During the 1938 season, Champaign fans and alumni in St. Louis and Peoria became increasingly critical of Zuppke's coaching. After the Dad's Day loss to Ohio State, the student newspaper reported that wolves on the heels of Bob Zuppke found new meat yesterday afternoon and that many on campus, in the Twin Cities, in the state, and throughout the country, blamed him for the disappointing season. Wendell Wilson hosted the first I-Men's Dinner. Former president Kinley recalled the fortunes of Illinois athletics and stated his continuing belief in Coach Zuppke. The coach vowed that he was willing to go up or down with his athletes and struck back at critical wolves. He knew his own limitations and declared that he was no "baby kisser" and "no quitter." He added that he wouldn't step out until his successor had a fair chance. On November 17, the *Chicago Herald-Examiner* reported that Zuppke had resigned and the rumor "rumbled around" the state. Zup denied any intention of resigning and closed the season with a victory over Chicago. At the Champaign football banquet on November 21, he "raked his critics fore and aft." Acknowledging the public criticism, he alleged that critics were only interested in winning. He urged the players to attend practice and defended his speaking record. He received a vote of confidence from the team and thanked them for playing in the most criticized season in all Illinois history.[19]

In November, depressed by consecutive losses to Notre Dame, Northwestern and Michigan, an alumni attack in the *St. Louis Globe-Democrat* and questioning at a Peoria alumni meeting, Zuppke had asked Wilson what he would get if he decided to quit coaching before he reached the age of 65 in 1944. Wilson contacted President Arthur Willard, who agreed to approve a retirement plan if it was acceptable to Zuppke. Wilson had the legal counsel draw up a contract, which called for his retirement in 1939 and becoming a

Zuppke (center) reading about his forced resignation, November 29, 1938. Courtesy *The News-Gazette.*

consultant at $7,500 a year until 1944. On the 25th, Wilson obtained the approval of a retirement agreement, by the Athletic Association Board of Directors. On the 27th, he reported that Zuppke would not sign the agreement as he had stated publicly that he would not resign. The Association Board then reduced the retirement salary to $6,000 and passed a resolution requesting Zuppke to sign the agreement. On the day before the November 29 Board of Trustees meeting in Chicago, Wilson advised him that the "wise thing to do would be to sign the agreement" because the $6,000 salary might be reduced to $3,000 if he didn't sign. Zuppke had his lawyer review the document and included a phrase allowing him to engage in other activities during retirement, and then he signed five copies on the evening of November 28.[20]

At the November 29 trustees meeting, Wilson presented the retirement agreement to a surprised Board. Meanwhile, a Chicago Kappa Sigma alumnus called Zuppke about speaking at a December 9 banquet. The coach said that "I don't know if I'll ever give another speech. I've resigned." The news spread like wildfire around Chicago and reached the Associated Press and

United Press wire services. Trustees president Harold Pogue telephoned former players. Reporters packed the lobby of the Blackstone Hotel until 2:45
P.M., when the trustees announced that the resignation was rejected by an
eight to one vote. The scene of jubilation then shifted to Zuppke's Champaign apartment, where the coach entertained the press until midnight. He
said that "it all started because three tramp athletes couldn't make my football team, rotten as it was." The following week, he spoke to the Oak Park
Rotary football banquet and joined Willard in speaking to the 900 attending the Chicago Illini Club annual football banquet. The Chicago affair was
"almost a Zuppke love feast," and the coach said he was ready to forgive and
forget. After receiving the club's gold watch from Grange, he said that the
Athletic Association only "meant to do a kindness to an old man." He concluded with the observation that being responsible to an irresponsible public is not easy. He also spoke to football meetings in Belleville, Canton,
LaSalle-Peru, Monticello, Springfield and Toulon, before returning to Champaign to respond to some of the 240 letters of support. The master of deceptive plays had won the final game of the season.[21]

19

Coaching in Limbo and Integration

Zuppke's victory at the trustees meeting did not silence his critics or end the coaching controversy. On December 1, the Alumni Association Board of Directors met with Fred Russell at the Palmer House to hear an "off the record" report of Russell's version of the retirement affair, which contradicted newspaper accounts. His "revealing narrative" was much appreciated by the directors. The *Daily Illini* reported that "a group of anti–Zuppke alumni had requested Mr. Russell to do all in his power to remove the coach." Most undergraduates were unaware of the controversy. Some of them objected because they were not consulted during the controversy. The lettermen's club was unanimous in its support of the coach, but law students petitioned for his resignation. Alumni in St. Louis, Peoria, Bloomington and Danville demanded an investigation. John Rabenau of the St. Louis Club urged the Alumni Association to investigate the Athletic Department. Insurance salesman Fred Luthy, president of the Peoria Illini Club, secured a resolution requesting that the university trustees investigate the athletic situation and "rectify the existing conditions." Copies of this anti–Zuppke resolution were sent to all Illini Clubs. On December 14, Professor Russell told the Pekin Rotary Club's football banquet that a new coach would need "salesmanship" and "showmanship" to organize the alumni and should speak forty-five to seventy times a year. At a December 17 meeting in Chicago, Russell and Wilson spoke at length to the Board of Trustees about the coach's status. Russell requested a reconsideration of the Board's November 29 rejection of the "resignation." Zuppke followed with a one-hour statement to the Board, which took no action. After the football season, he had filled eleven speaking engagements before he left in early January for a month in Phoenix. While the coach rested from his labors, trustee Harold Pogue investigated the status of the Athletic Association directors. Other alumni contrasted

Zuppke's reputation for honesty with the low moral ceiling of big-time athletics.[1]

Zup had always favored fast players. After three weeks in Arizona, he heard that the wolves were at work and rushed back to Champaign to keep an eye on the situation. He drove 1,968 miles in three days to meet with seventy-five enthusiastic and supportive football players assembled at a fraternity house by Captain Mel Brewer. On February 3, he attacked the wolves in a talk at the McLean County Illini Club. He said critics were "tackling a buzz saw" and argued for harmony. He boasted that he could take it and that he would get out when he thought the right man was there who was big enough to carry on in the job. He said that he could hire a team that would win, but he believed that Illinois did not want subsidized athletes and would not recruit beggars. He confided to Al Fuller at the Palmer House that he had quite a fight on his hands and that "the whole thing is not definitely settled, but seems to be developing altogether in my favor. However, you can never tell what kind of twists things may take." Colleagues in the Athletic Association staff supported him, but the uncooperative Athletic Association Board rejected his request for the appointment of George "Potsy" Clark and Jack Beynon as assistant coaches. The support of local newspapers was wavering. Zup believed that they would get along all right provided outsiders left them alone. The 1938 resignation affair had boosted the sales of *Zuppke of Illinois*, but by 1939, Kuhn's department store gave away copies with the purchase of an $8 suit.[2]

Russell's opposition was not confined to his membership on the Athletic Association Board. In the fall of 1938, he was also co-editor of the Foundation's *Illini News*, a bi-weekly newspaper for donors to the fund for the student union. In covering the 1939 football season, the headline for a report on the "sloppily and queerly played" loss to Ohio University read "Fans Disappointed at Performance of Touted Varsity Eleven." After the trustees rejection of Zuppke's resignation, the *Illini News* denied that there was a movement to oust him. It criticized newspaper reports and proclaimed that Clifford was a warm personal friend of Zuppke and that Wilson looked up to and respected the coach. Russell was identified as a popular professor who encouraged Zuppke's teams and sought players. Zuppke called the unfavorable comments to Willard's attention and Russell was no longer listed as an editor.[3]

The alumni and administrative wolves were not the only constituencies concerned about the football program. Professor Robert Browne, representing the Faculty Advisory Committee, acknowledged the conflict between Zuppke's "play with what you've got" philosophy and his critics' contention that he should "go out and get them." Browne suggested that it was easier to make athletes out of students than students out of athletes. He believed that the material was 85 percent of success and the coaching was 15 percent. More concerned about football's place in the university, he maintained that academic quality had little correlation with athletic success and contrasted the academic standing of Harvard and Chicago with the football reputation of Pittsburgh and Notre Dame. He did not think that universities should provide public entertainment, but did not draw the line to exclude commencement and homecoming. He also observed that the more money athletics took in, the more is spent on athletics. He opposed the pampering of athletes to keep them eligible and compared the athletic program's support of intramural sports to a charity ball. Other faculty committees objected to spring practices and travel absences. The Committee on Athletics criticized Zuppke for extending the return dates for the 1935 and 1939 games at Southern California.[4]

In addition to faculty concerns about the football program, the publicity following the November 1938 trustees meeting stimulated university discussions of the situation. On December 23, the Kampus Kibitzers Klub, composed of university journalists and public relations staff, staged a program on reorganization. A quartet sang a hymn of reorganization to "defrost, deflate and debunk the powers that be." Fred Schooley of WILL read a radio bulletin announcing that a Board of Trustees meeting at the Blackstone Hotel in Chicago had voted eight to one to appoint Zuppke as president with dictatorial powers. Bill Pfister played the role of Zuppke. Other bulletins announced that Zup had abolished the Board of Trustees and the Athletic Association Board and sold the football band. The new president appointed the Athletic Association Board members as vice presidents, Steward Staley as head football coach, and Lloyd Morey as head of the Physical Plant. The young alumni of Danville greeted Zuppke's elevation to the presidency as an opportunity to get a good football coach and awarded the president a DBBS degree (Double barreled Bull Shooter). The Kibitzers specialized in fantastic whimsy, but the football coaching issue remained a topic of campus conversations. In 1950, the university published a history by Chief Kibitzer Carl Stephens, which included a photo of Zuppke captioned "Five presidents of the University have served during my regime, and I have been proud of every one of them."[5]

The wolves continued to call for Zuppke's replacement. In May, the Athletic Association Board opposed a change in its membership, as it would only stir up another fuss. After a lengthy discussion on July 21, 1939, the trustees reappointed the five Athletic Association directors who had approved the 1938 resignation. An attempt to add Milton Olander failed to pass. Zuppke's position improved on September 30, when the trustees increased the Athletic Association Board from five to seven members by adding Milt Olander and

Charles M. Thompson. Olander was a former player and assistant coach. Thompson was dean of the College of Commerce and served as president of the Alumni Association and the fund-raising University Foundation. He had replaced George Huff as an alumni leader and political power broker and was not known to have been involved in the 1938 coaching controversy. The trustees hoped that a larger board would provide a broader basis and benefit from more counsel and ideas.[6]

Facing the 1939 season with few outstanding players, Zuppke doubted that they would win the majority of their games, which would give the wolves another opportunity to howl. He wrote Carl Voyles that the Trustees had told him that "I may coach as long as I want to." Voyles was interested in returning to the Illinois coaching staff, but Zup questioned the wisdom of leaving a $9,000 position at William and Mary for the turmoil in Champaign. Football practice began on February 6. In the spring, Zuppke made speaking engagements in Detroit, Chicago, Peoria, New York, Philadelphia, Memphis and George Ade's party at Brook, Indiana. Ade was a nationally known humorist and playwright and creator of the popular 1902 light opera *The Sultan of Sulu* and the 1904 football comedy *The College Widow*. His home was a social and political mecca. He was also a major contributor to the building of Purdue's football stadium. On May 24, at Ade's Hazelden Celebrity Night party in honor of visiting notables, Zuppke stood a hundred of the boys on their heads with his spellbinding oratory. When Ade's home was struck by a tornado, Zup wrote a letter of encouragement. His remarks at the dinner party with the New York Illini Club also brought national publicity.[7]

After a few weeks at Muskegon in July and August, Zuppke returned for fall practice in September. The problems that had plagued him since 1930 remained. In September, he told the Campus Businessmen's Association that Champaign "was not as gifted for proselytizing" as universities in big cities where jobs are easy to find and where there are men with money and time to get athletes. The businessmen did not enjoy hearing about the shortcomings of their community. The economic pressures of the depression, increased competition for the services of the best players, and demands of the wolves for a winning season limited his options.[8]

At the spring practice, he had noticed that Alphonse Anders, an African-American end from Rock Island, outran the entire team. Recalling the spectacular running of Iowa's Ozzie Simmons in 1935 and Northwestern's Bernard Jefferson in 1938, he planned to use African-American players. The first Illinois player had been George A. Flippin, who was a sophomore at the University's College of Physicians and Surgeons in Chicago in 1897. In his five years at the University of Nebraska, he had played against Illinois in 1892. He continued to play for the medical school, which met the university team in 1898 and 1900–01. Roy Young and Hiram Wheeler played for the Illini in 1904–05. From 1905 to 1938, there were no African-Americans on Illinois football, basketball and baseball teams. The causes or depth of racism in Illinois sports lay in public attitudes and the sensitivity of public universities to popular and legislative sentiments. The race riots of 1907 in Springfield, 1917 in East St. Louis and 1919 in Chicago only deepened racial frustration and prejudices. Champaign-Urbana was not a progressive community in racial relations. From 1920 to 1922, local businessmen staged "Bob Zuppke's Business Men's Minstrel Show" at the Rialto and Illinois theaters. Directed by a New York manager, eight local men presented black face acts. As an attraction, Zuppke was the Referee between the Promoter and the Interlocutor. Employment, commercial establishments, and fraternal organizations were segregated. The number of African-American students at the university reached 50 in 1913 and 100 in 1928. In 1939, there were 132. Most of them sought teaching and professional degrees. They had little time for sports and few athletic careers were open to them. The first organized housing was provided by black fraternities in 1917 and 1927. From 1923 to 1930, the University YMCA sponsored an Interracial Commission, but their educational program made slow progress. In the 1930s, minstrel shows were popular in small towns and as student entertainment at the university. A 1935 study of Negro students reported rumors of neglect of athletes trying out for freshman football.[9]

The Illini seldom met African-American players on opposing teams. Colgate did not use them in its 1916 conquest of the Illini in Urbana. The play of Iowa's Fred "Duke" Slater in 1919, 1920 and 1921 games with Illinois was a different matter. Illinois won in 1919, but the 202-pound Iowa tackle broke up plays behind the line and caught runners from behind. He was strong throughout the game, which the Illini won only by scoring on an onside kick recovery and run. In 1920, Slater played a strong defensive game in the first half before the Illinois offense outclassed the Hawkeyes 20–3. In Slater's final game at Iowa City, he opened up holes in Zuppke's line and stopped Illini backs for a 14–2 win. Conditions began to change in 1931 and 1932 when Illinois played against linemen Bill Bell of Ohio State and Fitzhugh Lyons of Indiana. In 1935, Ozzie and Don Simmons and B.T. Harris led Iowa to a 19–0 win over the Illini. Fullback Ozzie's beautiful dodging and outracing the defenders in a 75-yard touchdown run produced the first Iowa score. The game became rougher in the final quarter and there were many fumbles. Simmons got up smiling from a hard tackle. When he was stopped for a 12-yard loss in a drive near the Illinois goal line, the defenders were penalized for piling on. Iowa got the ball on their 2-yard line and scored. Fourteen years later, Illinois center Elvin Sayre recalled the "hell" that Zuppke gave him for "squatting" on Simmons. A stiff arm by Simmons also aroused the disappointed Illinois crowd. In 1936, the Illini thoroughly shackled Simmons despite his dancing, twisting and sidestepping runs, one of which was called back by a penalty. The game was a 0–0 tie. A week later, Illinois suffered a 13–2 loss in an encounter with Northwestern and its African-American halfbacks Clarence Hinton and Bernard Jefferson. In 1938, Jefferson started at halfback in another 13–0 win for the Wildcats. In 1935–38, Illinois was 1-4-1 in games with Iowa and Northwestern and the color barrier was about to be broken.[10]

Highly recommended by Moline High School coach George Senneff, Alphonse "Flip" Anders won the high school dashes at the 1937 interscholastic track meet and entered the university in 1938. His football career was plagued by eligibility questions. In the fall of 1938, Zuppke moved him from end to the backfield and then back to end as he sought to use Anders' speed and aggressive blocking and tackling. Eligibility problems prevented him from playing in the opening game with Bradley. He played thirty-seven minutes at Southern California and was involved in the play that set up the touchdown in the loss to Indiana. In the Homecoming upset of Michigan, he played thirty-three minutes and recovered a fumble to set up the second Illinois touchdown. He played thirty-three minutes in a win at Wisconsin and forty-two minutes in a loss at Ohio State. He started the final game at Chicago and was awarded a letter. Eligibility problems resulted in Anders transferring to Western Illinois University.[11]

The changed attitude toward African-American players was reflected in the career of freshman Bert Piggott who played several games against the 1939 varsity and ran plays of the future opponents. In 1940, Piggott played in the losses to Notre Dame, Michigan and Iowa. He earned a letter as a substitute fullback in 1946, graduated in 1947 and later played professional football. In 1940, Isaiah "Ike" Owens arrived from Gary, Indiana. He was recommended by his high school coach, who knew Ray Eliot. He met the academic and athletic challenges and was invited back for the training table and varsity practice in 1941. He found it pretty difficult to make an impression on Zuppke, but the coach was "aware that a change in race relations was due" and was making some progress toward that end. Owens played in six games before being drafted in the fall of 1941. He returned to play a leading role in the 1947 Rose Bowl victory and graduated with a degree in fine arts. Though there was no publicity and media attention, the color barrier for Illinois football had been broken.[12]

The year 1939 was Zuppke's first season after the attempt to replace him. It started with three losses and a tie. Illinois dominated the opening game with Bradley, but lacked the scoring punch in a 0–0 tie. Zuppke played five sophomores and found that the team was slow and erratic. Half of the players had classes until 4 P.M. Two weeks later, the team traveled to Los Angeles to meet Howard Jones's Southern California Trojans. Despite his perennial pessimism, Zup was the life of the party on the eight-day trip and demonstrated his knowledge of Arizona's natural wonders during practices at Tucson. The hosts outmanned the traveling Illini in 98-degree weather for a 26–0 win before 60,000 fans. During the season, Zuppke spoke at six banquets in Los Angeles, Chicago, Glen Ellyn, River Forest, Columbus and the twentieth reunion of the 1919 championship team in Champaign. On October 21, Illinois lost a 7–6 game to Indiana. On the 28th, they gave up two second-half touchdowns in a 13–0 loss to Northwestern. At their November 4 Homecoming game, they hosted a powerful Michigan team led by All-American Tom Harmon. Two Michigan backs were injured, so Zup was able to contain Harmon with a 5-4-2 defense. Anders recovered one of the Wolverines five fumbles. The Illinois touchdowns were Zup's specials. The second-period score came on a sideline sleeper pass. The fourth quarter score was on a faked missed signal or "talking play," where the quarterback and fullback divert the defense as the ball is snapped to a halfback. The 16–7 victory was Zup's last major upset. The result brought national acclaim from sportswriters and laudatory fan mail from former players, the president of the Board of Trustees, Michigan Illini and the Ohio State football coach. Nearly forty years later, Ray Eliot recalled Zuppke's advice: "When you're faced with one of those years, when your material is only fair and you're not going to win many games, put your eggs in one basket, pick out a tough team and lay for it. Knock it off and you've got yourself a season." Eliot, Zuppke's assistant in 1939, would later include an emotional account of the Michigan game in his inspirational speeches. In another home game, the Illini defeated Wisconsin 7–0. Wisconsin coach Harry Stuhldreher accused the crowd of unsportsmanlike conduct. Zuppke said that he had always "taken it," as no one could control an enthusiastic crowd. He added, "After the game is over the best thing to do is shut up." He avoided public complaints, but called Big Ten commissioner Griffith's attention to a faulty clock at Wisconsin and a twelve-and-a-half-minute halftime delay of the game at Northwestern. The commissioner responded by sending a memo to officials about enforcing the rules. Illinois closed out the season with a 21–0 loss at Ohio State and a 46–0 win at Chicago. A month later, Chicago discontinued intercollegiate football.[13]

After the victories over Michigan and Wisconsin, the Lettermen's Association adopted a resolution calling for a plan involving the Athletic and Alumni Associations in the development of a plan for involving the alumni in securing athletic material, the restoring of the coaching school and coordination of the Athletic Association and the Physical Education Department, bringing Illinois eligibility rules in line with the majority of Big Ten universities, finding jobs for student athletes, and providing proper assistance to deserving players. The Athletic Association had already secured an appropriation for tutoring athletes and established a training table that provided four evening meals a week to the varsity during the football season. On September 30, the Athletic Association directors responded to the Lettermen's resolutions by requesting a modification of the university's scholastic eligibility rules to permit students on probation to play, provided the Big Ten did not modify its rules to secure a uniform interpretation of scholastic eligibility. In reporting to the Board of Trustees on December 18, President Willard referred to the Athletic Association's practice of giving legitimate employment to athletes as ticket sellers, gate men, ushers and skating rink guards and the Student Employment Bureau's policy of considering scholastic standing and financial need in awarding the limited number of part-time jobs in the university and the community. He also said that jobs funded by the National Youth Administration should not be awarded to special groups.[14]

With three Big Ten victories for the first time since 1934 and a football profit of $108,695, the post-season celebrations were upbeat. At the November 28 football banquet, Zuppke credited the new 6 P.M. training table with affording working athletes two hours of practice time each day. He added that the Michigan victory meant more to the players than a conference championship. President Willard acknowledged that football success contributed to the success of the university in the view of the general public. At the December 7 banquet in Chicago, the coach credited a new team spirit for the three conference wins. He hailed the hearty support of President Willard and the perfect confidence of the Board of Trustees. Looking at the difficult 1940 schedule, he mentioned that the Illini might take on Germany and Russia in between games. For the Chicago guests, he located the university in "the corn fields which produce 56 gallons to the acre, and which is so damned provincial that sometimes I even get sore at myself." He promised that he would not buy a team, but build a great team because we have a great university.[15]

The successes against Michigan and Wisconsin enabled Zuppke to retain his folksy sense of humor, but he complained that his coaching duties required attendance at frequent meetings to satisfy the alumni. As the school's constantly traveling ambassador, he went to all sorts of speaking engagements and maintained that he did more for the university in fulfilling them than professors did in their lectures. There was a continuing demand for his speeches at high school football banquets. Such activities were often overlooked and involved uncompensated personal expenses. In a 1939 Athletic Association salary review, Seward Staley and Coleman Griffith concluded that Zuppke's $10,000 salary was unwarranted on the basis of service rendered, but agreed that under the "circumstances surrounding this position," nothing should be done. Staley's dissatisfaction was consistent with the longstanding rivalry and jealousy existing between physical education teachers and athletics coaches. After the termination of his athletic research program in 1930, Griffith had moved from sports psychology to educational administration as head of the Bureau of Institutional Research. He no longer had personal contact with Zuppke. His Memo 220 recommended a $2,520 reduction in university support of Athletic Association staff salaries. The principal transfers from the university to the Association budget were for Douglas Mills $700, Robert Zuppke $500 and Matthew Bullock $270. The Association's response that the coaches were doing university public relations work had little effect, but the shifts were delayed until 1940.[16]

Upon his return from Phoenix in February 1940, Zuppke's cold turned into influenza, which brought on laryngitis and medical appointments for high blood pressure and a strained back. By May 21, he was able to report that "my teeth are all back in and I again can bite in all directions from soup to nuts." In the fall, he was able to attend a dinner in Ann Arbor for Yost's retirement as athletics director. Yost wrote that Zuppke's speech "just about stole the show." The cumulative effect of his medical problems forced Zuppke to restrict his public speaking and give up golf. On his doctor's orders, he was forced to decline fifty-five invitations to speak in fourteen states. His health problems gave the wolves an additional argument for his replacement. The firing of Illinois football coaching graduates in Colorado and Vermont and the departures of Big Ten rivals Francis Schmidt at Ohio State and Clark Shaughnessy at Chicago added to Zuppke's cares.[17]

Deprived of his golf and recreational travel, Zuppke turned to writing. In the 1938 football season, he provided material for Christy Walsh's syndicated "Robert Zuppke Story." Late in 1939, he joined Grantland Rice in planning a book on competitive sports. A leading promoter of sports journalism since the 1920s, Rice supplied the enthusiasm with phrases such as "We are probing souls, heart and brains here" for a text that could reach 5,000,000 school and college players. By March 1940, Zuppke had submitted eight pages on Knute Rockne, aptitude, athletic performance, habits, instincts, and practice. His formula for competition "was to give the boys the opportunities, encourage them, and they will ... be driven by their instincts, which is the nest of their various talents, aptitudes, bents and desires." He also wrote that he "used to hear ... that this race has qualifications the other race does not possess.... We know differently now." Rice contacted Dick Simon of the Simon and Schuster publishing firm in New York. By May, the war situation had affected the publishing market and Zuppke was unable to give his attention to the project. Sports agent Christy Walsh cited radio and the depression as causes of the declining demand that caused him to drop his syndicated articles by sports coaches. He still retained Zuppke on his All-America Board of Football.[18]

As the European war spread across the Atlantic to America, German-Americans again encountered the loyalty issue. In August, Zuppke was the guest of the Justice Department's NBC *I'm An American* series of interviews of naturalized citizens. He stated that he was definitely opposed to the German ideology. "I believe the State exists for the people and not the people for the State." As a coach of athletes who participated voluntarily, he maintained that regimentation in physical education drained and dwarfed the imagination. He considered football as a thoroughly masculine sport in which young men are hardened both physically and mentally. Athletics made loyal and dependable citizens, and loyalty was essential for the family, the school and the country. He taught his boys that taxpayers paid for their education and to respect the local and national governments.[19]

20

The People's University

From 1904 to 1930, Presidents James and Kinley based their appeals for financial support on the concept of a people's university. In 1921, Zuppke told alumni that "every citizen of Illinois is a part owner of the University of Illinois." In his 1930 *President's Report*, Kinley wrote that the people own the University, and that the University belongs to the people, because they created it and support it. He praised the wise policy the people followed in trusting to the good judgment of their elected representatives, the Board of Trustees, and their appointed servants, the members of the faculty. Most legislators exercised good judgment in distributing scholarships and allowing the university's faculty to seek facts and truth. In 1939–40, $5,432,500, or 63.3 precent of the university's income, was appropriated by the Illinois legislature. The biennial appropriation bills reminded legislators of the people's ownership of the university. Legislators representing Champaign County and politically minded trustees became prime factors in ending Zuppke's coaching career.[1]

Public officials often owed their election to favorable publicity and the support of local business interests. Hotel keepers, shopkeepers and commercial businessmen, whose profits depended on the business generated by the football program, demanded victories. With a population of 36,000, excluding the 11,170 university students, Champaign-Urbana had four hotels, several restaurants and two sporting goods stores that relied on football crowds for income. While home attendance rebounded from the depression lows of 1933 and 1934, the average ranged from 21,394 to 35,160 in a stadium that could seat 70,000. From 1935 to 1940, Illinois finished from sixth to ninth in the conference. The Illini won four and lost sixteen games to traditional conference rivals Michigan, Northwestern and Ohio State. The home contests with Notre Dame in 1937 and 1940 and away dates with Southern California in 1935 and 1939 provided much of the additional income needed to fund four minor sports teams and intramural and recreational sports programs.

The depression also increased the commercial exploitation of college football. Newspaper coverage, sponsored radio broadcasts, syndicated columns and the development of advertising agencies contributed to the trend. Ads became an indicator of public taste and profit margins. Advertisers featured football and football players to reach valued consumer markets for their products and services. Businessmen placed football-related advertisements in metropolitan and student newspapers and sports programs. Illinois Homecoming programs indicated that local clothiers and restaurateurs placed the most program ads from 1913 to 1923. After 1933, cigarette firms were the dominant advertisers. The general trend was from local and institutional ads to the national marketing of products and brand names. When football attendance declined, national advertisers placed fewer ads in the programs. These national products had local vendors, whose voices were added to those of the businessmen whose jobs depended on the football crowds. Most of the $139,148 football profit in 1940 came from road games, which did not benefit the local economy. [2]

In April 1940, Zuppke thought that the situation had improved, when Commerce professor Frederic Russell, "the faculty instigator of all this mess," was no longer a member of the Athletic Association Board of Directors. The Board now included three former football players. At its May 8 meeting, Wilson announced that he would aid the athletic program by spending the summer at his boys camp in Wyoming and selling Illinois athletics to the campers. He asked that the coaches remain on campus to meet prospective players. In July, the situation changed again when Harold Pogue was not renominated for the university Board of Trustees and Ken Williamson, "one of Weenie's fraternity brothers" and a member of the "notorious Peoria ring in our squabble," was appointed as a trustee. Zuppke was also told that the football budget, which had been $104,000 in 1938 and $132,000 in 1939, would be $150,000 in 1940. He advised President Arthur Willard that the amount might not be practical in view of the critical years facing the university and a money schedule with three home games against Southern California, Notre Dame and Ohio State.[3]

In the fall of 1940, Zuppke faced the toughest schedule in the United States, which he alleged that the former Athletic Association directors had egged on him. He liked the spirit of the team, but deplored the lack of reserves needed to win games. The Illini opened the season before 13,500 Boy Scouts, 4,726 high school football players and 4,000 war veterans with a 31–0 win over Bradley. The rest of the season brought seven defeats in games with Southern California, Michigan, Notre Dame, Wisconsin, Northwestern, Ohio State and Iowa. In these games, the Illini relied on forward passing to compensate for the lack of a ground game. The offense scored six touchdowns and the defense gave up 144 points. In the Northwestern and Wisconsin games, Illinois lost the contest in the fourth quarter. Two one-touchdown losses to Wisconsin and Ohio State brought compliments from an official on the team's marvelous spirit. Zuppke relayed them to the team as they needed bolstering not scolding.[4]

After the season, a Peoria supporter mentioned five other big name coaches who he had listed in his 1938 reply to the Illini Club's criticism. Zuppke noted that three had lost their jobs, Lynn Waldorf "had trouble" at Northwestern and Elmer Layden was safe at Notre Dame, "which is without doubt the football capital of the United States." Losing six of eight games with Notre Dame and Southern California in the 1930–41 period was less damaging to Zuppke's reputation than losing eleven of twelve games with Ohio State and nine of twelve to Northwestern. He attributed the ups and downs of life at Illinois to their insistence on not producing a maladjustment between football and the true purpose of the university educational program. He acknowledged articles on sportsmanship with the sentiment that as long as he had anything to do with Illinois, they will play the game square and aboveboard. "Every boy here is required to study to his utmost." Though evening exams interfered with practice, "their school work comes first" and he hated "to squawk much."[5]

When the season ended, the press reported Illinois' "most disastrous season." At the Chicago Illini Club's December 5 football banquet, President Willard said the trustees, the Athletic Association Board and the staff all backed the coach. Within a few months, Willard was also hearing the wolves. The new Board of Trustees launched a survey of the university's business operations and hired consultants to determine the efficiency and economy of the operations of the university administration. At the Champaign banquet, Zup said that before he was through, we'll be dishing it out again at Illinois. After the banquets, he left on January 20, 1941, for a 600-mile motor trip to Mexico City with 1915 captain Jack Watson and his wife. After wintering in Phoenix, Zup returned to Champaign for the March 15 to April 26 spring practice. Following a May 22 team meeting, he spent the summer in Muskegon. Zuppke's coaching services had not required his presence in the summer. By 1940, his health had prevented a twelve-month commitment to coaching and speaking to alumni groups.[6]

The controversies and losing records in 1939 and 1940 did not improve Illinois' ability to recruit talented football players. Commenting on the 1940 season, *Chicago Tribune* columnist Arch Ward stated that Zuppke still had creative genius, but that rivals violated conference regulations, whereas Illinois wanted a winning team on a legitimate basis. The alumni were divided. Albert Lee, the President's Office clerk, believed that alumni before 1930 supported Zuppke, whereas those of later years opposed him. There were exceptions, but the coach's strongest support came from older alumni who remembered his winning years. Of thirty-seven communications to the Board of Trustees between April 24 and July 15, twenty-four favored keeping Zuppke, nine favored keeping Wilson, and four would favor dismissing both and starting over. The coach's strongest support came from former players, especially in Chicago. The Illinois Club of Chicago's 1935 *Year Book* was an "Athletic Edition." Three of the club's eight elected officers had played on Zuppke's teams. Twenty-three Chicago alumni and friends petitioned the trustees to retain him so he could complete his university service under the most favorable circumstances. Signers included Harold Pogue, George Halas, Ralph Chapman, Bob Fletcher, Red Grange, Gene Schobinger, and Ernie Lovejoy. George Huff's son wrote that his father would take the same viewpoint.[7]

The Athletic Association Board of Directors was divided. Commerce dean Thompson had resigned. The new board included three alumni who had played football for Zuppke: Milton Olander, Harry Hall and Robert Hickman. Two of them were attorneys. The faculty was represented by Dairy Husbandry professor W.W. Yapp, Law School professor George Goble and the faculty representative Frank Richart from the College of Engineering. The "alumni" favored terminating Wilson's service. The faculty circulated a condemnation of Zuppke's reluctance to meet with high school coaches and his mistreatment of players. They cited cases of coaches and potential players from St. Louis, Alton, Centralia, Spring Valley, Moline, Kewaunee, Joliet, Aurora and Danville who were ignored or mistreated by Zuppke. They also prepared a "statement of facts not for the press" that represented "the overwhelming sentiment of students, faculty, alumni, and townspeople of Champaign-Urbana." The statement claimed that Zuppke's conduct hurt relations with high school coaches, injured the university's influence with state officials in Springfield, and disorganized the coaching staff. At its May 5 meeting, the Board gave Assistant Coach Ray Eliot a $500 raise to keep him at Illinois if there was a change in the football staff.[8]

The underlying problem was the conflicting relationship between the athletic director and the football coach. Wilson's prior service as an assistant coach prompted him to continue scouting games and recruiting players. Zuppke resented Wilson's efforts to assume some of the coach's responsibilities and refused to discuss a need for an aggressive recruitment program. Wilson's support came from members of the St. Louis and Peoria Illini Clubs, hometown friends from Rockford, and Champaign County Republican legislators representing local businesses and political interests. While Illinois did not have an organized support group like Chicago's 55th Street Business Men's Association, local merchants supported efforts to develop a winning football team. As the president of the Campus Businessmen's Association, Shelby Himes was a key figure in providing financial aid for athletes. During the 1940 legislative session, State Senator Everett Peters and Athletics Director Wilson arranged a Springfield meeting to launch an "informal campaign" to give legislative scholarships to outstanding and top-ranking high school athletes. In 1941, two players received legislative scholarships. Peters called for Zuppke's immediate replacement and reminded the trustees that he had secured legislative scholarships and employment for prominent high school athletes. His many conversations with Wilson convinced him that the athletic director was doing everything that was possible to improve the program within Big Ten rules. As an example, he cited Wilson's summer camp for athletes in Wyoming's Teton Mountains. Wilson's idea was that high school graduates would be hired as instructors for the boys. Zuppke said that the camp had not supplied athletes for the football team. Edgar Bands '11, editor of the *Sporting News* and secretary of the St. Louis Illini Club, advised the trustees that both alumni clubs and prospective students were "not interested in the activities of a college which has nothing to offer except a scholastic curriculum, which in itself, interests only a few."[9]

Alumni and players who had supported Zuppke in 1938 remained loyal, but the decisions were now being made by trustees and faculty who were tired of the controversy and convinced that the coach should go. Park Livingston was one of four new Republican trustees elected in the November 1940 general election. Democrat Harold Pogue and four other trustees who had supported Zuppke in 1938 were no longer on the board. Only Homer Mat Adams and two other elected members remained from the Board that rejected his 1938 resignation. Livingston and Adams were the leading trustees in the oust Zuppke movement. Governor Dwight Green and the legislature cut the university's budget and the trustees opened their meetings to the press. Former trustee Oscar Mayer believed that the hue and cry for open meetings stemmed principally from the nuisance squabbles surrounding the athletic situation. On May 19, President Willard received a printed resolution of the St. Louis Illini Club calling for an investigation of the football program. Sponsored by Edgar Brands of the *Sporting News* and signed by fifteen other alumni, the resolution detailed the lack of football success in the preceding twelve years. In May, trouble flared again when Livingston asked for a report of the trustee's athletics committee on their response to the St. Louis petition. In a June 4 speech in the legislature, state senator John Fribley contended that football teams "advertise our state" and demanded that the university fire both Wilson and Zuppke. On June 12, the Athletic Association Board was deadlocked between the three faculty members and the three football alumni. The trustees asked Willard to confer with both men about their resignations.[10]

After the Athletic Association Board's three to three deadlock, Zuppke's tenure was in the hands of a hostile Board of Trustees. Sensing his situation, he went to his Lake Harbor cottage near Muskegon, a few miles from where he began his coaching career. On June 26 and 27, he gave his version of the athletic situation to *Chicago Tribune* reporter Edward Prell. He stated that he had coached the last five years "with a knife in my back" and that his position became more difficult each year. He named Wendell Wilson and Fred Russell as sources of criticism. Wilson had an "ambition to coach the football team" and his stand on proselytizing conflicted with the "amateurism ideals of G. Huff." Zup contended that the alumni who supported him in 1938 had reaffirmed their support at a June 13 golf festival. They were responsible for selling Illinois to the boys. He conceded that his position that the coach was not the head of an employment agency might have become an "impractical ideal." He cited his contributions to the university, refused to meet with President Willard about a resignation, and said that he would never resign. "They'll have to fire me."[11]

The coaching controversy continued until the July 15 trustees meeting in Chicago. On June 28, the *Daily Illini* called for the coach's resignation. Zuppke dismissed the summer *Illini* editorial. The Champaign newspaper speculation was that both the athletics director and the coach would be fired. Kansas City and Seattle alumni clubs announced their support of Zuppke. Grange threatened Wilson with a libel suit. On July 7, President Arthur Willard recommended that the athletic director should not be a member of the Athletic Board, that Wilson be given leave on September 1, 1941, and that Zuppke be reappointed for 1941–42 on condition that he retire between September 1942 and July 1944. As an Athletic Board meeting in Chicago on July 12 was still deadlocked, Willard's recommendations were referred to the Board of Trustees for action.[12]

The Board's Committee on Athletics was highly critical of Zuppke. In reviewing the situation, they suggested that he may have felt that he could ignore his former pupil who was later his assistant coach, but was now his superior as athletic director, and felt that he had enough alumni support and personal friendships with the faculty, president and trustees that he could ignore constituted authority. They noted that the probability was that neither Zuppke's character nor intentional attitude changed, but that he continued to assert his well-known rugged personality and eccentricities, with which George Huff had been able to deal directing them for the benefit not only of the football team but the university as well. The committee observed that losing football teams made it more difficult for his superiors, the student body, and some alumni to overlook these characteristics. They cited Zuppke's discontinuance of coaching school teaching and his limited public relations activities. It was their opinion that the Trustees' refusal to ratify his 1938 retirement plan merely aggravated the situation and that the 1940 appointment of three former football players as Athletic Association directors further contributed to the problem. The committee deleted the praise of Zuppke in Willard's report. They cited the absence of Zuppke and Wilson during the 1940 and 1941 summer sessions and their failure to engage in constructive work for the Athletic Association as reasons for the decision to terminate their services. The trustees' committee recommended that Wilson retire in September 1941 and that the sixty-two-year-old Zuppke confer with the administration regarding his future employment or retirement before March 1, 1942. Its report was adopted by the trustees. To comply with the conference requirement for faculty control, the trustees asked the president to accept the resignations of all seven members of the Athletic Association Board. None of the new members Willard recommended had played football at Illinois. The Board unanimously approved the one-year settlement.[13]

After one more season, Zuppke would deal with a purged Athletic Board and a hostile Board of Trustees. For the press, he expressed pleasure that he could "start all over again" and appreciation for the Athletic Association Board of Control members who had resigned. After their vote, trustees Adams, Davis, Grigsby, Livingston and Meyer stated their approval of Weenie Wilson and their unhappiness with the coach and his supporters. Representing the Illinois electorate, Democrat Homer Matt Adams and Republican Park Livingston agreed that a new coach was needed. Trustee Dr. Karl Meyer, a surgeon at Northwestern's hospital, declared that he would "hate to psychoanalyze Mr. Zuppke's actions." In return, Zup offered to psychoanalyze the doctor. Soon after the trustees' action, Zuppke walked into the Chicago Bears training camp at Delafield, Wisconsin. George Halas rushed to greet him and, after a private discussion, called his three assistants over to discuss coaching strategies. The discussions of coaching and football continued through dinner.[14]

In 1941, Zuppke faced his final season with a conscientious and very hard working team, but one that was not capable of playing Big Ten football. With the military draft taking older players, the team was overloaded with sophomores. Illinois opened with a 45–0 win over Miami University. Outweighed twenty pounds per man, they lost to Big Ten champion Minnesota 34–6. After a 40–0 win over Drake University, the Illini lost their last five games to Notre Dame, Michigan, Iowa, Ohio State and Northwestern. In the Notre Dame game, ten sophomores were on the field at one time. The losses to Michigan and Iowa were largely due to fumbles and a weak secondary. Before the Homecoming game with Michigan, President Willard said that Illinois did not have an anticipation of victory. Athletic director Doug Mills hesitated to talk about the present. The coach wrote that "our boys had to fight like fiends to keep from being annihilated every game they played."[15]

As the season drew to a close, Zup planned his departure. Before the November 15 Ohio State game, he conferred with Harold Pogue and Arch Ward for several hours. On November 18, he told Pogue of his intention to resign as football coach after the November 22 Northwestern game and asked him to notify President Willard and the Board of Trustees. Radio station WGN announced his resignation at 8 P.M. on November 17 and Arch Ward had the exclusive story in the morning *Chicago Tribune*. Illinois lost to North-western 27–0 as 35,000 fans watched "the last strong-hold of simon-pure university athletics in the middle west" fall before the Wildcats' offense. The crowd cheered Zup before the game and during a halftime awards appearance. In writing "Chapter Z," the *Champaign-Urbana News-Gazette* reported that Illinois was "down in the depths." On December 30, 1941, the trustees accepted Zuppke's resignation as of November 22, 1941. His opposition to the active recruiting of players, the deaths of his wife and George Huff in 1936, his medical problems, the increased alumni and political criticism in Champaign, Peoria and St. Louis and the unsuccessful attempt to secure his resignation in 1938 had all contributed to the problems of his last five years as the Illinois football coach.[16]

21

Retirement, Coaching and Honors

When Zuppke resigned, he had been head football coach for nearly twenty-nine years. During this time, Wisconsin had nine coaches, Indiana, Northwestern and Purdue seven each, Iowa six, Michigan and Minnesota five each, Ohio State four and Chicago two. Despite his losing record in the 1930s, Zuppke had only Ohio State and Michigan with wining records against his teams. He was 0–3–1 against Notre Dame, 14–7–2 in intersectional games and 41–5–3 in early-season games against midwestern teams from other conferences. Grantland Rice, the poet laureate of popular sports-writing, commemorated Zup's retirement with "So Long, Zup."

> Twenty-nine years in harness — and now it is journey's end, Always set for a battle, scrapping with foe or friend. Many's the night you held me to dawn came rolling in, But never a sad, dull moment, in spite of your vocal din. Painter, coach and philosopher, orator full of flame, Given an even scramble, you played the winning game. Pack with the rainbow's color — here is a friendly cup, Here's to one of the great ones, here's to your best health, Zup!

Zuppke said the poetry was better than the one you wrote to the "Lady in Red" many years ago in the Empire Room. Rice's column concluded with four stories reflecting the color, hilarity and human interest that Zuppke gave to sport. The last undocumented tale was Zup's 1913 response to President James's counsel on coaching football: "I appreciate ... what you have just told me, but there will be many presidents at this university who will come and go while I am still coaching." There were four.[1]

Zuppke had always advised other coaches to wait out their problems and resign only when they could beat them to the draw. The public perception of his resignation was presented by Arch Ward in an exclusive *Chicago Tribune* story. "The man who speaks his mind" explained to President Willard that he had made his decision for the best interest of the university. "There has been too much dissension among alumni and political factions in the last year or two." "The welfare of Illinois comes ahead of any personal ambition.

I am removing myself ... in the hope of re-establishing harmony." He told the president that he wanted to retire when he felt the university's athletic affairs were in good hands. He had attained that objective. Wendell Wilson had been ousted. In Doug Mills, the university had an athletic director whose feet were on the ground. His retirement would clear the way for his job of reorganization. He planned to devote more of his time to farming and painting.[2]

The Illinois press provided extensive coverage of his resignation. In 1914, the *Illini* cartoonist portrayed Zuppke as Napoleon. After his resignation, Sombal of the *Chicago Tribune* portrayed him as the slouched Indian on horseback with a lowered lance as depicted in Fraser's *The End of the Trail*. Zuppke did not care for either representation. Writers hailed his accomplishments, but often referred to his departure as inevitable. Some papers mentioned his refusal to bend from a line of strict amateurism and suggested that he should have stepped out a little sooner. The *Los Angeles Times*, *New York Times*, *Philadelphia Evening Bulletin* and *Inquirer*, and *St. Louis Post-Dispatch* ran articles and editorials on his career. Observing that Zuppke's resignation was overdue because he heeded the advice of friends who urged him to fight on, Lloyd Lewis of the *Chicago Daily News* concluded that "his weaknesses were but part of his very strengths."[3]

In responding to dozens of letters from his supporters, he used a form letter to express his appreciation and willingness to cooperate. "I will never forget the good things Illinois has done for me in my quarter century of service and wish it the greatest success. I will do all I can to help." In private, he was bitter about the controversy, the allegations and his financial settlement. He cited his contributions to the athletic program, the Stadium Drive, the organization of the Illini Clubs and the scheduling of the Army and Southern California games. He complained that Russell, Wilson and Willard did not know of, or appreciate, his activities for the university. He recalled two years of travel for the Stadium Drive before envy began to appear and I was blamed for everything. "I made it my business to stimulate G. Huff. He always consulted me. After his death, no one did." He summed up his retirement by stating that "I began to think I was an Illinois man. Finally, I found out that I was only a hired man." The retirement provided that Zuppke received $6,000 for the year ending August 31, 1942. He then received a $4,000-a-year retirement allowance, $3,000 of which came from the Athletic Association.[4]

A month after his retirement, Zuppke's coaching colleagues honored him with a testimonial dinner at the December 31, 1941, American Football Coaches Association meeting in Detroit. Harold Pogue introduced his old coach by referring to the national reputation of Zuppke football and Zup's vision, efforts and ability, which secured a modern athletic plant at Illinois. Thanks largely to him, it was paid for as it was built, and Illinois' athletic policy was unhampered by interest coupons and maturing bonds. Zuppke was a fighter, utterly fearless, honest, honorable, and tough minded, who rejected adulation when he won and blame when he lost. Characterized by an intense masculinity and a most colorful personality, his lack of tact and diplomacy caused criticism and annoyance. He treated his players as men who should do their best. Zuppke closed with quips about his relationships with Fielding Yost. Regarding his future, he said that he was probably through with the game, but that he would like very much to stay with it and would seriously consider any opportunity that is offered to me.[5]

The university did not regard the retirement agreement as preventing independent part-time work for another university or employer. The United States entered World War II two weeks after his resignation and enlistments and draft calls for military service limited civilian coaching opportunities. College football was again sponsored by federal military training programs. Zuppke cited his health and retirement compensation arrangements in declining coaching positions at Camp Grant and Grand Rapids University and responding to an inquiry from Yale. In February 1942, he declined an invitation to speak at an All-Illini banquet for Athletic Director Douglas Mills and football coach Ray Eliot, but accepted Harry Stuhldreher's invitation to lead two sessions at a May 1–2 high school coaches clinic at his alma mater in Madison.[6]

A 1942 offer from the *Chicago Tribune's* Arch Ward brought Zuppke back to coach his last game. In 1934, Ward had begun promotion of an annual game in late August between the National Football League champions and College All-Stars. The *Tribune* provided extensive publicity in the weeks before the game, and the profits went to *Tribune* charities. The college players were selected on the basis of votes by fans. By 1941, the professionals had won three straight All-Star games and George Halas's Chicago Bears had won twelve of their thirteen National Football League games. By March 5, Zuppke had agreed to coach the college team.[7]

The brilliant strategist from Illinois had two weeks to accomplish the tremendous task of preparing the collection of college players to play against the Bears. Zuppke and his assistants had twenty-seven drills and scrimmages to sort and shape the sixty-two-man squad into a competitive team. Amos Stagg visited the All-Star camp at Northwestern and pronounced the team physically fit. On August 28, before 101,100 spectators in Soldier Field, the All-Stars gave up touchdowns in the first three periods for a 21–0 loss. Two deep in all positions, the experienced Bears dominated the collegians in the line play. In the second half, a Lake Michigan fog obscured the players and deprived Bears quarterback Sid Luckman of the chance to run up the score. In his final game, Zup at last had good material, but he did not have the time to prepare them to defeat a veteran professional team. Most of the players in Chicago were headed for active military duty. Their participation in the huge spectacle produced $160,000 for the Army and Navy Relief Funds. While the college All-Stars were in training, Lieutenant Commander Gene Tunney criticized the publicity given to military personnel playing in benefit games and claimed that All-Star sports events detracted from military training. Zuppke responded with an attack on Tunney's qualifications to evaluate football and doubted that physical education programs were more effective in preparing men to cooperate in groups and developing stamina.[8]

A few weeks after the All-Star game, Zuppke had surgery. While he was able to attend an Illinois game late in the 1942 season, he could not consider a coaching position at Great Lakes Naval Training Station. He attended the 1943 All-Star game, but gasoline rationing limited his out-of-town travel. He remained an avid reader of the sports pages, but seldom watched a game in person. His doctor suggested forgetting about football for a year and Zuppke declined another offer to coach at Camp Grant. On Saturday, October 30, Davis Walsh of the *Chicago Herald-American* interviewed him in Champaign. Zup still had a sharp, agile mind, but dwelt more on his enjoyment in changing formations and tactics in his early coaching days. He wasn't going to the Michigan game. If he had gone to the game, he would have seen the best Wisconsin and Minnesota players, who were in military training at Michigan, defeat the Illini, 42–6. On November 8, he was the featured speaker at the Herald-American's Monday Quarterback Club. He reviewed intercollegiate sports since 1852 and concluded that there was always an open season for attacks on football. He defined proselytizing as enticing a boy to enter a school he doesn't want to go to or learning when he doesn't want to. After discussing the early history of the T formation and the development of the flea-flicker, he said that the hidden ball trick was a prohibition era outgrowth of the hidden bottle. He concluded with a plea that his audience should support collegiate football after the war.[9]

Zuppke spent most of 1944 at his apartment in Champaign. He devoted part of each morning to writing letters to former Illinois players in the military service. In March 1942, Lieutenant Robert Ingle, a guard on the 1938 team, was killed in a bomber crash in Texas. In 1944, Frank Rokusek and Jim McDonald, captains of the 1924 and 1938 teams, were killed in the war. Zup's war effort also involved the production of food on the home front. He took frequent breaks to visit his farms in Mahomet with his German shepherd dog named Grange. Red also had a new dog named Zup, who was a brother of Grange. In the fall, Zuppke visited his brother Paul in Minneapolis. On his sixty-fifth birthday in July, a reporter interviewed the coach about his football and art careers. The final question about "the high spot of your 65 years" brought an immediate response — "Mrs. Zuppke."[10]

Most wartime visitors were interested in football. In April 1944, Zuppke urged increased participation in school athletics to promote military fitness. In May, Arch Ward of the *Chicago Tribune* interviewed him about college and professional football, competition and rules. He appreciated the compliment in Doug Mills' classroom use of his sixteen points for coaching. He responded to inquiries about great football players and teams, but declined two offers to be an assistant coach. On November 4, the *Chicago Daily News* featured him in its rotogravure section. He was pictured coaching neighborhood boys, painting, admiring a bull, writing letters and reading. On November 24, he attended a Chicago reunion of his championship 1914 and 1919 teams.[11]

In the postwar years, Zuppke's football career still claimed public attention. On July 2, 1945, he spent his sixty-sixth birthday in Auburn, Alabama, helping former Illini coach Carl Voyles develop a new offense. In late September, he accepted a posiition as an unpaid guest coach of the freshman football team at the University of Havana. He was overjoyed by the prospect of coaching, visiting Athletics Director James Kendrigan, and painting in the Cuban winter. The inexperienced Cuban football players were fast and embraced the trick plays devised by their advisory coach. They defeated an American army base in Havana 32–0, but fell victim to Johnny Lujack and the Fort Pierce Florida Amphibs. Arriving in October, he enjoyed six months of fine living. He officiated at track meets, made a hundred sketches for paintings, socialized with playwright and editor Joseph P. McEvoy, fished on Ernest Hemingway's yacht and attended Hemingway's wedding. His host had entered Oak Park High School in the year in which Zuppke left for Illinois. Zuppke had a vague recollection of an active boy who might have been able to make the football team. Hemingway sent autographed copies of eight of his books to Zup, who acknowledged Hemingway's most interesting and wonderful hospitality with a letter and a sketch of "The Master."[12]

Refreshed by his Cuban visit, Zuppke returned to Champaign in April 1946. The university campus was overflowing with students. Wartime dislocations had moved college football players to military services or universities with military training programs. Peacetime brought a flow of talented athletes, whose education was funded by the G.I. Bill of Rights. After the disappointing 1935 to 1942 seasons, Zup often said that he wouldn't resign until his successor had a chance. His resignation two weeks before Pearl Harbor satisfied critics. His satisfaction was that his former players and assistant coaches took over from their teacher. He praised the appointments of Doug

Mills and Ray Eliot. Mills, the new Athletic Director, was a quarterback on Zup's 1927–29 teams. Eliot, the new head football coach, was a guard on his 1930–31 teams. Like Zup, Eliot had no experience as a university head coach. Born Ray Nusspickel, he was also the son of a German immigrant. Like Zup, he became known as an inspirational speaker. His speeches were delivered even more rapidly than Zup's. By 1946, he had fashioned another championship team built around three players from Zuppke's 1941 team, three players from the 1941 freshman team and players from his own 1942–45 teams. After a slow start, they won a Big Ten title with a 6–1 record and a 45–14 upset victory over U.C.L.A. in the Rose Bowl. After the Illini won the Big Ten championship, Zup was asked for his opinions. He admired the competitive spirit of the Illinis team and remarked about the number of quality athletes on the team.[13]

After World War II, college football faced increased market competition from the professional game. Returning veterans followed the precedents of their fathers, who had organized professional football in 1920. College players had joined professionals on service teams. Inspired by the huge talent pool and the prospects of television revenues, Arch Ward and investors established the All-American Football Conference. In 1945, the Bears had a 3–7 record, which was their worst season in the National Football League. In September 1946 and August 1947, George Halas brought Zup to the Chicago Bears training camp as an advisory coach. With Coach Halas and the veterans from the 1941 team, the 1946 Bears won the NFL championship.[14]

In September 1946, Zup joined Ray Eliot and the Illinois coaching staff at a Bears pre-season charity game with the New York Giants. At halftime he was introduced as an All-American coach for the Chicago Herald-American's All-American team. After a Bears victory over Philadelphia, a locker-room questioner asked about the "Board of Trustees." The question referred to "the occupants of the piggery on Zup's farm." Zup replied that "Truman had liberated them" and that they "were in Chicago right now."[15]

For one who hated to write for publication, Zuppke carried on an extensive correspondence, which was often supplemented with crayon sketches and diagrams of football plays. While he approved sketches and statements about football, he seldom wrote them. In drafting a tribute to Fielding Yost, he wrote that "I am not much of a writer, in fact I hate to write." An exception was a 1947 tribute to Yost, whom he regarded as a friend. He said that Michigan would have to "hurry up" forever to hold the pace set by Yost. Yost had a high regard for George Huff, who had referred him to the Michigan position in 1901. He had also contributed to the Illinois Stadium Fund.[16]

Zuppke made a southern trip with the Beloit basketball team in the winter of 1946–47. Public appearances then became more difficult. His health forced him to rest until the Bears training camp opened in August. In May, he declined Red Grange's invitation to attend a Chicago luncheon of the Illinois scholarship committee because of his health and because he did not believe in athletic scholarships. In 1948, he supplied advice and plays to Carl Voyles, who was coaching Branch Rickey's Brooklyn Dodgers in the All-American Conference. In March 1950, he vacationed in Vero Beach, Florida, as a guest of Rickey at the Dodgers training camp. In August, he again helped at the Bears summer camp in Indiana and golfed in Wisconsin, before returning to Champaign on September 9. In the fall, he watched the World Series on his new television set, enjoyed Illinois' 14–7 win over Ohio State, and saw the Bears defeat the New York Yanks in Chicago.[17]

At seventy, player reunions and honors ceremonies were his primary activities. In 1949, he spent two weeks with Harry Hall in Fox Lake, Wisconsin and the rest of the summer in Muskegon. In August, he attended the All-Star game and was appointed a member of the National Football Shrine and Hall of Fame. On October 27, the Athletic Association held a Zuppke Testimonial Dinner to celebrate the twenty-fifth anniversary of the dedication of Memorial Stadium. The football captains from 1913 to 1941 returned for the four hours of "continuous adulation" during a Mutual Broadcasting System radio broadcast, two banquets and a talk to the team. Red Grange was the master of ceremonies during a Mutual Broadcasting System radio program. He credited Zuppke with the strategies used in the 1924 Michigan game and the 1925 Pennsylvania game. Ex-president Arthur Willard praised Zup as one of my best friends and a man who never said it can't be done. Zup thanked the speakers for their praise and hailed the Big Ten as the heart and the uncle of American football. He talked to the team before the game and was interviewed by Bill Stern for his NBC Colgate *Sports Newsreel*. At the game, former players presented Zuppke with a combination television, radio and phonograph. After a dinner with flea-flicker appetizers and a razzle-dazzle steak, the guests received Dutch Master cigars and listened to "the same old Zup, flashing from humor to seriousness, defending his sport, and making his points with words snatched from his fluid vocabulary." With a keen innate sense of timing and humor, he recalled the golden stadia era and argued for the preservation of amateurism. The 1924 backfield of Harry Hall, Wally McIlwain, Earl Britton and "Red" Grange reminisced at Zuppke's testimonial dinner. Popular with the New York press, on December 1, 1949, he accepted a Touchdown Club award. In 1950, he was honored in the Helms Hall College Football Hall of Fame.[18]

In 1951, Zuppke listed the innovations that he made between 1906 and 1923. While he claimed that many of them were made at Illinois, he acknowledged that he lacked documentary evidence and agreed that many were

The 1924 backfield of (left to right) Harry Hall, Wally McIlwain, Earl Britton and Harold Grange returned for the Zuppke testimonial, October 27, 1949. Courtesy *The News-Gazette.*

adapted from formations and plays developed by Warner, Yost, Williams and others. He also acknowledged that he had obtained valuable information from participants in the Illinois School for Coaches. Approached by a sportswriter for material on *Football's Greatest Coaches*, he said that the balanced or T formation was in general use before 1906. A researcher noted that timing in the sense of knowing when to use a play was Zuppke's major contribution and concluded that he was up to his tricks and stretching the rules to the end of his career.[19]

By the 1950s, Zup did not need a syndicated column to express his football views. He was frequently quoted by John Carmichael of the *Chicago Daily News* and Jack Prowell of the *Champaign-Urbana News-Gazette*. His views of the game were good copy. He deplored the blandishments of recruiting and was concerned about the specialization of the two-platoon system. He took a dim view of "high-pressure recruiting and said that the NCAA's Sanity Code was unrealistic as the nation no longer worshipped amateurism. The development of offensive and defensive specialization and the legitimization of athletic scholarships were changing the game. Most of his comments related to the two-platoon substitution rule, all-star teams, historic games, and comparisons of current players and teams with those of the 1913–41 era. As the postwar enthusiasm for the return of football abated, perennial controversies concerning intercollegiate athletics returned. In 1951, the *Chicago Daily News* ran articles by Chicago president Robert M. Hutchins on the evils of athletics. Reporter Bob Russell then interviewed Zuppke for his views on the evils of sports. Zup did not attack the critics, but he conceded that recruiting depended on the character of the alumni, citing over-emphasis and betting as continuing problems. He viewed television as the greatest future influence on football. He admitted that conditions had improved since the good old days and cited tramp athletes, betting, riots, vandalism, untrained officials and poorly conditioned athletes as problems that were now uncommon. As modern problems, he identified illegal subsidies, bigger gate receipts and television demands that football become an entertainment show.[20]

Zuppke proposed a solution to college football's problems that was as radical as Hutchins' 1938 ten-cent admissions charge. In a November *Christian Science Monitor* interview, he outlined his "seniors only" competition proposal. To curb the emphasis on alumni recruiting, he proposed that conferences adopt a rule that intercollegiate competition would be between seniors. Schools with the best intramural systems, not the best recruiting systems, would come up with the best senior football teams. He maintained that no one is going to offer a high school kid the whole campus plus a few bucks extra if he knows the boy has got to spend three years getting eligible to play. It would make the boy realize, too, that the main idea of going to college is to get an education. The plan would lessen the ardor to win *at any price*. It was his final solution for the "very tainted situation" produced by "show athletics."[21]

When his health permitted, Zup continued to write and attend ceremonies. At its fall homecoming in 1951, Muskegon's "M" Club honored Zupppke with a plaque and praise as the "Father of Muskegon High School Football." In 1953, he contributed a sketch of Red Grange for the Saturday Evening Post's "The Best Player I Ever Coached" series. In 1955, he received the American Football Coaches Association's Amos Alonzo Stagg Award for services in advancing football. On August 8, 1955, Zuppke agreed that Fred Young of the Bloomington *Pantagraph* could write his life story. Material was solicited, collected, and edited, but only a few rough drafts were produced in 1956. As time passed, Zuppke took a more philosophical view of his retirement. He recalled a story about a circus fat woman who married a midget. She smothered him in an embrace but kept him in her room for mourning. Enraged when the landlady closed the door, she was told that the cats had had him down in the coal bin three times already. Zupp added that was about

Zuppke in retirement, 1952. Courtesy University of Illinois Archives.

the position he was in. Reflecting on his early days, he wanted to arrange an attractive schedule and play intersectional games. G. Huff did not agree. He wanted to sit here and leave things as they were. "As I look back on it..., I think I agree with him."[22]

Zup's health enabled him to attend the January 18, 1957, dinner of the Touchdown Club in Columbus, Ohio, where his witty remarks stole the show. The Zuppke Award for the best college football team playing the toughest schedule went to the University of Iowa. Bob's departure for Arizona caused him to miss a January 25 testimonial dinner for George Halas. He received a friend's report that three quarters of Halas's superb talk was allocated to you, your background, your history and your many contributions to the game. In 1956, the Illinois Athletic Association and the Foundation joined the Alumni Association in establishing a Grants-in-Aid program for students in extracurricular activities. In an April 1957 interview with an Albuquerque sports editor, Zuppke declared that there were "honest and commercial" football squads. One "tries to avoid under-the-table operations and can't." The other comes out and says "What it's paying boys's and keeps football under the athletic association, which is separate from the school. He said that he did not like either idea and that he never recruited, but took boys from Illinois and made something of them. For him, football was more than the natural enthusiasm of youth for competition and physical fitness. It was a part of life, which was more complex.[23]

22

The Dutch Master and His Avocations

Twentieth-century intercollegiate football was both a performing and a competitive art. The head coaches were key figures in staging these Saturday afternoon competitions. The artistic stage for football as a sports spectacle featured a hundred-yard gridiron field, colorful uniforms, intricate formations and shifts, forward and lateral passes, punts and field goals, timing, and consistent rules enforcement. Zuppke directed the performing artists on the football field and attracted national coverage in media interviews. Each year, he selected a new cast for seven or eight performances. Students and spectators were involved, but the players were selected and cast in their roles by the coaches who directed the productions.

When the football and banquet seasons were over, Coach Zuppke turned to the arts of sketching and painting. Art was a lifetime avocation for him. He wrote his baccalaureate thesis at Wisconsin on Tommaso Masaccio, a Florentine Renaissance painter renowned for his vivid realism and stress on light and shadow. Throughout his career, the Dutch Master used brush, pen, pencil and crayon to sketch landscapes and people. Sign painting in Milwaukee, marginal decorations on his class notes, sketches for normal school and university yearbooks, crayon drawings on letters to friends, penciled sketches and paintings in his studio were both a means of expression and a form of recreation. He painted hundreds of oils and pastels. His art was characterized by bold, free and impressionist landscapes. Trees, mountains, water scenes and the desert were favorite subjects. He seldom painted football scenes. An exception was a charcoal sketch of a coach and three "scrubs." He stressed that skills in touch, precision, accuracy, timing, rhythm, movement, distance and coordination were important in both football and art. He maintained that the values of all portraits, "whether in pigskin or pigment, lies in their resemblance to life — in the extent of their warmth and movement." He laid in the draw-

ing in charcoal and completed an oil painting in four hours. He was a lover
of "untampered nature" and more interested in color than form. He stated
that he had not studied painting in the technical sense, but painted "because
I really love it."[1]

While the 1906 offer of a coaching and teaching position in Muskegon
ended Zuppke's career as a professional artist for a Grand Rapids advertising
agency, he maintained a lifelong devotion to amateur art. In Oak Park, he
took a summer course at the Chicago Art Institute. He entered his work in
1911 and 1912 exhibitions at the Institute. His 1912 entry in the Western Artists
exhibit was *Solitude*. After a 1913 showing in Toledo, his coaching and speaking responsibilities at Illinois placed heavy demands on his time. Much of his
art was based on summer scenes sketched at Muskegon and painted at Urbana
in January and February. In July 1917, he left for a month of painting and
fishing in Muskegon. In April 1920, he exhibited paintings of Lake Michigan
storms in Champaign stores. In 1922, he displayed the firm, definite and
forceful strokes of his brush in a Daubers art show in the Auditorium. A Zuppke sketch of a woodland scene was used as the frontispiece for the 1922 *Illio*.
Fannie could draw upon personal experience for her October 19 talk on "America's Landscape Artists." Bob was elected as an associate member of the
Daubers art fraternity. On their 1923 trip to California, Bob sketched Arizona's and New Mexico's skies and sunsets and California's clouds and waves.
When the Zuppkes moved from Urbana to Champaign in 1926, their new
apartment had a room that would become Bob's studio. When they traveled,
he visited art galleries in America and abroad and filled many sketchbooks
on vacation trips to Europe, Alaska, California, Cuba and Arizona. In his winter months in Arizona, he painted desert and mountain scenes.[2]

As his painting's became known, he received more requests for exhibit-
ing his works. In 1929–30, he exhibited paintings at the Southern States Art
Exposition, where his *Quaking Aspens in Colorado* won second prize. In 1931,
he contributed eight paintings to a joint exhibit at the Stanford Art Gallery
with Stanford coach Glenn "Pop" Warner, who also painted. He sent *Quaking Aspens* and *Desert Plains* to exhibitions at the Chicago No-Jury Society of
Artists and Knox College. In 1934, he exhibited at Monmouth College and
the Chicago No-Jury Society. In January 1935, the Zuppkes spent a week at
the Wigwam Inn in Litchfield Park, Arizona, where Bob played golf and led
a group of amateur artists on painting trips to the desert. In the summer
months at Muskegon, he painted lakes and dunes. Each April, he sent paintings to the University of Illinois Faculty Art Exhibition. In 1934, he submitted four landscapes. In 1935, his six entries were Arizona studies, of which
three were *Along the Apache Trail*, *Mountain Top* and *Solitude*. In 1936, four
of his five Arizona works were *Desert Scene*, *Valley of the Sun*, *Fish Creek Canyon*

Zuppke the painter, with three of his landscapes displayed around his 1948 Amos A. Stagg Award, March 1954. Courtesy University of Illinois Archives.

and *Litchfield Park*. In 1937, he entered several pastels, including *The Gold Knoll*, *Sunset*, *Moonlight* and *Palisades*. In 1938, his entries were *Ladies of the Woods*, *Rim Country*, *Toyland* and *Yellow Pine*.[3]

Zuppke's artistic ability was publicized in the 1925 yearbook of the *Busi-*

ness Men's Art Club of Chicago, the *School Arts Magazine* and *Everyday Art* in March 1932, *Esquire* in October 1936, *Literary Digest* in June 1937 and many newspaper feature articles. Chicagoans hailed him as an amateur painter of great ability. A Stanford writer thought his work was bold and free, possibly influenced by modern impressionism, but still obviously the expression of a vivid personality. His sensitive feeling for color and spontaneity caused critics to believe that he worked rapidly with an insistent inspiration. In the *Esquire* interview, he described his 1925 football team. "I sketched a team" around Red Grange like the "complementary background of a painting." He wrote that as an artist created a picture on canvas, a football coach created a mobile image of an array of raw physical masses. Painters' strokes resembled men in motion. He knew his players by their movements, not their numbers. The coach must understand the temperament of his men, as the painter understand's his brush and pigments. He kept a sketchbook record of his wanderings in Europe, and his landscapes showed a steady increase in power and artistic skill. A *Chicago Post* writer found *Quaking Aspens of Colorado* hanging on the Zuppkes' dining room wall and notes for paintings of Swiss landscapes on his worktable. He worked in the mornings and at night by lamplight and produced about thirty paintings a year. Though his paintings were not in the art tradition of the twentieth century, Zuppke found fulfillment in his art and gave most of his works to his friends.[4]

After Fannie's death on July 31, 1936, and the football season had ended, Zuppke turned to painting to compensate for his personal loss. He drove to Camelback Inn in Phoenix and sketched for twelve hours a day in the Arizona desert. By April, he had produced twenty-one paintings. In May 1937 and 1938, Zuppke sent twenty-one pastels to one-man shows at the Colonial Art Gallery in Chicago's Palmer House. The Tribune's art critic praised his work as "well drawn, well composed and excellent in color" and added that he had stepped from the football stadium to the painter's palette gracefully. In October 1937, the Hackley Art Gallery in Muskegon exhibited twenty-five of his works. Half were Arizona scenes. Five other states, Alaska and Germany were included in the landscapes. Zuppke wrote to the director that he had "puttered around off and on for the last twenty-five years" and decided that he could not stay away from painting and would now take it seriously. By 1938, he had given to friends or sold about 150 paintings. Strangers were charged $150. He advised Palmer House advertising director Al Fuller not to put the price too high. In May 1940, Zuppke sent twenty-one paintings to an exhibition at the Palmer House. Thirteen of them were southwestern landscapes. In 1941, he exhibited at the *Milwaukee Journal* Hobby Show and sent thirty pastels to an exhibit at the Davenport, Iowa, Art Institute.[5]

Two New York sportswriters provided the most publicized critiques of

Zup's paintings. In November 1937, he sent the paintings to an exhibit at the Western Studios in New York. In the *New York Times*, John Kieran praised the art of the perennial football coach of the Illini as far superior to much work of the moderns. The artist's lavish use of purples and yellows in his landscapes were gorgeous. His trees, waters, mountains and sunsets were recognizable as scenes from Arizona, Alaska, Bavaria, Florida, and the Rocky Mountains. John Lardner noted that "old Zup" was asking $100 for the oils, and had sold *Grazing Plains* and *Lower Alaska Coast* at that price. Zuppke didn't care whether he sold them or not, as painting was strictly a hobby that he liked. Some critics said his technique was too brutal, but the coach said he painted forests as they were. Lardner's favorite picture was Grange at Pennsylvania, which was worth $14 to him at 7 to 5. Noting that the true value of paintings was determined after the boys had gone to their reward, he quoted winter book odds of 6 to 1 against the 1980 value of the Zuppke entry." Adding that Hopi chief Eagle Plume had approved of Zuppke's representations, And Lardner said he would invest when he could scratch the price together.[6]

In retirement, Zuppke had more time to paint in his studio. Painting remained primarily a hobby or recreational activity, and he continued to obtain favorable publicity. Under doctor's orders to take it easy in 1943, he departed from landscapes and painted Red Grange in action. Former players in Champaign for football games would visit his studio and often selected a painting. A complimentary letter from a young lady brought his response that it should be given to her for expenses, which were twenty-five dollars. In 1945, Rock Springs, Wyoming, high school students sent him $135 for two paintings. He returned the money. After his 1946 Cuban trip, he wrote Hemingway that, while he had exhibited twenty-six paintings, he only had strength enough to paint two sailfish soaring above stormy waters. "I like the two highballs I am allowed to drink ... then I think of you, Mary and the Finca Vigia of Papa Hemingway at San Francisco de Paula."[7]

In 1946, Zup had another opportunity to reflect on problems affecting his artistic career. Samson Raphaelson, the student manager of the 1921 stadium campaign, had moved on to write the *The Jazz Singer* in 1929 and to have a successful 1930s career as a Hollywood screenwriter. In November 1946, he returned to Illinois to teach a writing course. Zuppke enjoyed Raphaelson's company to the utmost. "It was refreshing to talk about something else besides football and limburger cheese. Most everyone I meet asks me something about football or training food." When the "physical education season is done with," he looked forward to turning his attention to "what may, or may not, be called art." Unfortunately, the Illinois Rose Bowl season was interfering with the life movements of the muse of art. "These P.E. football teams have a way of developing campus hysteria, causing temporary maladjustment between true scholarship and show athletics, a la Hollywood." While the sports mania may have something to do with the zest for life, excess energy, exuberant health, restlessness, lack of poise or a competitive urge, it is all out of harmony with the quiet and thoughtful life of the studio. "As soon as I start to paint, there goes the football phone." "I will try to conquer this mad atmosphere of a college town and concentrate on my studies. My grades are low. Who cares, for the town and gown are happy."[8]

In 1947, he exhibited paintings at Beloit College and the Southern Hotel in Columbus, Ohio. In 1950, he sent Walter "Red" Barber a *Cuban Scene* painting. Barber responded in his newspaper column with an Easter Sunday tribute to Bob. In an answer to a request for biographical information for a November 8–28, 1953, exhibit of his paintings in Galesburg, Illinois, he said that he did not paint to sell, but to express himself in color on canvas. Noting that viewers reactions varied, he said that "they all looked good to me until I see the finished job, then my enthusiasm wanes and I start another, hoping for the big one. Twenty-one viewers commented on his Galesburg exhibit. They praised his colors of the desert, mountains, snow, waters and sky. For them, the landscapes revealed a sense of action, imagination and humor. Their favorite paintings depicted Morro Castle in Havana, the moonlight saguaro cactus and Pigeon Hill in Muskegon.[9]

Painting was not Zuppke's only retirement avocation. In 1939, a friend advised him that farmland near Mahomet, Illinois, would be a good investment. In December, he bought 115 acres at the southern edge of Mahomet. In July 1941, he purchased 178 acres a mile and a half north of the town. The farms were operated by his housekeeper's brother. Though he had no experience in rural life or farming, he made frequent visits to the farms and was photographed as he surveyed his agricultural investment. In 1940, an Ohio friend traded two Hampshire sows for some paintings. Zup named them Illinois and Ohio State. Minnesota, Grange and Tobin came later. With large litters, he soon had 250 hogs. Farmer Bob denied that he had named "several portly swine" for the university trustees who voted for his retirement. The *Chicago Tribune's* Thomas Morrow reported that Zuppke did not fear a suit by enraged hogs, but was afraid that he might gore the feelings of a used trustee. He admitted naming a hog or two after people, but declined to give names as using pigs and people in humor required great care. In 1943, he named five new lambs the Whiz Kids after the successful Illinois basketball team. Jersey cows obtained in exchange for paintings were also added to his livestock. Under doctor's orders to avoid labor, he consulted agricultural staff and observed farm activities. He sold the farms in July and October 1947.[10]

In retirement, Zuppke's seasonal activities continued. Spring practices and autumn schedules were replaced by longer winters in warmer climates and in an increasing number of visits to professional and college training camps and games. Burt Hurd at the First National Bank in Champaign continued to handle Zuppke's financial, investment and tax matters. By 1954, Zuppke paid about $4,400 in federal income taxes. In 1937, he had bought an interest in the Camelback. In 1938, he rented a cottage at Lake Harbor near Muskegon for July, traveled to New York and Canada in August, and spent six or seven weeks at the Camelback Inn in Phoenix for the "best winter climate." In 1947, he rented the Peterson house at Lake Harbor. At Christmas, he visited the Harry Hall family in Waukegan. In 1950, he bought a new Cadillac. In June, he and Leona Ray went to Fox Lake for two weeks and then to Muskegon. On April 16, he attended a testimonial dinner for Arch Ward in Chicago. He spoke at the Class of 1925's twenty-fifth reunion, the I-Men's dinner, a dinner party for Butch Nowack in LaSalle and the All-State Football Banquet. He spent Christmas with Harry Hall's family in Waukegan and visited Jack Stewart at the Camelback Inn in January 1951. In 1952, he wintered in Vero Beach and summered at Fox Lake and Muskegon. He restricted personal appearances, but produced paintings for friends and responded to football inquiries. In October, he attended two memorial services for Butch Nowack, spoke to the Quarterback Club in Rockford and attended the Illinois-Wisconsin game in Madison. In 1953, he spent the summer at a cottage on Mona Lake, near Muskegon. In September, he joined Red Grange in attending a Marquette football banquet, where Zuppke received the civic service award from Marquette and the Milwaukee Eagles.[11]

Zup took up golf in 1915 and played with coaches, neighbors and businessmen. He belonged to the Champaign Rotary Club and the Champaign County and Muskegon County Country Clubs. In 1922, he joined the other coaches in playing a two-hole course on Illinois Field. In a 1923 match between Champaign and Clinton, he shot an 81. While most of his golfing was in Champaign and Muskegon, he also played on summer vacations. In the summer of 1934, Bob had a June 2 to July 8 golfing reunion with his brothers in Minneapolis. At a June 5, 1937, Chicago golf outing, he won a prize for the most "beefing" on holes. As a golfer, he shot in the 80 to 102 range and responded to a "why" question with "once a dub, always a dub." In 1953, he recalled a Muskegon tournament, where he ousted a Wisconsin state champion. Health problems forced him to quit golfing in 1951. He turned to chess and painting and said that he had spent too much time knocking paint off golf balls instead of putting it on canvas.[12]

Zuppke began 1954 with a hospitalization for high blood pressure. He followed instructions to slow down but made exceptions for old friends. On February 4, he joined George Halas for a "Sports Scrapbook" appearance. In April, he went to a Milwaukee party honoring Chris Steinmetz, which featured a reunion of three surviving members of the 1905 Wisconsin basketball team — Steinmetz, Zuppke and Emil Breitkreutz. Grateful Badgers provided Zup with a supply of beer and Swiss cheese. He responded with a sketch of him enjoying the Wisconsin products. In June, he went to the Chicago Illini Club's golf outing, where he walked the course without playing. He returned via the Rockford wedding of Bob Reitsch's daughter. In July, he went to Chicago for an appearance on Red Grange's television show. In October, he attended the 1914 and 1919 team reunions. From August to November, he was ill again and mourned the loss of two old friends: Pop Warner and Grantland Rice.[13]

In 1955, he provided information to Edwin Pope of the *Atlanta Journal*, who was writing a book on *Football's Greatest Coaches*. Zup carefully explained that the T formation had been known as the balanced formation when he used it at Muskegon and Oak Park and the "Princeton formation" when Phil King brought it to Wisconsin in the 1890s. His recollections of formations and plays filled sports columns. He attended the I-Men's Banquet and the Rotary football dinner. The year also brought trips to the hospital. Two severe strokes and a dramatic recovery in December brought additional publicity.[14]

Zup was not active in campus affairs and politics. In 1950, two former football players ran against each other for a seat on the university Board of Trustees. Democrat Harold Pogue was a candidate for re-election. He was defeated by the Republican nominee, Red Grange. While photographed with a "Grange for Trustee" badge, Zuppke was neutral in the race between two close friends. In 1953, Grange joined a Republican majority in firing university president George D. Stoddard. In an interview, Zuppke supported Stoddard as "one of the greatest educators," but not a politician. His only fault was his unpopularity. He said that Grange had been "used by politicians," but maintained that his criticisms of Grange had been garbled in the newspaper report. When approached about university recognition of Grange, Zuppke replied that Stoddard's dismissal divided university opinion for and against Red and that the wounds of that affair would have to heal before any action in his favor.[15]

Zuppke's eclectic views on politics were similar to his views on religion. Religious beliefs were a personal matter. He was not an active member of any religious body. Based on his parentage, he listed himself as a Lutheran. When he left Milwaukee, sixty-five percent of the people were Roman Catholics. Fannie was a member of the Episcopal Church in Muskegon. He and Fannie were married by a Methodist minister. She attended the Episcopal church in Champaign. Leona Ray was a Presbyterian. His funeral services were held in the Presbyterian church. He bequeathed funds to the Champaign Episcopal and Presbyterian churches and the Methodist Cunningham Children's Home in Urbana.[16]

At home, housing, investments and medical expenses were the major budget items. In his seventies, Zuppke had major surgery for prostate cancer in 1950. With coronary problems, he was hospitalized six times between April and October, 1951. He had further surgery in 1953. On December 18, 1955, he suffered a stroke and was hospitalized in serious condition. He recovered in the summer of 1956 at his summer cottage in Lake Harbor. On September 10, 1956, he married Leona P. Ray, who had been his housekeeper since 1936. He had provided an annuity for her and paid her a monthly salary of $100. Zuppke said that he had been thinking about the marriage for a long time. The largest expense in 1956 was $3,296 for her wedding ring. The newlyweds were able to travel to Phoenix for the winter, but his stroke had impaired his circulation and arthritis added to his cancer problems. By August, he had further surgery and made five trips to the hospital. By October 24, he was bedfast. On December 22, 1957, Zuppke died.[17]

The funeral eulogy was given by Rev. Malcolm Nygren and printed on the first page of the Champaign newspaper. The clergyman remarked that the legendary coach had been "a hero in his youth" and that "there was always something bigger-than-life" about him. He praised Zuppke's "brilliant mind and strong personality," and lauded the coach's vision that considered that men were more important than the game. He found that Zuppke stood up for his principles and his convictions and thanked God "for a man with great talent" who used it to improve the world.[18]

Many players testified to their affection for their coach. Red Grange drew on his memory for a tribute to Zuppke:

I can see him now, still out in the cold at 7 P.M., and that big sheepskin coat — on such a little guy — almost dragging the ground. Yeh, 7 p,m,, and some of us would start loafing, figuring Zup wouldn't notice. But that little Dutchman could see in the dark — from the back of his head!... What a guy, ferocious and kind. Understood men; knew who to pat and who to kick in the pants. Many times, after I'd scored a touchdown or two, he'd take me out and raise the devil about some mistake I made. And I did lots of wind sprints for mistakes in practice. Darn, I can hear Zup now, calling McIlwain "Sir Lancelot," calling Mitterwallner "Middle Waller," and calling me G-r-a-i-n-c-h.

I'll always remember those Friday nights the team spent at the Champaign country club, with ol' Zup reminiscing in front of the fire. He'd tell us about football's old days, and most always mention the Illinois upset of Minnesota in 1916. He'd intersperse remarks about the next day's game in his reminiscing. His voice was like syrup, and it was a wonderful way to relax us. You know Zup could fire up a scrub player to kill an All-American. I'll guarantee this: no matter how inadequate it was, no Zuppke team ever took the field thinking it was beaten! Zup was an idealist. To him, proselytizing was a deadly sin. Zup believed that the honor of attending Illinois should be sufficient inducement for an athlete. Gee, Zup was a salesman. He was months setting up that great afternoon we had against Michigan. All summer long he wrote every player, warning us of Michigan's greatness and Yost's trick-

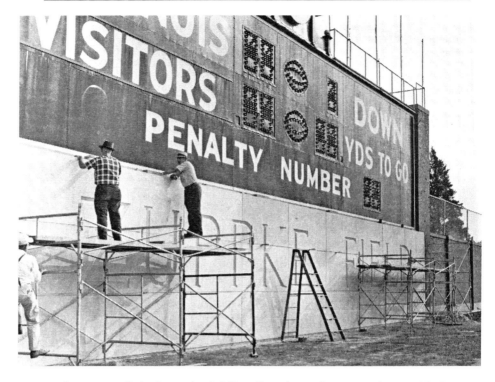

Workmen install the "Zuppke field" wall in the stadium, October, 1966. Courtesy *The News-Gazette*.

ery. So we were keyed up to beat anybody that hot Saturday. I have to laugh remembering the freezing winter morning our football special chugged into some whistle stop. We all stepped out to stretch our legs, and Zup, bareheaded, was the last off. His wife reminded him that he should be wearing a hat. Zup said he wasn't cold. And his wife said: "Robert! You get right back on that train and put on your hat!" Zup sheepishly went for his hat, and all of us players began laughing. We couldn't believe that anyone had actually talked back to Zup. What a guy, Zup. He'd have gone to the end of the world for one of his players.[19]

Trainer Matt Bullock had provided a significant tribute in 1949, when he said that he admired Zup most for his work with teams that were not champions, even with teams that didn't win a game. Fellows on winning teams had it good, but, in other years, he knew a patient and kind Zup who helped boys along when the going was tough. In 1940, when he faced his last two winless seasons, Zuppke taught fight, stamina, courage and buoyancy.[20]

Ray Eliot, who succeeded Zuppke as head football coach, praised his friend and a constant inspiration for his contributions to football and his lessons about the game of life. As a player on two of Zupp's losing teams, Eliot recalled that winning was important, but not everything. He credited the Zuppke philosophy that a man should play for the love of the game with permeating the alumni and administration at Illinois. Athletics Director Doug Mills, who played for three of Zuppke's winning teams, described his coach as a rugged individualist and a genius who enriched the lives of those who played for him and served Illinois far beyond his activities as a coach.[21]

On April 4, 1958, Zuppke's ashes were buried next to the grave of George Huff in Roselawn Cemetery across the street from the 50-yard line of Memorial Stadium. After George Huff's death, the trustees had named the gymnasium for him. Soon after Zuppke's death, alumni and newspapermen suggested naming a proposed assembly hall for Zuppke. In 1966, three years after the Assembly Hall was opened, the playing field at the Memorial Stadium was named Zuppke Field. He left an estate in excess of $400,000, which went to Leona, his nephews and nieces, three medical charities, his investments counselor, local charities and the University Foundation.[22]

23

Legacies

In the twenty-two seasons between 1920 and 1941, Zuppke's Illini played before more than five million spectators. Millions more heard radio broadcasts of the games. The popularity of intercollegiate football as a performing art and a profitable entertainment commodity that generated publicity for public universities formed the basis for many successful coaching careers. This cultural phenomenon was also responsible for the professionalization of coaching and the establishment of the popular image of the coach as an inspirational and innovative figure. An assessment of Zuppke's unique achievements must be based on specific contributions made during his entire career at Muskegon, Oak Park and Illinois.[1]

Football history is replete with legends and lore about the first coach to use a particular formation or play. Grantland Rice, Hugh Fullerton, Allison Danzig, Edwin Pope and other writers have glorified the big names among college football coaches. Sports historians have usually identified Bob Zuppke with an innovative coaching style that included surprise or trick plays and a razzle-dazzle offense. He was a keen observer of the plays of other coaches and teams and skilled in adapting and applying his knowledge to the preparation of his players. Before World War I, he made significant contributions to the development of the forward-passing game. Most of his formations and plays were suitable for smaller and faster teams. His players used the huddle, shifts and combinations of forward and lateral passes. His flea-flicker pass and lateral is still in use. A careful student of rules changes, he adapted his offensive and defensive styles to the talents of his players and his assessments of his opponents. His ability to evaluate players also enabled him to select the coaching staffs that prepared championship players.

Records and the keeping of records have been an integral part of American sports and intercollegiate football. Sportswriters, alumni and fans are concerned about championships, ratings, All-Americans, won-lost records, yardage gained, pass completions, tackles and recruiting competitions. In the twenty-nine years from 1913 to 1941, the Big Ten was a well-balanced conference. Eight teams won or shared at least one conference championship. Michigan with nine, Illinois with seven, and Minnesota with six were the leaders. The overall record of Zuppke's Illini was seventy-six wins, sixty-six losses and eight ties. Illinois played more Big Ten games than the other seven state universities and nearly equaled the two private universities in Chicago and Evanston. From 1913 to 1929, his teams won fifty-six games and lost twenty-four in a highly competitive conference, winning 70 percent of their games. From 1930 to 1941, they won 32 percent and he demonstrated that he could *take it* on the gridiron while the country *took it* in a depressed economy.

Both the players in the winning years and those in the losing years appreciated Zup's influence in their lives. Though not an aggressive recruiter, he was a keen judge of talent and skilled in distributing players among the fraternities. He had the longest tenure among state university coaches in the Big Ten. Yost coached for twenty-six years and Williams for twenty-two. He was also the most successful football coach. In a hundred and fourteen years, Illinois football teams have won or shared Big Ten conference championships fifteen times. In the first seventeen years, they won in 1910 while playing a four-game schedule. In the twenty-nine years coached by Bob Zuppke, they won or shared seven championships. In Ray Eliot's eighteen seasons, they won on three occasions. In the forty-eight seasons since 1960, under eight coaches, they have won or shared four titles. The only two coaches who won Big Ten championships between 1955 and 1990 were dismissed for rules violations. Zuppke's twenty-nine years at Illinois contrasted with that of many coaches who moved from one position to another. John Heisman coached eight different teams. Pop Warner and Bo McMillin coached seven.

Bob Zuppke was adept in cultivating the press and inspiring alumni loyalty in a state university. His colorful personality and oratorical skills inspired loyalty to the university and its football teams. His coaching career coincided with the emergence of college football as a major source of publicity for colleges and universities. University administrators at Yale, Chicago and Michigan played leading roles in the early development of football enthusiasm. At Illinois, George Huff and Bob Zuppke exploited the university's needs for newspaper and radio publicity, legislative support, alumni contributions and attracting students. Football became the most publicized and visible activity at the University of Illinois. Administrators were pleased by the recognition it accorded to their institution and its association with other universities of similar background and status. Intercollegiate football became both a sporting event and an institutional program. As sports spectacles, football games were also prized highly by trustees and administrators as seasonal reminders of state and alumni loyalty. Spectators were entertained at the games with marching bands and pageantry and enjoyed visits to the campus. Propaganda and criticism, profits and deficits, victories and losses tended to obscure football's lasting contributions. With its heroics and scandals, college football remained a vital expression of the national enthusiasm for competitive sports.

Zuppke was an advocate for football as an educational medium. He taught hundreds of audiences that football provided valuable lessons in courage, perseverance and sportsmanship for both players and spectators. He coached every team to win the next game. However, for him football games were a helpful incident in college life and a series of starts toward a goal of self-control and perseverance in difficult situations. Football was justified by the positive publicity and seasonal reminders to thousands of alumni and taxpayers of the learning and labor of their youth at the state university. His position that football as a performing art had a strong and enduring popularity has been affirmed.

In addition to innovative plays, football records and university publicity, Zuppke's legacies included tangible contributions. A hundred years after Zuppke watched the teams of Stagg, Williams and Yost perform at Camp Randall Stadium in Madison Wisconsin, huge stadiums were filled with spectators and extensive television coverage blanketed the country. There has been a dramatic increase in university investments in athletic programs and facilities for sports and public entertainment. Zuppke was a driving force in the 1922 construction of the Memorial Stadium. In 2002, the Chicago Bears played their home games on Zuppke Field in Memorial Stadium, which was decorated with four huge pictures of past "Illini" Bears adorning the north end zone. They included two of Zuppke's student athletes: George Halas and Red Grange. Huff and Zuppke also played major roles in the development of an intramural program at the university. After World War I, the new athletic facilities and football profits supported amateur recreational activity and inspired student participation in intramural and additional intercollegiate sports. In a rural community, where student numbers equaled the population of Urbana, football and recreational sports were part of a larger cultural and educational experience. The loyalty and determination of the Dutch Master was an example for two generations of students. In his 1957 will, he left $50,000 to the University Foundation.

Zuppke's long tenure as a coach and his greatest legacies were rooted in the transitory annual experiences of preparing football teams for intercollegiate competition, and teaching college and high school coaches in the coaching school. In teaching players how to develop the motivation, skill, speed, strength and effort required to play football, he organized practice drills and scrimmages and provided the offensive and defensive formations for games. He prepared his teams in locker-room chalk talks; in practice with body contact exercises, blocking sleds and calisthenics; in signal drills with formations and plays; in scrimmages; and in games. The physical preparation was supplemented by his application of sports psychology, where he drew upon his studies at Wisconsin and his collaboration with sports psychologist Coleman Griffith at Illinois. His reputation as a coach rested as much on his upsets of Minnesota in 1916, Ohio State in 1921, Michigan in 1924, Pennsylvania in 1925 and Michigan in 1939 as it did on his won-loss record. In addition to shaping the performance of his teams, his football classes were a major attraction of the coaching schools, where he taught college and high school coaches from 1914 to 1932. Vince Lombardi was quoted as saying that winning was "the only thing." Bob Zuppke said that "all quitters are good losers," but his favorite quote was that "football is only an incident in life and not as important as life after college." He also said that taking it, by losing, was as important as winning. By no means a graceful loser, he recognized that teaching young men to survive disappointment also prepared them for life after college. The lasting effect of his work with players was evident in their performance, their post-college careers and the lifelong affection between Zuppke and his players. This legacy was carved on his tombstone: "He so lived that those whose lives touched his were a little better for having known him."

As head football coach, Zuppke established a strong rapport with players, alumni and administrators. He possessed unique oratorical skills, which enabled him to capitalize on the popularity of intercollegiate football. Seasoned with philosophy and wit, his strong arguments for the college game were coupled with his ability to drive himself and his players. His teams and classes supplied coaches and players who were instrumental in establishing and popularizing high school, college and professional football. An acute observer and adept in motivating both players and the media, he played a significant role in leading football from his after-school games on the lots of Milwaukee to the massive Memorial Stadium on the prairie to coaching the players and coaches who established the National Football League.

Chapter Notes

Preface

1. John S. Watterson, *College Football* (Baltimore: Johns Hopkins University Press, 2000), 27–28, 86, 170–176, 193; Michael Oriard, *King Football* (Chapel Hill: University of North Carolina Press, 2001), 18–19; John R. Thelin, *Games Colleges Play* (Baltimore: Johns Hopkins University Press, 1994), 3–7, 197–203.

2. Robin Lester, *Stagg's University* (Urbana: University of Illinois Press, 1955), xxi.

Chapter 1

1. Citations of Zuppke correspondence, manuscripts and memoranda are to items in the Robert C. Zuppke Papers, University of Illinois Archives, RS 28/3/20; Harold E. Grange, *Zuppke of Illinois* (Chicago, IL: A.L. Glaser, 1937), 1; Irving Dilliard, "Robert Carl Zuppke," in *Dictionary of American Biography, Supplement Six, 1956–1960*, edited by John Garraty (New York: Charles Scribner's Sons, 1980), 728; United States Bureau of the Census, *Historical Statistics of the United States, Colonial Times to 1970* (Washington, DC: GPO, 1975), C89–101: 1937; *1880 United States Census, Social Statistics of Cities*, 660, 676; Bayrd Still, *Milwaukee* (Madison: State Historical Society of Wisconsin, 1965), 192–193, 259, 262, 264–265, 574–575, 577–578.

2. University of Illinois Athletic Association, Art Press Release, 1937; Robert Zuppke to Dorothy Donnell, April 4, 1941, "I'm an American — Robert C. Zuppke," United States Department of Justice, Script 68, August 31, 1941; "Zuppke Biographical Manuscript," ca. 1956.

3. *The Milwaukee Directory for 1883* (Milwaukee, WI: Alfred G. Wright, 1883) 710; *Milwaukee City Directory* (Milwaukee, WI: Alfred G. Wright, 1898), 1068; Franz Zuppke Naturalization Record, October 7, 1896, Milwaukee County Historical Society; Still, *Milwaukee*, 578–579; *Champaign-Urbana News-Gazette*, December 5, 1929; *Chicago Tribune*, May 11, 1938; Grange, *Zuppke*, 2; Zuppke, "memorandum," June 18, 1937.

4. "Salute to Robert C. Zuppke," October 27, 1949, Disk T595, Sound Recordings, RS 13/6/5; Grange, *Zuppke*, 3, 7; William H. Currie to Zuppke, November 20, 1941; *Chicago Tribune*, December 23, 1957; West Division High School, Milwaukee, WI, *Hesper 98*, 10, 55, 70, 74, 76, 91, 106; M.J. Kelling to Zuppke, December 2, 1938; *Milwaukee Journal*, ca. January 5, 1939; Chris Steinmetz to Zuppke, March 21, 1939; Zuppke, "memorandum," June 18, 1937.

5. Milwaukee Normal School, *Echo*, 1900, *passim*, 1901, *passim*; "Norman Conquest," 1899–1900, Medieval History Sources, 1900–1901, RS 28/3/20–11; A.J. Hedding to Zuppke, January 9, 1939; *Echo 1901*, 18, 31, 54, 86, 90, 93; Ronald A. Smith, "Athletics in the Wisconsin State University System, 1867–1913," *Wisconsin Magazine of History* 55, no. 1 (Autumn 1971): 11.

6. Milwaukee Normal School, *Echo*, 1900, 170–174; *Echo*, 1901, 107–108; Zuppke to Hasso K. Pestalozzi, May 29, 1941; *Illinois Alumni News*, May 1932, 319.

7. Zuppke, "memorandum," June 18, 1937; Robert Zuppke, "Intercollegiate Athletics in Its Relation to a Program of Health and Physical Education," 1931, RS 28/3/20; Chris

Steinmetz, "Bob Zuppke Stories," ca, 1956; *Echo 1902*, 240.

8. Merle Curti and Vernon Carstensen, *The University of Wisconsin* (Madison: University of Wisconsin Press, 1949), 1:545, 642, 2:311, 486; University of Wisconsin, Official Transcript, 1905; "American History," Carl R. Fish, 1903, "European History," "Abnormal Psychology," "Comparative Psychology"; Stephen S. Visher, *Scientists Starred 1903–1943 in "American Men of Science"* (Baltimore: Johns Hopkins Press, 1947) 143; Zuppke, "I'm an American," August 31, 1941; *St. Louis Post-Dispatch*, December 8, 1937; *The Jubilee Badger 1905*, 15, 35, 143, 147, 149, 185, 394; *Badger 1906*, 13, 54, 121–129, 272, 280–281, 301, 339, 358, 361; *The Sphinx*, September 28, 1904, October 19, 1904, November 10, 1904, July 15, 1905; University of Wisconsin, 52nd Commencement Program, June 22, 1905, 2, 20, University of Wisconsin Archives.

9. Curti and Carstensen, *University of Wisconsin*, 2:535, 537, 540; Amos Alonzo Stagg and Henry L. Williams were co-authors of *A Scientific and Practical Treatise on American Football for Schools and Colleges* (Hartford, CT: Press of the case, Lockwood & Bainard, 1893; New York: D. Appleton, 1994); George W. Pierson, *Yale College, An Educational History, 1871–1921* (New Haven, CT: Yale Press, 1952), 96; Grange, *Zuppke of Illinois*, 7, 9–10; Colleen Shaw to Zuppke, December 5, 1953; Zuppke to Shaw, January 7, 1954.

10. *Badger 1905*, 153, 174; *Badger 1906*, 396–397, 414–415; Grange, *Zuppke*, 9–10; *Chicago Tribune*, October 27, 1953; *Champaign-Urbana Courier*, July 2, 1953; Chris Steinmetz, "Bob Zuppke Stories," ca. 1956; John L. Griffith, ed., *The Big Ten Book of Athletic Events* (Chicago, IL: C.D. Hobson, 1929), 166; Zuppke to Bill Fox, December 23, 1940.

Chapter 2

1. Biographical Manuscript, ca. 1956; *Chicago Tribune*, November 2, 1952; *Champaign-Urbana Courier*, April 24, 1953; Art Statement, ca. 1935; Grange, *Zuppke of Illinois*, 10–14, 17; Zuppke, "memorandum," June 18, 1937; *Champaign-Urbana News-Gazette*, November 28, 1926.

2. *Optimist*, 1910, 24, 71–72, 1911, 90, 93–94; George S. Cowley to Zuppke, November 15, 1949; Zuppke to James Kenefick, March 8, 10, April 4, 1910, 4.1/44, Director of Athletics File, 1909–29, Notre Dame University Archives; James Kenefick to Zuppke, March 9, April 1, 1910; Fred H. Jacks to Fred H. Young, August 2, 1956; Fielding H. Yost, *Football for Player and Spectator* (Ann Arbor, MI: University Publishing, 1905); *Muskegon Chronicle*, May 18, 1910; *Chicago Tribune*, October 27, 1953.

3. Grange, *Zuppke*, 16; Harry E. Potter to Zuppke, September 12, 1950; *Champaign-Urbana Courier*, December 23, 1957; *Grand Rapids Herald*, July 19, 1953; *Muskegon Chronicle*, August 13, 1987.

4. *Muskegon Chronicle*, May 18, 1910; Grange, *Zuppke*, 18–21; Winton U. Solberg, *The University of Illinois, 1894–1904* (Urbana: University of Illinois Press, 2000), 359; *Champaign-Urbana Courier*, December 23, 1957; *Grand Rapids Herald*, July 19, 1953; John D. McCallum, *Big Ten Football Since 1895* (Radnor, PA: Chilton Book, 1976), 18; *Chicago Tribune*, May 18, 1911.

5. Robin Lester, *Stagg's University* (Urbana: University of Illinois Press, 1995), 47, 111–112; *Chicago Tribune*, October 27, 1953.

6. For Wisconsin data on high school growth, see Ronald Smith, "Athletics in the Wisconsin State University System," 8. Friends spelled Zuppke's nickname "Zup" or "Zupp." For consistency, we use the first spelling. In 1943, Oak Park's winning streak was still accepted as the state high school record. Illinois Superintendent of Public Instruction, *Eighteenth Biennial Report for 1888–1890* (Springfield, IL: H.W. Rokker, 1891), xiv; *Statistical Abstract of the United States for 1920* (Washington, DC: GPO, 1921), 112; Oriard, *King Football*, 3; Division of Intercollegiate Athletics, University of Illinois, "Four Year Course in Athletic Coaching," *University of Illinois Bulletin*, 22, no. 19 (January 5, 1925), 19; *Champaign-Urbana Courier*, December 23, 1957; Robert Zuppke, "Portraits in Pigskin," *Esquire*, October 1936, 124; "Oak Park High School Student Rosters and Sports Participation"; Ray Berry to Zuppke, November 21, 1941.

7. *Chicago Tribune*, November 1, 6–7, 1910; *Champaign-Urbana News-Gazette*, November 28, 1926.

8. Lester, *Stagg's University*, 28–31; *Boston Globe*, November 30, 1912; *Chicago Tribune*,

24, 28 November 1910, 1, 10, 14, 18, 22–31 December 1910, 1, 3–6 January 1911.

9. *Chicago Tribune*, 7, 11, 13 February 1911, 18 May 1911.

10. For a negative view of Eckersall's academic shortcomings, bad debts and ""loose morals," see Lester, *Stagg's University*, 55–63. *Chicago Tribune*, 27 September 1911, 2, 5, 15, 20, 27, 29 November 1911, 3 December 1911.

11. *Chicago Tribune*, September 15, October 25, November 2–3, 10, 22–23, 26, 28, 30, December 1, 1912; *Boston Globe*, December 1, 1912; Press release from *The Austinite*, October 6, 1937; Charles Bruce to Zuppke, December 2, 1912.

12. *Chicago Tribune*, December 4, 14, 1912, January 12, 1913; Lowell B. Smith to Zuppke, November 30, 1937.

13. *Muskegon Chronicle*, October 28, 1903, June 27, 1908, November 7, 1912; *United States Census Schedules*, Muskegon, Muskegon County, Michigan, Webster Street, 9–74–6, 1900, Jefferson Street, 7–88–24, 1910; Damien E. Rostar to Maynard Brichford, December 21, 2004; *Illinois Alumni News*, October 1936, 21; Biographical Manuscript, ca. 1956; Ray Berry to Zuppke, November 21, 1941.

Chapter 3

1. J. Douglas Toma, *Football U, Spectator Sports in the Life of the American University* (Ann Arbor: University of Michigan Press, 2003), 20, 26, 29.

2. Winton U. Solberg, *The University of Illinois 1867–1894* (Urbana: University of Illinois Press, 1968), 227, 230.

3. Oriard, *King Football*, 79.

4. Michael Oriard, *Reading Football* (Chapel Hill: University of North Carolina Press, 1993), 35–133; Michael Pearson, *Illini Legends, Lists & Lore* (Champaign, IL: Sagamore, 1995), viii; Watterson, *College Football*, 140, 156, 191; Lester, *Stagg's University*, 88–91; *University of Illinois Song Book* (New York: Hinds, Noble & Eldredge, 1908), 24–25; *Fortnightly Notes*, November 1, 1912, 6 and November 15, 1913, 98–99; *Alumni Quarterly and Fortnightly News* (hereafter cited as *AQFN*) November 1, 1919, 25; *Paxton Record*, October 10, 1919.

5. In 1891, the Illinois faculty obtained control of the Student Athletic Association.

Board of Trustees 16th Report, April 10, 1891; John M. Carroll, "The Rise of Organized Sports," in *Sports in Modern America*, ed. William J. Baker and John M. Carroll, 11–12 (St. Louis, MO: River City Publishers, 1981); Pierson, *Yale College*, 255; Griffith, "*Big Ten Book,*" 5, 7.

6. Lester, *Stagg's University*, 87–91, 211; Watterson, *College Football*, 87–129.

7. Michael Oriard's *Reading Football* and *King Football* contain extensive coverage of the influence of magazines, newspapers, newsreels, motion pictures and radio broadcasting.

8. For the competitive and financial travails of early Illinois football, see Winton Solberg, *The University of Illinois 1894–1904*, 364–374; Griffith, *Big Ten Book*, 49, 63, 105; Lester, *Stagg's University*, 48–49; Robin Lester, "Michigan-Chicago 1905: The First Greatest Game of the Century," *Journal of Sport History* 18, no. 2 (Summer 1991): 267–273; Mike Pearson, *Illini Legends and Lore* (Champaign, IL: Sports Publishing, 2002), 31; Solberg, *Illinois, 1894–1904*, 375; Robert Pruter, "High School Intersectional Games Between Boston and Chicago, 1911–1914," North American Society for Sport History, May 30, 2005.

9. The details of Zuppke's original contract are not well documented. The Athletic Board of Control recommended his appointment to the Athletic Association. The first mention of his service in the Trustees' *Proceedings* is a payment of $225 for a June 8, 1914 summer session appointment. Zuppke coached freshman basketball from 1913 to 1920. For the Northwestern offer, see George R. Carr to Frank Scott, December 18, 1912, Zuppke File, RS 26/4/1. Franklin W. Scott, ed., *The Semi-Centennial Alumni Record of the University of Illinois* (Chicago, IL: R.R. Donnelley & Sons, 1918), 66, 968; *Board of Trustees Transactions, 21st Report*, June 11, 1901, 82; *Board of Trustees, 27th Report*, July 5, 1912, 84 and July 23, 1913, 609–619; Roger Ebert, ed., *An Illini Century* (Urbana: University of Illinois Press, 1967), 92–93; Robert C. Zuppke File, Record Series 2/2/15–363; Grange, *Zuppke*, 4, 23–24; "Athletic Coaching," 19; Special Council Meeting, December 12, 1912, Council of Administration Minutes, 1894–1931, RS 3/1/1-XI; Contract, December 13, 1912, RS 28/3/20–1; David Kinley, "Impres-

sions of Illinois Athletic History," August 3, 1937, Carl Stephens Papers, RS 26/1/20–8; Zuppke to R.D. Peterson, November 3, 1937, RS 28/3/20–2; *Chicago Tribune,* December 15, 1912; *Chicago Daily News,* December 23, 1957.

Chapter 4

1. *Champaign-Urbana Courier,* 24 April 1953, 2 July 1953; *Chicago Tribune,* October 17, 1953.

2. *Alumni Quarterly,* January 1913, 7:1:17–18, 7:2:136, 7:3:229; *Fortnightly Notes,* January 1, 1913, 5, April 1, 1913, 47, May 1, 1913, 50–51; *Chicago Tribune,* 22 December 1912, 29 March 1913, 18 May 1913, 12 June 1913, 21 September 1913; Robert Leckie, *The Story of Football* (New York: Random House, 1965), 14, 31–33.

3. *The Illinois,* October 1913, 5:2:57–59, RS 15/7/810.

4. Griffith, "*Big Ten Book,*" *passim;* Lester, *Stagg's University,* 48, 102; *Chicago Tribune,* October 28, 1953; *Fortnightly Notes,* November 1, 1913, 94–96, November 15, 1913, 97–98, 103–104; *Illio,* 1914, 161.

5. Gene Schobinger to Bob Cromie, ca. August 1956; *Fortnightly Notes,* November 1, 1914, 93; *Boston Globe,* December 1, 1912.

6. Another account has Zuppke invited to Boston by Harvard coach Percy Haughton in 1913, where he explained the open offense that was used by Harvard in 1915 and Holy Cross in 1921. *Daily Illini,* December 4, 1921; *Illio,* 1915, 308: "He Was a Judge of Men," 1957; *Champaign-Urbana News-Gazette,* March 10, 1953; *Siren,* November 1914; *Alumni Quarterly,* July 1915, 9:1:40; Contract, December 16, 1914; Biographical Manuscript, ca. 1956; *Bloomington Bulletin,* June 29, 1915.

7. The championship was shared with Minnesota, which had a 3-0-1 record. Robert C. Zuppke, "Will Illinois Repeat?" *Illinois Magazine* 7, no. 1 (October 1915):, 5–6; Oriard, *King Football,* 50; Zuppke to Walter Camp, November 22, 1915; Microfilm Roll 21, Walter Camp Papers, Yale University (microfilm copy at Notre Dame University); G.K. Squier to Zuppke, November 25, 1937, RS 28/3/20–2.

8. Allison Danzig, *The History of American Football* (Englewood Cliffs, NJ: Prentice-Hall, 1956), 211; Wiley L. Umphlett, *Creating*

the Big Game (Westport, CT: Greenwood, 1992), 129; Zuppke, *Football Techniques and Tactics,* 228; Murray Sperber, *Shake Down the Thunder* (New York: Henry Holt, 1993) 39; Lester, *Stagg's University,* 103–104; *Milwaukee Journal,* December 3, 1937; *Champaign-Urbana Courier,* April 24, 1953; *Muskegon Chronicle,* August 11, 1953; *Champaign-Urbana News-Gazette,* December 14, 1950; Biographical Manuscript, ca. 1956; Zuppke to Mike Tobin, January 22, 1940; John Doyle to Tobin, March 4, 1941; Zuppke to Arch Ward, November 30, 1950; *Athletic Journal* 5, no. 2 (October 1924): 3; *Grand Rapids Herald,* July 19, 1953; Zuppke to Christy Walsh, September 22, 1949; Zuppke to Edwin Pope, April 8, 1955; Edwin Pope, *Football's Greatest Coaches* (Atlanta, GA: Tupper and Love, 1955), 291.

9. Interscholastic Programs, 1913–30, RS 28/5/814; *Daily Illini,* 15 November 1916, 8 February 1918, 30 October 1919, 9 December 1921, 8 April 1923; *Ill.io,* 1916, 232–241; *Illio,* 1917, 39–120, 371–372; *Athletic Association Book,* 1915–1916; *Annual Register, 1915–1916,* 455–519, RS 25/3/801; Burton Ingwersen Papers, RS 28/3/22; Ernie Lovejoy to Robert Cromie, December 14, 1957; Zuppke to R.D. Peterson, November 3, 1937; Zuppke to Harry Dillinger, February 19, 1938, RS 28/3/20–2; *Chicago Tribune,* December 24, 1957; William J. Barber, *George Huff, A Short Biography* (privately printed, 1951); Lon Eubanks, *The Fighting Illini* (Huntsville, AL: Strode Publishers, 1976), 61.

10. Thomas A. Clark, *The Sunday Eight O'Clock* (Urbana, IL: Illini, 1916), 63–65.

11. Alumni Association Minutes, 3 May 1913, 30 October 1915, 16 November 1916, 1 June 1919, 20 June 1919, 31 May 1920, 6 December 1920, RS 26/1/2–1; *Board of Trustees 29th Report,* June 12, 1917, 353; Carl Stephens to George Huff, December 13, 1920, RS 26/1/2–1.

Chapter 5

1. Macomber's account of the 1916 Minnesota game and Zuppke's ingenious game plan was enclosed in Ernie Lovejoy to Robert Cromie, December 14, 1957; *Champaign-Urbana News-Gazette,* September 13, 1943; Council of Administration Minutes, 14:147, September 26, 1916, 15:18, November 14,

1916, RS 3/1/1; *Fortnightly Notes*, May 1, 1915, 51; *AQFN*, October 15, 1915, 56–57, November 15, 1915, 100–101, December 1, 1915, 114–117, 124, December 15, 1915, 134–135; *Daily Illini*, November 4, 16, 1916; *Urbana Courier*, September 25, 1916; Zuppke to Walter Camp, November 23, 1916, Walter Camp Papers.

2. Carl A. Voltmer, *A Brief History of the Intercollegiate Conference of Faculty Representatives* (New York: George Banta, 1935), 28–29; *Daily Illini*, July 6, 1916; *Urbana Courier*, December 16, 1917.

3. Athletic Association Record Books, 1917; *Illio 1919*, 248, 250–251; *Rules, Regulations and Opinions of the Intercollegiate Conference of Faculty Representatives* (1925), 5.

4. *Daily Illini*, February 20, 1918; *AQFN*, June 1, 1918, 303.

5. Watterson, *College Football*, 139–140; Grange, *Zuppke*, 58; Pearson, *Illini Legends and Lore*, 52; *President's Report, 1922–23*, 151; *Daily Illini*, 7 February 1918, 27 February 1919.

6. Michael Rosenthal, *The Character Factory* (New York: Pantheon Books, 1986), 67, 69, 98; William Pencak, *For God & Country: The American Legion, 1919–1941* (Boston: Northeastern University Press, 1989), 34; *Daily Illini*, December 9, 1919; *Revised Handbook for Boys* (New York: Boy Scouts of America, 1927), 38–41, 338–347. 588–596; *Daily Illini*, 14 May 1921, 14 March 1922; *Champaign-Urbana News*, 6 December 1919, 12 February 1921.

7. *AQFN*, October 15, 1919, 18, November 1, 1919, 26, 30–31, November 15, 1919, 43–44; *Daily Illini*, November 1, 1919; Athletic Association Record Books, 1919; *1921 Illio*, 154, 161; *Columbus Dispatch*, October 19, 1919; *St. Paul Pioneer Press*, October 29, 1919; *Chicago Tribune*, November 11, 1919; *Rockford Star*, November 11, 1919; *Chicago News*, November 17, 1919.

8. *Columbus Journal*, November 21, 1919; *Daily Illini*, November 22, 1919, November 25, 1919; *Urbana Courier*, November 24, 1919; *Chicago Post*, November 24, 1919; Council of Administration Minutes, 29 May 1917, 24 July 1917, 2 October 1917, 11 March 1918, 8 January 1919, RS 3/1/1.

9. Athletic Association Record Books, 1919; *Peoria Journal*, December 3, 1919; *AQFN*, December 1, 1919, 49–50; Jack

Watson-Bob Zuppke Radio Script, May 26, 1937; *Daily Illini*, November 23, 1919, November 26, 1919; *Chicago Tribune*, December 15, 1919; *Chicago Examiner*, December 7, 1919; *Pittsburgh Leader*, December 6, 1919; *Milwaukee Sentinel*, December 27, 1919.

10. McCallum, *Big Ten Football*, 246–296; *1991 University of Illinois at Urbana-Champaign Football Guide*, 140–142.

11. *Daily Illini*, February 20, 1917; *AQFN*, April 15, 1920, 138, May 1, 1920, 149; Joseph Wright to David Kinley, March 31, 1920 in RS 2/6/1–50; *Urbana Courier*, 29 April 1920, 23 May 1920.

12. Athletic Record Books, 1879–1925, vols. I–III. Division of Intercollegiate Athletics; Intramural Scrapbook, 1918–21, RS 16/7/5–1; *Daily Illini*, 15 November 1919, 14 February 1922, 9 July 1922.

13. The "Athletic Coaching" majors were the "great-grandfathers" of the current "Sports Management" majors. *Board of Trustees Transactions 1918–20*, March 15, 1919, 266; *Catalog, 1919–20*, 581; *Catalog, 1920–21*, 593.

Chapter 6

1. Watterson. *College Football*, 45; Toma, *Football U*, 150.

2. Scott. *Alumni Record 1918*, v, vi, xxi, xxii, 894; Richard A. Swanson, "Edmund J. James, 1855–1925: A Conservative Progressive in American Higher Education," (Ph.D. diss., University of Illinois 1966), 233; Ebert, *Illini Century*, 77; Edmund James to George Huff, December 19, 1913; Huff to James, December 24, 1913, RS 2/5/6–36; James to Huff, July 26, 1916, RS 2/5/3–18.

3. Clarence J. Roseberry, ed., *The University of Illinois Directory for 1929* (Danville: Illinois Publishing Co., 1929), xiii.

4. *AQFN*, October 15, 1919, 16; Scott, *Alumni Record 1918*, 901; David Kinley, *The Autobiography of David Kinley* (Urbana: University of Illinois Press, 1949), 15, 22; *Daily Illini*, December 17, 1916.

5. David Kinley to Robert C. Zuppke. November 29, 1919; Zuppke to Kinley, December 2, 1919, RS 2/6/1–25, University Archives; *Urbana Courier*, November 6, 1919; Kinley to Zuppke, September 24, 1928, RS 2/6/1–52.

6. Council of Administraton Minutes. 21:296, May 21, 1921, RS 3/1/1; *Daily Illini*,

March 14, 1922; Homecoming Program, October 21, 1922; Merle Trees to David Kinley, 19 November 1923, 22 November 1923; Kinley to Trees, 20 November 1923, 27 November, 1923, 2 December 1923, RS 2/6/1–109; Henry C. Johnson and Erwin V. Johanningmeier, *Teachers for the Prairie* (Urbana: University of Illinois Press, 1972), 226–233, 252–257, 260–263.

7. *Illinois Alumni News*, October 1923, 6; Carl Stephens, *Illini Years: A Picture History* (Champaign: University of Illinois Press, 1950), 77; Football Ticket Requests, Kinley Subject File, RS 2/5/6–1.

8. *Illio*, 1922, 4.

9. Richard Whittingham, *What a Game They Played* (New York: Simon & Schuster, 1984), 6; Roger Treat, *The Encyclopedia of Football* (New York: A.S. Barnes, 1979), 23–28; Grange, *Zuppke*, 44; Bruce Evensen, "George Halas," in *The Scribner Encyclopedia of American Lives, Sports Figures*, ed. Arnold Markoe, 337–379 (New York: Charles Scribner's Sons, 2002), vol. 1.

10. Eubanks. *Fighting Illini*, 62–64, 66–67,78–81; *Daily Illini*, 24 October 1920, 25, October 1920.

11. Football Publicity Materials, 1921, 1911–65, RS 28/5/805; Athletic Association Record Books, 1921; *Champaign-Urbana Courier*, April 24, 1953; *Chicago Tribune*, November 18, 1941; Grange, *Zuppke*, 64–66.

12. *AQFN*, December 1, 1920, 70; Watterson, *College Football*, 151–152; George Halas (with Gwen Morgan and Arthur Veysey), *Halas by Halas* (New York: McGraw-Hill, 1979), 58–59, 84, 136; Sperber, *Shake Down the Thunder*, 120–121, 124; Whittingham, *What a Game They Played*, 5; Howard Roberts, *The Chicago Bears* (New York: Putnam, 1947), 3, 21; Eubanks, *Fighting Illini*, 80, 82–85; Kenneth L. Wilson and Jerry Brondfield, *The Big Ten* (Englewood Cliffs, NJ: Prentice-Hall, 1967), 186–189; *Taylorville Daily Breeze*, October 3, 13, 20, November 4, 7, 26, 1921, January 28, 30, 1922.

13. *Taylorville Daily Breeze*, November 26, 28–29, 1921, January 30, 1922.

14. *AQFN*, February 1, 1922, 116, February 15, 1922, 136; *Daily Illini*, January 7, 1921, Janaury 28, 29, 31, 1922, February 1, 1922; Roberts, *Chicago Bears*, 24; *Collyer's Eye*, February 2, 1922.

15. Richard Whittingham, *The Chicago Bears* (Chicago, IL: Rand McNally & Co., 1979), 14–15; *Daily Illini*, October 30, 1920; *AQFN*, January 1, 1921, 97; *Columbus Journal*, November 24, 1919; H. Gordon Hullfish to Oscar G. Mayer, December 2, 1938, RS 1/1/1–22; Wilson, *Big Ten*, 135–137.

16. *Collyer's Eye*, February 4, 1922.

17. *Alumni Quarterly*, January 1914, 43; *Fort Wayne Journal-Gazette*, August 26, 1919; *Chicago Tribune*, October 4, 1919; *Daily Illini*, January 29, 1922.

18. Halas, *Halas by Halas*, vii–xiv, 34–35, 59, 66, 107; Roberts, *The Chicago Bears*, 22; Whittingham, *The Chicago Bears*, 81–83; *2004 Orange & Blue Book* (Champaign: University of Illinois, 2004), 365–366, 368.

19. *Illinois Alumni News*, January 1933, 113; Roberts, *Chicago Bears*, 91–93; *2004 Orange & Blue Book*, 365, 368; *Daily Illini*, December 19, 1933.

Chapter 7

1. "Synopsis of Charter of the Athletic Association," 1922, Physical Education Historical Documents, RS 16/1/50; Eubanks, *Fighting Illini*, 47; *Daily Illini*, March 11, 1925; *New York Times*, December 7, 1944; *Champaign-Urbana Courier*, September 4, 1962; David Kinley's "Athletic History Impressions," August 3, 1937, RS 26/1/20–8; George Huff to E.M. Phillips, February 9, 1921, March 10, 1921, May 23, 1921; Phillips to Huff, March 4, May 21, 1921; David Kinley to Harold Tunnell, June 13, 1925, Legislative File, 1921–29, RS 2/6/3–3.

2. Frank Murphy Papers, 1969, RS 28/2/20; *Daily Illini*, September 14, 1923; Charles Bowen File, RS 25/4/2; Chuck Bennis and Jim Barnhart, *Illinois, Zup and I* (n.p., IL: Smith Printing, 1991) 44; *Champaign-Urbana Courier*, March 6, 1966.

3. *AQFN*, December 1, 1920, 70; Watterson, *College Football*, 151–152; Halas, *Halas by Halas*, 58–59, 84, 136; Sperber, *Shake Down the Thunder*, 120–121, 124; Whittingham, *What a Game They Played*, 5, 81–83; Roberts, *Chicago Bears*, 3, 21; Eubanks, *Fighting Illini*, 80, 82–85; Wilson, *Big Ten*, 186–189.

4. Ralph Cannon, "Football's Forgotten Men," *Esquire*, October 1936, 64, 122; Bennis, *Zup and I*, 55; Grange, *Zuppke*, 87; Burt Ingwersen Papers, 1967, RS 28/3/21.

5. Lex J. Bullock to Maynard Brichford, December 27, 2005, March 3, 2006; U.S. Patent 1,641,733, September 6, 1927; Football Program, November 29, 1929, RS 28/5/811; Bennis, *Zup and I*, 45; Grange, *Zuppke*, 4, 36; *Champaign-Urbana News-Gazette*, 17 October 1937, 3 and 4 October 1962.

6. Coleman Griffith to Zuppke, December 4, 1922, Zuppke to Griffith, December 6, 1922, Coleman Griffith Papers, 1919–63, RS 5/1/21–1; Grange, *Zuppke*, 47, 51; *Chicago Tribune*, December 15, 1929; Whittingham, *What a Game They Played*, 18.

7. Griffith to Louis M. Tobin, May 30, 1930, Course in Athletic Coaching File, 1926–30, RS 28/3/10; Knute Rockne to Griffith, February 10, 1925, Coleman Griffith Papers, RS 5/1/21–1, 5, 15; Ira Morton, *The Galloping Ghost* (Wheaton, IL: DuPage Heritage Gallery, 1981), 68; Wilson, *Big Ten*, 91.

8. Murray Sperber discussed the "gee whiz" and "aw nuts" reporters in his biography of Knute Rockne. The "gee whiz" journalists praised the exploits of the local team. The "aw nuts" journalists were often syndicated columnists or urban pundits. Both were dependent on coaches and sports information offices. Cary C. Burford, *"We're Loyal to You, Illinois"* (Danville, IL: The Interstate, 1952), 172; Louis M. Tobin File, Alumni Records, RS 26/2/20; Jerome Rodnitzky, *A History of Public Relations at the University of Illinois, 1904–1930* (Ph.D. diss., University of Illinois at Urbana-Champaign,1967), 233; Zuppke to Wesley W. Stout, January 23, 1934, RS 28/3/1; Bennis, *Zup and I*, 46; Ernest W. Vatthauer to Zuppke, November 30, 1938.

9. *Urbana Courier*, January 22, 1916; Joseph Wright to David Kinley, November 24, 1920 in RS 2/6/1–50; W.H. Beatty clipping in Guy Thompson Scrapbook, University Archives, RG 41; Zuppke to Frank M. Lindsay, April 1956; Zuppke to Eddie Jacquin, November 27, 1956; *Milwaukee Journal*, November 25, 1941; Oriard, *King Football*, 134–135.

10. *Daily Illini*, December 4, 1920, October 15, 1921.

11. The Athletic Association retained control of intramural sports until 1962, and intercollegiate sports until 1989, when it was merged with the university and became the Division of Intercollegiate Athletics. Faculty involvement had been minimal and control negligible. *Rules, Regulations and Opinions of the Intercollegiate Conference of Faculty Representatives*, 1925:10 and 1937:8, 11; Ira O. Baker and Everett E. King, *A History of the College of Engineering, of the University of Illinois, 1868–1945*, 2 vols. (Urbana: University of Illinois, 1945), 1:247–248, 346–347, 426.

12. Council of Administration Minutes, 1868–1931, December 4, 1923, RS 3/1/1; *Illio*, 1931, 37:201; *Board of Trustees 36th Report*, October 30, 1931, June 11, 1932, 474, 609; University of Illinois Physical Education Graduates, 1935–36; *Board of Trustees 39th Report*, October 26, 1936, February 27, 1937, 78–79, 185.

Chapter 8

1. Danzig, *American Football*, 210; *Milwaukee Journal*, January 20, 1930, *Champaign-Urbana Courier*, October 28, 1949; Champaign-Urbana newspaper clipping, December 10, 1922; *AQFN*, January 1, 1920, 70; Jacob Goldstein to Lena Wolkow, November 10, 1929, RS 41/20/165.

2. For an extensive discussion of the imagery of masculinity, see Oriard, *King Football*, 328–363; *Catalogs, 1920, 1925, 1930, 1935, 1940*, RS 25/3/801.

3. *Daily Illini*, February 9, 1917.

4. Danzig, *American Football*, 210.

5. Grange, *Zuppke*, 49–50.

Chapter 9

1. John Kieran, "Zuppke Comes Up with the Ball," *New York Times*, July 16, 1941; Robert S. Gallagher, "The Galloping Ghost" *American Heritage* 26, no. 1 (December 1974): 23–24; *Chicago Tribune*, October 5, 1925.

2. The salaries are as reported by the Board of Trustees. The Zuppke Papers include signed Athletic Association five-year contracts for $7,000 a year beginning September 15, 1920 and $10,000 a year beginning September 15, 1925. Zuppke to Northwestern Athletics Director, December 8, 1919; *AQFN*, January 1, 1920, 70; *Board of Trustees 23rd Report*, Nov. 22, 1924, 20, 357; *28th Report*, July 18, 1929, 322; "Report of Board of Trustees Committee on Athletics," September 16, 1964, RS 2/5/15–363; George Huff to Arthur T. Evans, April 7, 1024, RS

2/6/1–102; George Huff to Charles E. Chadsey, May 6, 1925, RS 2/6/1–113.

3. *Fortnightly Notes*, December 15, 1913, 116–117; January 1, 1914, 10; *Annual Register 1915–1916*, 213, 385; George Little to Zuppke, July 13, 1955; *The Athletic Journal* 4, no. 9 (May 1924): 27; 3, no. 8 (April 1923): 25; 4 no. 9 (May 1924): 27; 5, no. 8 (April 1925): 33, 35, 37, 52; 5, no. 9 (May 1925): 23, 33, 36; 5, no. 10 (June 1925): 23; "Athletic Coaching," 4, 21; *Daily Illini*, July 1, 1921, June 20, 1923; July 16, 1926; Frank McCormick, RS 2/5/15–40; Robert Zuppke, introduction to *Football Techniques and Tactics* (Champaign, IL: Bailey and Himes, 1924); School for Coaches Photograph, Bucknell University, July 10, 1928.

4. George Huff to Edmund James, January 31, 1916, RS 2/5/3–88; "Four Year Course in Athletic Coaching," (1920), 8–11, 28–29; "Athletic Coaching," 3–5, 10–12, 14–15, 20–21; *Illinois Alumni News*, February 10, 1930, 219; *Chicago Post*, August 6, 1919; Johnson and Johanningmeier, *Teachers for the Prairie*, 254; *Chicago Tribune*, December 12, 1929; George Huff to Waldo Ball, July 7, 1929, Course in Athletic Coaching File, 1926–30, RS 28/3/10.

5. Robert C. Zuppke, *Football Technique and Tactics* (Urbana, IL: Zuppke and Bearg, 1922); *Daily Illini*, September 29, 1921, October 9, 1921, December 8, 1921, September 17, November 2, 1922.

6. Robert C. Zuppke, *Football Technique and Tactics* (Champaign, IL: Bailey and Himes, 1924).

7. *Illinois Alumni News*, November 1928, 85; Snavely-Newland Football Tests Bibliography, Bucknell University, September 1933; *Athletic Journal*, 5, no. 1 (September 1924): 54; Robert C. Zuppke, *Coaching Football* (Champaign: Bailey and Himes, 1930); "The Psychology of Football," 1935.

8. Howard J. Savage, *American College Athletics*, Carnegie Foundation for the Advancement of Teaching, Bulletin 23 (New York, 1929), 121–122. (Hereafter cited as *Carnegie* Report); David O. Levine, *The American College and the Culture of Aspiration, 1915–1940* (Ithaca, NY: Cornell University Press, 1986), 67, 69–70.

9. *Athletic Journal* 5, no. 8 (April 1925): 31; "Rawlings and Zuppke Hard to Beat," April 1, 1928; Rawlings Catalog, ca. 1926, 10–12;

Chicago Daily News, September 25, 30, 1925; Football Programs, RS 28/5/811.

10. *Athletic Journal* 1, no. 1 (March 1921): 8, 23; 3, no.1 (September 1922): 14, 42; 3, no. 4 (December 1922): 44; 7, no. 1 (September 1926): 6–8; Gus Kirby to Avery Brundage, December 28, 1928, Avery Brundage Collection, RS 26/20/37–28.

11. A dramatic rendering of the 1924 AFCA presidential election is in Grange, *Zuppke*, 5–7; *Daily Illini*, December 30, 1923; Jack Falla, *NCAA: The Voice of College Sports* (Mission, KS: NCAA, 1981), 237; Champaign-Urbana newspaper clipping, December 20, 1924; *American Football Coaches Association* (Hanover, NH: A.F.C.A., 1947), 3–4, 13; J.H. Nichols to Coleman Griffith, January 10, 1925, Coleman Griffith Papers, RS 15/1/21–1; Zuppke to Knute Rockne, April 24, 1925, 22/30, Director of Athletics File, 1909–29, Notre Dame University Archives.

12. Knute Rockne to Zuppke, February 2, 1928, 22/30, Director of Athletics File, 1909–29, Notre Dame University Archives; *Chicago Tribune*, September 14, 1913, December 30, 31, 1957, January 1, 1958; *Milwaukee Journal*, ca. January 5, 1939; *Los Angeles Times*, December 23, 1957; Howard Jones to Zuppke, February 18, 1934, RS 28/3/1; McCallum, *Big Ten Football*, 214.

13. *Urbana Daily Courier*, April 26, 1922; *Daily Illini*, May 2, 1923, April 27, 1930.

Chapter 10

1. *Carnegie Report*, 29; *AQFN*, November 1, 1919, 31, November 15, 1920, 52, December 1, 1920, 66, December 15, 1920, 79–81; Alva W. Stewart, *College Football Stadiums* (Jefferson, NC: McFarland, 2000), 75, 79, 145, *Daily Illini*, December 5, 1920, January 20, 1921; July 29, 1921.

2. Raphaelson recalled that Huff was a wonderful, solid, slow-moving, slightly heavy, marvelous, quiet, gentle person, who offered him $100,000 to handle publicity. McCallum, *Big Ten Football*, 233; Kinley, *Autobiography*, 112; *Daily Illini*, December 1, 9–10, 22, 1920, January 7, 20, 23, 25, 1921, February 2, 11, 16–17, 1921, March 9, 13, 22, 1921, April 1, 4, 5, 8–9, 14–15, 1921, May 22, 1921; Football Program, November 11–12, 1921; *Board of Trustees 31st Report*, February

8, 1922, 157; Samson Raphaelson Oral History Interview, 188, Samson Raphaelson Papers, RS 26/20/38–1.

3. *Daily Illini*, April 22, 24, 26–30, May 1, 1921; *AQFN*, May 1, 1921, 222; May 15, 1921, 235–236; Guy Thompson Scrapbook, University Archives, RG 41; Samson Raphaelson, *Story of the Stadium*, 16–22 in Stadium Drive Publications, RS 2/6/805; *The Illinois Stadium "for Fighting Illini,"* 11, 20, RS 2/6/805; p. 188, Oral History Interview in the Samson Raphaelson Papers, RS 26/20/38–1.

4. *Daily Illini*, April 26–27, 1921; *Urbana Courier*, April 26, 1921; Guy Thompson Scrapbook, University Archives, RG 41; Grange, *Zuppke*, 80–81.

5. February 17, 1921, May 31, 1921, Alumni Association Minutes, 1912–73, RS 26/1/2–1; *Urbana Courier*, April 21, 1921; Catalog *1920–21*, 542–547, RS 25/3/801; *AQFN*, July 15, 1921, 282–291, October 1, 1921, 4; *Daily Illini*, April 28, May 5, 11, 13, 27, July 25, 1921; *Illinois Alumni News*, March 1924, 177. *"Fight, Illini! The Stadium Song,"* RS 0/1/804.

6. Grange, *Zuppke*, 68–69; *AQFN*, January 1, 1922, 88–89, January 15, 1922, 102, April 1, 1922, 184–185; *Daily Illini*, July 29, 1921, March 4, 1922, November 9, 14, 1922; Alumni Association Minutes, November 13, 1921, RS 26/1/2; *Board of Trustees 31st Report*, February 8, 1922, 157–158; *Illinois Alumni News*, October 1, 1922, 8–9, 12–13; December 1922, 84, March 1923, 175.

7. *Illinois Alumni News*, June 1923, 261, October 1923, 12, June 1924, 309; *Board of Trustees 32nd Report*, October 20, 1922, 67; *Memorial Stadium Notes*, May 1923, April 1925, August 1925, August 1927, RS 2/6/805; Football Ticket Information, 1929, RS 28/5/805; Lloyd Morey to J.M. Brooks, December 10, 1931, RS 6/3/11; DIA Record Books, Football, 1926–29.

8. Athletic Association finances before 1925 were very informal. The football income, expense and profit figures in this table are based on Athletic Association Audit and Financial Correspondence File, 1918–90, RS 6/3/11. See also *Illinois Alumni News*, February 1927, 183–184.

9. Alumni Association Minutes, May 31, 1921, June 8, 12, 1922, October 21, 1922, April 13, 1923, June 9, 30, 1923, May 31, 1924, June 20, 1924, June 11, 1925, May 11, 1926, RS 26/1/2–1; Football program, October 31, 1931, RS 28/5/811.

10. *Report of Commission on Athletics and Physical Education*, November 23, 1923, RS 2/6/5–1; David Kinley to George Huff, September 18, 1923, RS 2/6/1–102.

11. *Board of Trustees 32nd Report*, June 9, 1924, 577–579; *36th Report*, October 17, 1930, 108; *Illinois Alumni News*, February 1927, 183–184; Football program, October 31, 1931, RS 28/5/811.

12. *Board of Trustees 32nd Report*, September 22, 1922, 24; Edward C. English File and Edward C. English to Carl Stephens, October 6, 1922, RS 26/4/1.

13. Burford, *We're Loya*, 371–414; *Daily Illini*, November 10, 1920; Grange, *Zuppke*, 73; Zuppke to Norman Callow, May 11, 1948.

14. In 1989, Chief Illiniwek became a controversial figure. He was symbolizing a stereotypical male dominant, conservative and ethnocentric American culture to Samuel McGlathery and an esteemed tradition to Jim Fay. Samuel L. McGlathery, "Chief Illiniwek: A Case Study in American Masculinity and Ethnocentrism," March 9, 1992 and Jim Fay, "The Roots of Chief Illiniwek, Tradition at the University of Illinois," 1998, University Archives Reference File. On February 9, 2007, the president of the Board of Trustees announced that Chief Illiniwek would not perform at future University athletic events. The University was responding to an NCAA finding that the Chief's performance was "hostile and abusive" and its ban on the university's hosting postseason intercollegiate athletic events. *The Illini*, January 1874; *1910 Illio*, 188; *1912 Illio*, 179; Council of Administration Minutes, 1868–1931, December 4, 1923, RS 3/1/1; *Illinois Alumni News*, October, 1976; Florence Dvorak to William Schowalter, April 8, 1991; Clarence W. Alvord to *Illini* Editor, November 17, 1919.

Chapter 11

1. Ira Morton, *Galloping Ghost*, 18; McCallum, *Big Ten Football*, 252; *Illinois Alumni News*, October 1, 1922, 12–13, November 1922, 40–42, January 1923, 110, March 1924, 176; *Daily Illini*, November 22, 1922; Zuppke to Walter Camp, November 27, 1922, Walter Camp Papers; Grange, *Zuppke*, 67–69.

2. *Illinois Alumni News*, February 1923, 147, April 1923, 212, June 1923, 273; *Daily Illini*, November 30,1922, December 3, 5, 1922, February 4, 1923, March 10, 1923, April 5, 21, 1923; George Huff to Arthur T. Evans, April 7, 1924, RS 2/6/1–102.

3. *Daily Illini*, February 4, 1923, November 11, 1923; Grange, *Zuppke*, 68–69; *Illinois Alumni News*, October 1923, 13, November 1923, 44, December 1923, 72–79; Edith L. Lemarr Scrapbook, RS 41/20/94; Carey Trimble to David Kinley, September 28, 1923, RS 2/6/1.

4. *Illinois Alumni News*, January 1924, 111–114.

5. Division of Intercollegiate Athletics, Record Books, Football, 1923.

6. Jack Brickhouse and Red Grange Video Interview, WGN-TV, 1979; *Illinois Alumni News*, November 1924, 45, 56; December 80, 82–83, 1924,; March 1925, 175; James A. Peterson, *Grange of Illinois* (Chicago, IL: Hinckley & Schmitt, 1956) 6, 14, 16, 18–19, 22, 24; McCallum, *Big Ten Football*, 122; *Champaign-Urbana Courier*, October 14, 1943; Lester, *Stagg's University*, 122–124; Stephens, *Illini Years*, 80; DIA Record Books, Football, 1924.

7. For the Big Ten games, 300 to 400 complimentary tickets were used for the team, band, and ushers. DIA Record Books, Football, 1924.

8. Dwight W. Follett to Zuppke, November 27, 1937, RS 28/3/20–2.

9. *Illinois Alumni News*, December 1924, 80–81, January 1925, 116, April 1925, 223, May 1925, 257; *Daily Illini*, November 26, 1924, December 6, 1924; George Huff to Charles Chadsey, May 6, 1925, RS 2/6/1–113; "Press Comments on Zuppke Talks," RS 28/5/5.

10. Complimentary Tickets, 1925, RS 2/6/5; Peterson, *Grange of Illinois*, 37–39; Grange, *Zuppke*, 10; John M. Carroll, *Red Grange and the Rise of Modern Football* (Urbana: University of Illinois Press, 1999), 88, 123–124, 129–132, 142–143, 152–154, 183–184, 193–194, 201; Charles L. Allen, ed., *Illinois' Greatest Football Game* (1925), 4, 12, 31, 34; Halas, *Halas by Halas*, 46; *Illinois Alumni News*, July 1925, 332, October 7, 1925, 41–42, November 1925, 57–58, November 4, 1925, 89–94, November 25, 1925, 97–100; *Urbana Courier*, November 19,

1925; "Zuppke on Football," September 22, 1934; *Catalog, 1925–26*, 87, 444; Whittingham, *Chicago Bears*, 36, 38.

11. Athletic Association Minutes, January 31, 1926, RS 28/1/3; *Literary Digest*, December 26, 1925; *New York Times*, December 8, 1925; Dudley Butler to David Kinley, November 19, 1925; David Kinley to Edward Keator, December 16, 1925, RS 2/9/1–129.

12. Grange's statements that Zuppke would not speak to him after he turned professional were not accurate. *Urbana Courier*, November 25, 1925; *Illinois Alumni News*, January 1926, 138, February 1926, 180–183, March 1926, 215, June 1933, 313; Rodnitzky, *Public Relations*, 235–236; Oriard, *King Football*, 235.

Chapter 12

1. *Illinois Alumni News*, March 1926, 217, May 1926, 291, June 1926, 324; *Daily Illini*, June 16–17, 1926.

2. *Illinois Alumni News*, October 20, 27, 1926, 49–56; November 1, 10, 1926, 89–96; *Collyer's Eye*, November 6, 1926; *President's Report, 1926–27*, 38.

3. *Illinois Alumni News*, January 1927, 145; *Daily Illini*, November 23, 1926.

4. Gallagher, "*Galloping Ghost*," 23; Albon Holden, "Ten Personalities in the Football Coaching Game," *Big Ten Weekly*, September 30, 1926, 6, 11; Hugh Fullerton, "All-America Football Coaches," *Liberty*, February 12, 1927, 21–27; *1996 Football Guide*, 169; *Champaign-Urbana News-Gazette*, December 10, 1929; *Carnegie Report*, i, xx, 81, 133–134, 161–189, 253–254, 265; *President's Annual Report*, 1927.

5. *Daily Illini*, September 15–18, 20–22, 1927.

6. Grange, *Zuppke*, 123, 125–126; *Illinois Alumni News*, October 1927, 16, 42, January 1928, 159; DIA Record Books, Football, 1927; Football Concession Report, 1927, Fred H. Turner Papers, RS 41/1/20–10.

7. *Illinois Alumni News*, December 1927, 134–136.

8. *Illinois Alumni News*, January 1928, 161–163, 167.

9. Zuppke to Rockne, January 24, 1928, February 24, 1928, September 30, 1929, October 10, 1929, December 10, 1929; Rockne to Zuppke, November 5, 1925, Feb-

ruary 2, 1928, October 4, 12, 1929, November 19, 1929, December 16, 1929, 22/30, 22/31, Director of Athletics File, 1909–29, Notre Dame University Archives; "Knute Rockne as a Radio Speaker," Internet, November 24, 2003.

10. *Daily Illini*, December 7, 1927.

11. *Illinois Alumni News*, June 1925, 289, February 1928, 213, March 1928, 247–249.

12. *Illinois Alumni News*, October 1928, 18; *1930 Illio*, 204, 206; DIA Record Books, Football, 1928.

13. *Illinois Alumni News*, February 1930, 191.

14. Data based on three year averages, except for Minnesota, which is for 1927–28 only. Eight university administrators to Shirley Smith, March 18–21, 1931, RS 6/3/11–1. In 1927, Notre Dame projected a $500,000 return on its games with Southern California, Army, Navy, Minnesota and Georgia Tech, *Collyer's Eye*, December 31, 1927.

15. *Illinois Alumni News*, November 26, 140, 1928, December 5, 1928, December, 145–146, 1928; *Illinois State Register*, December 18, 1928.

16. *Illio*, 1930, 197, 201; George Huff to G.D. Stopp, June 14, 1919; Huff to Edmund James, March 11, 1919, RS 2/5/3–8; Huff to Kinley, April 20, 1927, RS 2/6/1–130.

Chapter 13

1. *National Collegiate Athletic Association Proceedings*, 17th Annual Convention, December 28, 1922, 67–74; *NCAA Proceedings*, 18th Annual Convention, December 28, 1923, 73–82.

2. The AAUP committee was chaired by a faculty member from the University of Chicago. *Carnegie Report*, vii; *New York Times*, May 26–28, 1926.

3. *New York Times*, May 24–25, 30, November 28–30, 1926; *Forum*, November 1926, 682–695, December 1926, 830–844.

4. *New York Times*, May 26–28, 1926; James R. Angell, "The Over-Population of the College," *Harpers Magazine*, October 1927, 529–530; Abraham Flexner, *Universities: American, English and German* (New York: Oxford University Press, 1930), 65–66.

5. Officials in the Amateur Athletic Union and Intercollegiate Association of Amateur Athletes of America maintained that Griffith believed in "commercializing everything," had no quarrel with professional baseball and football and cited his involvement in organizing sporting goods manufacturers — Gustavus Kirby to Avery Brundage, December 28, 1928, Avery Brundage Papers, RS 26/20/37. "Interest in Amateurism," May 25, 1925; Agreement on "Equal Competition" and "Illegitimate Recruiting," September 1, 1926; Griffith to Athletics Directors, September 29, 1926, April 10, 1927, RS 2/6/1–130.

6. *Daily Illini*, February 19, 1927; Report of Scholarships and Employment held by Athletes in Big Ten Schools, 1926–27, RS 2/6/1–130.

7. Kendric Babcock to Ralph Chapman, January 24, 1927; Special Committee of Sixty Minutes, January 28, 1927, RS 2/6/1–130; *Chicago Tribune*, October 29, 1953; Voltmer, *Brief History*, 35; J. Frank Lindsey to David Kinley, April 12, 1927, RS 2/6/1–130.

8. *Carnegie Report*, xiii, 92, 174, 242, 300–305; Flexner, *Universities*, 206.

9. Robert Zuppke, "Why Intercollegiate Athletics Should Persist," ca. 1935, RS 28/3/20–2; Ronald McIntyre, *Milwaukee Sentinel*, November 30, 1937; Carroll, *Grange*, 95–96; Halas, *Halas by Halas*, 114, 117–119.

10. Oriard, *King Football*, 106–108; Mervin D. Hyman and Gordon S. White, *Big Ten Football* (New York: Macmillan, 1977), 31–32.

11. Donald Chu, *The Character of American Higher Education and Intercollegiate Sports* (Albany: State University of New York Press, 1989), 22–24; Levine, *American College*, 19, 46–47.

12. Lester, *Stagg's University*, 117; Sperber, *Shake Down the Thunder*, 146, 265; Thomas J. Schlereth, *The University of Notre Dame* (Notre Dame, IN: University of Notre Dame Press, 1976), 147, 149; McCallum, *Big Ten Football*, 248–308; *Illinois Alumni News*, June 1928, 392.

13. *Report on Eligibility Rules*, May 8, 1912; *Report of Special Senate Committee*, 1915; *Committee on Athletics and Public Welfare Report*, 1923; Senate Committee of Nine on General Educational Organization and Administration, 1931–32; Clarence Berdahl to A.J. Harno, January 19, 1931; Cloyde M. Smith to Harrison E. Cunningham, January 20, 1931, RS 4/5/12.

14. *Report of Subcommittee on Physical Welfare*, April 23, 1931; *Report of Subcommittee on the Relation of Alumni and Ex-students to the University*, July 13, 1931, RS 4/5/12.

15. Coleman R. Griffith, "This Football Business; A Study in the Philosophy of Education," ca. 1930, RS 15/1/21–15.

16. *Illinois Alumni News*, January 1932, 181, February 1932, 216; Howard J. Savage, *Fruit of an Impulse* (New York: Harcourt, Brace, 1953), 158–159; Lester, *Stagg's University*, 162, 167–186; Levine, *The American College*, 120.

Chapter 14

1. *American College Football*, 236–240; *1937 Big Ten Rules*, 18; *Daily Illini*, December 2, 16, 1921.

2. Robert Dunkelberger, "Football Recruiting Trends at Major Midwestern Universities, 1910–2000, A Statistical Study," 4, 7, 13; *1914–1941 Illios*; *Student Directories, 1914–1941*.

3. *Carnegie Report*, xvii; *Register of the University of Illinois 1925–1926*, 57, 62, 152; University of Illinois Catalogs (Registers) 1920–1940.

4. *Illinois Alumni News*, June 1928, 392; Fred H. Turner, "Athletes Lead in Brains," *Big Ten Weekly*, April 1, 1926.

5. In 1939, President Willard's report on the eligibility and employment of athletes was referred to the Board's Athletic Activities Committee. Grange, *Zuppke*, 105; *Illinois Alumni News*, May 1932, 391; Zuppke to C.G. Easterwood, July 20, 1940; Zuppke to Anthony J. Janata, May 29, 1940; *Carnegie Report*, 245; *Champaign-Urbana News-Gazette*, August 4, 1940; *Milwaukee Journal*, January 18, 1930.

6. *AQFN*, July 15, 1920, 170, 176; Ebert, *An Illini Century*, 108–109; *Illinois Alumni News*, July 1924, 309.

7. Henry Pritchett was a Pritchett College graduate. Howard Savage taught English at Harvard. Harold Bentley taught Spanish at Columbia. John McGovern and Dean Smiley were in track and medicine at Cornell. *Carnegie Report*, 239–240.

8. *Illinois Alumni News*, May 1925, 257; Alpha Sigma Phi, "The Illini Etagram," 1930–41, RS 41/71/812; Delta Tau Delta,

"Beta Upsilon Booster," December 1932, January 1939, RS 41/71/834.

9. *Illios, 1916–1942*, RS 41/8/803; Leland F. Leland, *The Golden Book of Tau Kappa Epsilon 1899–1940* (St. Paul, MN: Fraternity Press, 1949), 145; Stewart Howe Collection, RS 26/20/30; Peterson, *Grange of Illinois*, 6, 8.

10. Savage, *American College Football*, 239; *Illinois Alumni News*, April 1927, 262; May 1936, 10; Kappa Epsilon, *The Alpha Gamma Messenger*, October 1933.

11.

Kappa Sigma, *Alpha Gamma Messenger*, October 1931, May, 1933, October 1933, October, 1935, December 1935, RS 41/71/843; Zuppke to Hersel Ekin, February 13, 1939; Edward S. Axline to Harrison E. Cunningham, January 13, 1938, RS 1/1/1–22; Mike Tobin to A.R. Kinsey, March 22, 1938.

12. *1929 Illio*, 406; *1939 Illio*, 360.

13. The financial support of boosters existed in the Zuppke era and developed rapidly after 1965. By the 1980s, fifty-eight universities reported annual private funding for sports averaging $1.34 million. By 2007, season ticket holders were boosters or investors in the football program. Toma, *Football U*, 129, 133, 137–166; Chu, *Higher Education*, 31, 33, 53–56; Coleman Griffith, "This Football Business," RS 5/1/21–15.

14. DIA Record Books, Football, 1933; *Daily Illini*, March 6, 1923; *Illinois Alumni News*, December 1, 1919, 51; Harry Monier and L.M. Rovelstad to Zuppke, November 18, 1933; L.M. Rovelstad to Friend, May 24, 1935; Athletic Relations Committee Minutes and Membership List, November 17, 1933, George Chapin Papers, Illinois Historical Survey; *Champaign-Urbana City Directory*, 1935.

Chapter 15

1. Robert C. Zuppke, "Playing the Game," *The Executives' Club News*, 1930; *Milwaukee Journal*, January 20, 1930; National Newspaper Service Release, September 7, 1930; *New York Herald-Tribune*, March 20, 1931.

2. Stagg also drove an electric car at Chicago. *Board of Trustees 34th Report*, December 14, 1926, 186; *Illinois Alumni News*, May 1927, 304; *The Spokesman*, August 25,

1926; *Los Angeles Times*, September 9, 1928; *Illinois Alumni News*, October 1931, 15.

3. *Daily Illini*, September 22, 1929; *Salt Lake Tribune*, June 14, 1929; *Dallas Morning News*, January 1, 1931; *The Havana Post*, January 9, 1931; *Miami Herald*, January 21, 1931; *Illinois Alumni News*, March 20, 1930, 429; June 20, 1930, 429; *Denver Post*, July 10, 1930, August 6, 1930.

4. Burford, *We're Loyal to You*, 121–125; Champaign-Urbana newspaper clipping, July 8, 1925; "Intercollegiate Athletics in Its Relation to a Program of Health and Physical Education," Zuppke Papers, RS 28/3/20–1; *Carnegie Report*, 81–82; Toma, *Football U*, 165, 168, 174.

5. Joseph R. DeMartini, "Student Protest During Two Periods in the History of the University of Illinois, 1867–94 and 1929–42," (Ph.D. diss., University of Illinois at Urbana-Champaign, 1974), 271, 303–304; Karl Grisso, "David Kinley" (Ph.D. diss., University of Illinois at Urbana-Champaign, 1964), 599; *Illinois Alumni News*, October 23, 1929, 45–48, October 30, 1929, 53, November 1929, 63; November 6, 1929, 101, 104–105; McCallum, *Big Ten Football*, 48; Rockne to Zuppke, December 16, 1929, 22/31, Director of Athletics File, 1909–29, Notre Dame University Archives.

6. *Illinois Alumni News*, November 20, 1929, 110–113, December 1929, 129–130.

7. This emphasis on defense was also evident in professional football. In 1935, the national champion Chicago Bears averaged eleven points a game and their opponents averaged three. *Illinois Alumni News*, February 1931, 189; Football Season Coupon Book Sales, April 15, 192, RS 2/7/5; *Chicago Tribune*, November 22, 1941; *Champaign-Urbana News-Gazette*, September 13, 1943; Whittingham, *Chicago Bears*, 86.

8. *Illinois Alumni News*, November 27, 1929, 116, January 1930, 158, February 1930, 199.

9. *Carnegie Report*, 168–174; *Illinois Alumni News*, January 1931, 160–161.

10. Frank Murphy Interview, November 3, 1969, RS 28/2/30; Reports of Distribution of Complimentary Tickets, 1937, RS 2/9/5–4.

11. Lester, *Stagg's University*, 136; Watterson, *College Football*, 162–164; Harold F. Williamson and Payson S. Wild, *Northwestern University, A History, 1850–1975* (Evanston,

IL: Northwestern University, 1976), 172; Kenneth L. Wilson, RS 26/4/1; Wilson, *Big Ten*, 116–117, 160–170.

12. Merle Trees to Arthur H. Daniels, June 21, 1935; Arthur Daniels to Merle Trees, June 22, 1935, RS 6/3/8–1.

13. Athletic Association Audit Report, September 22, 1925, March 1, 1927; Special Report on Purchasing Procedures of the Athletic Association, September 14, 1930; Lloyd Morey to J.D. Phillips et al., December 9, 1930.

14. *Illinois Alumni News*, July 1930, 457; October 18, 1930, 41–42; October 22, 1930, 45–47; October 29, 1930, 49–51; November 1930, 57; DIA Record Books, Football, 1930.

15. *Illinois Alumni News*, December 1930, 130; January 1931, 160–161; *Daily Illini*, December 24, 1930.

16. In 1929, thirty of the fifty-four players on the Army team had attended other colleges. *Illinois Alumni News*, November 5, 1930, 100, November 12, 1930, 101–104, January 1930, 121–122; Athletic Association Budget, 1931–32, RS 6/3/11–1.

17. *Illinois Alumni News*, October 8, 1930, 40; Ronald A. Smith, *Play by Play* (Baltimore: Johns Hopkins Press, 2001), 32–33.

18. Robert Zuppke, "Intercollegiate Athletics," " 1931, RS 28/3/20; *Milwaukee Journal*, February 26, 1931.

19. *New York Herald-Tribune*, March 20, 1931.

Chapter 16

1. Athletic Association, Financial File, RS 6/3/11; Public Information Subject File, 1919–84, RS 39/1/1–2.

2. *Illinois Alumni News*, November 18, 1931, 117–119, November 25, 1931, 121–124; *Chicago Tribune*, October 1932, 2, 5.

3. *Illinois Alumni News*, November 25, 1931, 24.

4. Budget, 1931–32, RS 6/3/11–1; Football Publicity Materials, 1932, RS 28/5/805; *Illinois Alumni News*, October 1932, 2, 5; DIA Record Books, Football, 1931–41; Athletic Association Scrapbooks, RS 28/1/10–1.

5. A.M. Buswell to A.J. Harno, October 22, 1931; Method for Intercollegiate Athletics Business, 1932; Harry W. Chase to George Huff, January 27, 1933; Lloyd Morey to

Chase, January 18, 19, 1933; Merle Trees to Arthur H. Daniels, July 26, 1933, RS 2/7/5.

6. Johnson, *Teachers for the Prairie*, 274–276; *Illinois Alumni News*, January 1933, 124–125; Harry W. Chase to George Huff, January 17, 1933; RS 2/7/5.

7. *Illinois Alumni News*, May 1932, 318–319.

8. DIA Record Books, Football, 1932; *Illinois Alumni News*, January 1933, 114–115.

9. *Illinois Alumni News*, April 1933, 230, 238–240, May 1933, 278–281, June 1933, 326–328; Kensort Williams to Zuppke, September 9, 1933.

10. Claude O. Ellis, "Did You Know" and "Beg Pardon," 1933; University Notes and Comments, April 1, 1933; O.S. Hitchner to Arthur Willard, ca. December 24, 1934, RS 0/1/801.

11. *Illinois Alumni News*, July 1927–July 1933; December 1935, 21; *Catalogs*, 1920–1940; Zuppke to A.K. Nelson, October 12, 1933, RS 28/3/1.

12. Milt Olander to Zuppke, August 1933.

13. Athletic Association Books, 1935–36, RS 28/1/10–1.

14. Zuppke to William V. Pauley, June 12, 1933; J.T. Smith to Zuppke, August 18, 1933; *Illinois Alumni News*, November 1933, 57–61, November 23, 1933, 50, December 1933, 95–100; *New York Herald-Tribune*, October 16, 1933.

15. *Illinois Alumni News*, December 1933, 95, January 1934, 122–123; *Chicago Daily News*, December 19, 1933; Stewart D. Owen to Zuppke, November 26, 1933, RS 28/3/1.

16. "Zuppke Speeches, 1933–1934" in R$ 28/3/1–1; *Illinois Alumni News*, February 1934, 161; Art Janz to Zuppke, December 2, 1933; H.D. McBride to Zuppke, January 1934; *Baker's Helper*, March 24, 1934, 462–464; *Champaign-Urbana News-Gazette*, January 2, 1958; *Champaign-Urbana Courier*, December 30, 1957; Zuppke to Bert C. Nelson, January 23, 1934.

17. Based on the Consumer Price Index, $10,000 in 1930 would be the equivalent of $1,058,200 in 2001. *Board of Trustees 32nd through 39th Reports*, 1932–1939; Zuppke Speech, ca. 1935.

Chapter 17

1. McCallum, *Big Ten Football*, 268–274, 280–297; *1991 Football Guide*, 30, 142–143; Godfrey Sperling, "Zup's formula for 'pure' college athletics," http://search.csmonitor.com.

2. Charles E. Bowen to Arthur C. Willard, March 8, 1937, RS 2/9/1–16; Zuppke to Paul T. Maulding, November 15, 1933; Zuppke to Paul M. Green, April 13, 1934, RS 28/3/1.

3. *Illinois Alumni News*, October 1934, 13, November 1934, 46, 60–63; December 1934, 96–98, 101; *Champaign-Urbana News-Gazette*, October 14, 1934; *Daily Illini*, November 9, 1934.

4. *Illinois Alumni News*, December 1934, 96, 101–104: *1933 Illio*, 168.

5. Zuppke to Howard Jones, September 22, 1933, RS 28/3/1; *Illinois Alumni News*, February 1935, 172; *Phoenix Gazette*, January 26, 1935; Jack Stewart to Zuppke, November 19, 1956.

6. Bennis, *Zup and I*, 15–17, 23–26, 28, 43, 49, 54–55.

7. Football Program, November 14, 1931, RS 16/1/21; Lester, *Stagg's University*, 149, 227; *Illinois Alumni News*, October 1934, 8, 10.

8. For a discussion of Simmons' career at Iowa, see Oriard, *King Football*, 302–307. *Illinois Alumni News*, October 1935, 19, November 1935, 6–7, 9, 18, December 1935, 5–6, 17–22; DIA Record Books, Football, 1935.

9. *Daily Illini*, November 13, 1935; *Illinois Alumni News*, December 1935, 15–16.

10. *1935 Illio*, 266; *Illinois Alumni News*, July 1937, 29, October 1937, 19, October 1939, 17; *Catalogs, 1920–21, 1940–41*, RS 25/2/801.

11. Burt C. Hurd to Zuppke, January 10, 1950; Petroleum Management Statement, April 1930, May 1931, RS 28/3/20–2; Zuppke to Harrison Cunningham, July 28, 1932, RS 2/5/15–363; F. Baldwin to Zuppke, April 15, 1938; Zuppke to W.F. Collar, Sept. 8, 1938; E.D. Griffin to Zuppke, November 3, 1937; "Football by Bob Zuppke," 1930–34; Robert C. Zuppke, *10 Things a Boy Should Know How to Do!* (Milwaukee, WI: Albert Richard, 1934); Ted Ashby to Zuppke, June 1, 1939; Zuppke to Harrison Harding, March 5, 1940; Zuppke to Ted Ashby, April 6, 1934, RS 28/3/1; *Des Moines Register* Syndicate to Koester, August 1, 1933, RS 28/3/1; 42; Grifith O. Ellis, *American Boy Sports Stories* (New York: Sun Dial Press, 1937), ix.

12. National Newspaper Service, Robert
Zuppke, "Football" and "Zuppke's Guesses,"
September 19, 1932–January 14, 1933; *Illinois
Alumni News*, October 1937, 18; *Champaign-
Urbana News-Gazette*, September 23–Octo-
ber 14, 1931; *Des Moines Register*, December
1938; Robert Zuppke, "Talks about late 20th
century..."; Howard Jones to Zuppke, February 18, 1934; "Football by Bob Zuppke," September 24,—December 1, 1934; Christy
Walsh, *Adios to Ghosts!* (published privately,1935), 28, 42; Illinois-Iowa Football
Program, November 26, 1935; Griffith O.
Ellis, ed., *American Boy Short Stories* (New
York: Sun Dial Press,1937), ix.
13. *Rules, Regulations and Opinions of the
Intercollegiate Conference of Faculty Representatives* (1937) 26–27; W.E. Bischoff to Zuppke, April 14, 1938; Zuppke to Bischoff, April
29, 1940.
14. *Illinois Alumni News*, April 1934, 230.
15. *Daily Illini*, October 15, 1916, July 16,
1926, December 16, 1926, October 7, 1923;
Urbana Courier, September 16, 1916; Edna
Erwin to Zuppke, November 19, 1945,
December 14, 29, 1948; Herma Heck to Zuppke, November 26, 1949.
16. *Champaign-Urbana News-Gazette*,
November 28, 1926, November 8, 1931,
August 1, 1936, September 3, 1936, October
28, 1949; *Urbana Courier*, December 11, 1916;
Champaign & Urbana City Directory, 1914,
539, 1925, 379, 1927, 361, 1957, 604; Mrs.
Glenwood Tanton to Zuppke, October 9,
1940; Zuppke to Tanton, November 7, 1940;
Biographical Manuscript, ca.1956; *Daily
Illini*, October 5, 1921, December 10, 1921,
December 9, 17, 1922, January 7, 1923, May
3, 1923, July 28, 1923, October 3, 1923; Elvin
Sayre to Zuppke, November 8, 1940;
Eubanks, *Fighting Illini*, 150; *Daily Illini*,
February 22, 1923, April 14, 1923; *Cham-
paign-Urbana Courier*, December 26, 1957;
Lex Bullock to Maynard Brichford, Decem-
ber 27, 2005; Grange, *Zuppke*, 161–163; Zup-
pke to Associated Press, March 11, 1938; *New
York Sun*, November 14, 1932; *Rockford
Register-Republic*, May 7, 1931.
17. "Bill Stern, the Colgate Shave Cream
Man" was the first line of a jingle sung at the
beginning of Stern's sports radio program.
Muskegon Chronicle, July 31, 1936, August 1,
1936, December 23, 1957; *Illinois Alumni
News*, October 1936, 21; "Reel Four! Profile

of an Empty Room," Bill Stern, 1941; Grange,
Zuppke, 141–142, 163.
18. *Chicago Daily News*, July 19, 1941;
Champaign-Urbana News-Gazette, July 18,
1941; *Milwaukee Journal*, November 25, 1941;
Bennis, *Zup and I*, 23.

Chapter 18

1. In 1949, Sayre recalled the tribulations
of his sophomore year and the instillation of
Zuppke's common sense, good judgment and
sense of fair play. Elvin Sayre to Zuppke,
November 8, 1949; *Illinois Alumni News*,
October 1936, 21; December 1936, 14–15;
Daily Maroon, November 24, 1936; Fred
Richart to John Griffith, December 18, 1936,
RS 4/2/12–2.
2. "In Memoriam, George A. Huff" in
The Caduceus of Kappa Sigma 52, no. 2
(November 1936); 156–158; *Champaign-
Urbana Courier*, October 1, 1926;
Champaign-Urbana News-Gazette, October
2, 1936; *Board of Trustees 39th Report*, Sept.
30, 1936, 27.
3. *Board of Trustees 39th Report*, Febru-
ary 27, 1937, 185; Trustees Committee on
Athletics Activities Report, July 15, 1941, RS
16/1/50–1; *Illinois Alumni News*, November
1936, 13, April 1937, 2, 11, January 1939, 3;
Champaign-Urbana News-Gazette, September 23, 1933; *Daily Illini*, July 15, 1941; Fred
A. Russell to Zuppke, March 28, 1937.
4. *Illinois Alumni News*, January 1937,
6–7, April 1937, 9; Bennis, *Zup and I*, 27;
George Goble Papers, RS 14/2/20–6.
5. Ebert, *Illini Century*, 118–119; *1912–13
Catalog*, 550; *1937–38 Catalog*, 612; *Illinois
Alumni News*, April 1937, 9.
6. Alumni Association Annual Meetings
File, 1935–63, RS 32/1/804; *Illinois Alumni
News*, February 1937, 8, April 1937, 10, June
1937, 17; Watson-Zuppke Radio Script, May
26, 1937.
7. *Illinois Alumni News*, February 1937,
9; April 1, 1941, February 2, 1942; *Champaign-Urbana News-Gazette*, December 15,
1938; *Illini News*, September 20, 1937.
8. Football Responses, 1933–34, Public
Information Subject File, 1919–84, RS
39/1/1–4; Athletic Association Budgets, 1937,
RS 4/2/12–1, 1937–38, 1939–40, RS 6/3/11–1;
"Radio Broadcasting," June 1939, RS 2/
9/1–38; *Board of Trustees 32nd Report*, 60,

338, 543; Douglas O. Baldwin, ed., *Sports in North America, A Documentary History, Sports in the Depression, 1930–1940* (Gulf Breeze, FL: Academic International Press, 2000), 161; *Champaign-Urbana News-Gazette,* November 30, 1938; Henry C. Klein to Zuppke, June 7, 1937; Zuppke to Klein, June 8, 1937; *Illinois Alumni News,* July 1937, 30, George Goble Papers, RS 14/2/20–6.

9. Lester, *Stagg's University,* 171–172; John Griffith to William Moenkhaus, William Marshall and Fred Richart, August 10, 1937, RS 4/2/12–2.

10. Watson-Zuppke Radio Script, May 26, 1937; *Illinois Alumni News,* November 1937, 20, December 1937, 12–13, 20, January 1938, 20; Division of Intercollegiate Athletics Sports Records, Football, 1937; DIA Record Books, Football, 1937.

11. *Champaign-Urbana News-Gazette,* March 29, 1937; WHN "Gridiron Smoker," October 29, 1937.

12. *Illinois Alumni News,* November 1937, 10; Mark Hindsley, *My Bands and I* (Urbana, IL: privately printed, 1984), 55; "Among My Letters," RS 28/3/20; Albert L. Lindell to Zuppke, December 1, 1937; Rev. John A. O'Brien to Zuppke, December 4, 1937.

13. On October 27, 1939, the publisher had 3,500 copies of *Zuppke of Illinois* on hand. Grange, *Zuppke,* ix–xi, 84,174; *Illinois Alumni News,* October 1937, 3, 18; November 1937, 20.

14. Football Dinner Program, November 22, 1937; *Illinois Alumni News,* December 1937, 13–14.

15. *Champaign-Urbana News-Gazette,* December 3–4, 1937; *Illini News,* December 6, 1937.

16. *Illini News,* November 18, 1937.

17. Griffith to Big Ten Athletic Directors, April 16, 1937; Griffith to Fielding Yost, July 27, 1937; Griffith to Kenneth S. Wilson, September 12, 1938; Frank Richart to Griffith, September 22, 1938; Griffith to W.J. Moenckhaus, William Marshall and Frank Richart, October 1, 1938, RS 4/2/12–2; *St. Louis Globe-Democrat,* September 19, 1938, October 6, 1938.

18. DIA Record Books, Football, 1938–39; Football Publicty Material, 1938, RS 28/5/805; *Illinois Alumni News,* December 1938, 17–18; *1939 Illio,* 188–189.

19. *Daily Illini,* November 13, 18, 23,

1938; *Illinois Alumni News,* December 1938, 3, 18.

20. Athletic Association Minutes, December 25, 27, 28, 1938 in Athletic Committee Chairman's File, 1907–68, RS 4/1/12–2; Biographical Manuscript, ca. 1956; *Illinois Alumni News,* December 1938, 3, 19.

21. *Daily Illini,* November 30, 1938; *Champaign-Urbana Courier,* Nov. 29, 30, 1938; *Chicago Tribune,* November 30, 1938; *Champaign-Urbana News-Gazette,* November 30, 1938, November 18, 1941; *Daily Illini,* December 2, 1938; Zuppke to A.W. Gross, December 12, 1938.

Chapter 19

1. Alumni Association Minutes, December 1, 1938, RS 26/1/2–15; *Daily Illini,* December 2, 7, 1938; *Illinois Alumni News,* December 1938, 3; Fred Luthy to Fellow Illini, December 6, 1938; Luthy to Frank Richart, December 7, 1938; *Polk's Peoria City Directory 1939* (Peoria, IL: R.L. Polk & Co., 1939), 281; *Chicago Daily News,* December 15, 1938; *Board of Trustees 40th Report,* November 29, 1938, December 17, 1938, 145, 178; Harold A. Pogue to Harrison E. Cunningham, December 19, 1938, January 23, 1939, RS 1/1/1–22; H. Gordon Hullfish to Oscar G. Mayer, December 2, 1938, RS 1/1/1–22.

2. *Champaign-Urbana Courier,* December 18, 1938; Fred Young to Mike Tobin, February 7, 1939; Zuppke to Al Fuller, February 10, 1939; Zuppke to Dan Morrisey, January 23, 1939; Athletic Association Minutes, February 14, 1939; *Champaign-Urbana News-Gazette,* March 29, 1939.

3. *Illini News,* September 28, 1938, October 1, 26, 1938, November 23, 1938, December 21, 1938, February 5, 1939; Willard to Zuppke, January 30, 1939.

4. In 1914, Chicago President Henry P. Judson had proclaimed that it was not the function of the University to provide at great cost spectacular entertainment for enormous crowds of people, while the capacity of the stadium was being increased from 11,500 to 32,000. *Illinois Alumni News,* October 1939, 16; Lester, *Stagg's University,* 99; Zuppke to Arthur C. Willard, October 29, 1939; Willard to Zuppke, October 26, 1939.

5. Carl Stephens Papers, RS 26/1/2–23; Stephens, *Illini Years,* 69.

6. Athletic Association Minutes, May 26, 1939; *Board of Trustees 40th Report,* July 21, September 30, 1939, 491, 567; *Daily Illini,* October 1, 1939.

7. Zuppke to Carl Voyles, March 2, 1939; Zuppke to Paul Gauger, May 18, 1939; George Ade to Zuppke, June 7, 1939; Zuppke to Ade, June 17, 1939; Donald Moffett to Zuppke, April 26, 1939; Zuppke to Potsy Clark, May 3, 1939; *Indianapolis Star,* November 1, 1970.

8. Zuppke to Molly Ducey, May 22, 1939; Ebert, *Illini Century,* 155.

9. Alan H. Levy, *Tackling Jim Crow* (Jefferson, NC: McFarland, 2003), 1–2, 14; Athletics Record Books, 1904, 29, 1905, 31; *Illini,* October 7, 1898; *Urbana Courier,* April 13, 1920; *Daily Illini,* April 23, 1921; *Champaign-Urbana News-Gazette,* November 6, 1988; Albert H. Lee, "Data on Negro Students, 1895–1940," University Archives Reference File; "Negro Students at the University of Illinois," RS 2/9/1–2.

10. Athletics Record Books, Football, October 14, 1916, October 18, 1919, October 16, 1920, October 10, 1921, October 26, 1935, October 17, 1936; *Illinois Alumni News,* December 1931, 121–123; December 1932, 92; Elvin Sayre to Zuppke, January 10, 1949.

11. George Senneff to Zuppke, November 19, 1937; *Daily Illini,* September 19–21, 24, 26–29, 1939, October 4–5, 8, 15, 22, 29, 1939; *Champaign-Urbana News-Gazette,* August 21, 1988.

12. It would be another nineteen years before the "barrier" was removed in basketball and about twenty-five years before much progress was made in the community. Athletics Record Books, October 22, 1928, October 18, 1941; Levy, *Tackling Jim Crow,* 98; *Illinois Alumni News,* November 1938, 23; *Daily Illini,* August 1, 1945; *Champaign-Urbana Courier,* February 26, 1967; Athletic Association Record Books, 1941.

13. Most of Eliot's dramatic account of the Michigan game is in McCallum, *Big Ten Football,* 81–82. *Daily Illini,* October 10–13, 15, 1939, November 3–5, 1939; Richard Oliver to Zuppke, September 15, 1939; Zuppke to Henry Schuettner, October 4, 1939; Zuppke to Austin Fox, October 5, 23, 1939; Earl Anderson to Zuppke, November 21, 1939; E.I. Burke to Zuppke, November 7,

1939; Charles J. Moynihan to Zuppke, November 13, 1939; Zuppke to Betty Michael, November 14, 1939; Jack W. Wilce to Zuppke, November 9, 1939; Zuppke to Harry H. Scott, November 15, 1939; Zuppke to John L. Griffith, November 7, 1939; Griffith to Zuppke, November 13, 1939; Zuppke to Ernest Lovejoy, April 11, 1939; Lovejoy to Zuppke, November 24, 1939; McCallum, *Big Ten Football,* 81–82; *Daily Illini,* September 7, 1978; David N. Nelson, *The Anatomy of the Game* (Newark, DE: University of Delaware, 1994), 162.

14. *Illinois Alumni News,* December 1939, 16–17; Charles E. Bowen to Arthur C. Willard, March 30, 1939; Athletic Association Budget, 1938–39, RS 6/3/11–1; *Board of Trustees 40th Report,* December 18, 1939, 678–680.

15. Athletic Association Audit Report, 1939–40, Trustees Correspondence, RS 1/1/1–25; *Illinois Alumni News,* January 1940, 13–15.

16. Coleman Griffith, Memo 220, January 25, 1939; Lloyd Morey to Arthur Willard, January 31, 1939, February 23, 1939; Willard to Wendell Wilson, February 6, 1939, March 2, 1939; Wilson to Willard, February 16, 1939, RS 6/3/8–1; Athletic Association Board Minutes, April 5, 1930, RS 28/1/3.

17. *Milwaukee Journal,* November 15, 1941; Dr. Ford to Edward Cochrane, September 23, 1940; L.M. Tobin to Milton Olander, November 8, 1940; Ray Hanson to Zuppke, May 21, 1940; Zuppke to Hanson, May 23, 1940; Zuppke to Lawrence A. Rust, May 29, 1940; Yost to Zuppke, October 30, 1940; Zuppke to Harry Hall, May 29, 1940, December 20, 1940; Lloyd Morey to Arthur Willard, May 3, 1939, RS 6/3/11; Zuppke to Bunny Oakes, April 2, 1940, May 25, 1940; Johnny Sabo to Zuppke, April 16, 24, 1940; Zuppke to Francis Schmidt, December 10, 1940; Clark Shaughnessy to Zuppke, February 7, 1940.

18. For evaluations of Rice and Walsh, see Sperber, *Shake Down the Thunder,* 175–177, 195. All-America Football, "Robert Zuppke Story," September 1—December 2, 1938; Interview with Grantland Rice, 1940; Rice to Zuppke, March 11, 27, 1940, May 9, 1940; Zuppke to Rice, March 4, 1940, May 15, 1940; Christy Walsh to Zuppke, February 26, November 8, 1940.

19. *Milwaukee Journal*, November 25, 1941; "I'm an American," August 31, 1941.

Chapter 20

1. *President's Report, 1929–30*, 9–10; *Daily Illini*, March 9, 1921; Comptroller's Report, 1939–40, 19, RS 6/1/801.

2. E.E. Stafford to R.B. Browne, January 12, 1937, Illinois Union Records, 1931–41, RS 37/7/7–2; Athletic Association Audit Report, 1940–41, Trustees Correspondence, RS 1/1/1–25.

3. *Board of Trustees 40th Report*, March 14, 1940, 788; Zuppke to Harold Pogue, July 3, 1940; Board of Directors Minutes, May 8, 1940, George Goble Papers, RS 14/2/20–6.

4. Zuppke to Harold Pogue, July 3, 1940; Zuppke to Edward Cochrane, September 24, 1940; John L. Griffith to Zuppke, November 7, 13, 1940; Zuppke to Griffith, November 14, 1940; Tom Johnson to Zuppke, November 18, 1940; Zuppke to Johnson, November 20, 1940; DIA Record Books, Football, 1940; *Illinois Alumni News*, September 1, 1941.

5. Carl Keith to Zuppke, December 3, 1940; Zuppke to Keith, June 22, 1940; Zuppke to H.A. Webber, November 19, 1940.

6. *Board of Trustees 41st Report*, December 16, 1941, 726–727; *Illinois Alumni News*, December 1, 1940, January 1, March 1, May 1, June 1, 1941; Jack Watson File, RS 26/4/1.

7. *Chicago Tribune*, December 4, 1940; Albert Lee, "Presidents I Have Known," 15, RS 2/6/21–6; Athletic Association File, Trustees Correspondence, 1940–41, RS 1/1/1–25: *University of Illinois Alumni Year Book* (Chicago, IL: Rockwell F. Clancy, 1935), 12.

8. *Board of Trustees 41st Report*, March 11, 1941, 222; Athletic Board of Directors Minutes, May 5, 1941, "On Getting Football Material," "Statement of Facts," July 15, 1941, George Goble Papers, RS 14/2/20–6.

9. Lester, *Stagg's University*, 184; *Illinois Alumni News*, July 1, 1940, March 1, 1941, February 1, 1942; Everett Peters to James M. Cleary, June 12, 1941; *Chicago Tribune*, June 27, 1941; *Champaign-Urbana News-Gazette*, April 23, 1978; Edgar G. Brands to Arthur C. Willard, April 24, 1941.

10. The close relationship between college sports and politics is discussed in my "Sports and Politics: Pro Patria and Alma Mater" given at the 6th ISHPES Congress, Budapest, July 18, 1999. St. Louis Illini Club resolution, March 19, 1941, George Goble Papers, RS 14/2/20–6; *Chicago Tribune*, June 4, 27, 1941; *Champaign-Urbana News-Gazette*, July 1–3, 1941; *Daily Illini*, May 16, 28, 1941, June 25, 28–29, 1941, July 9, 1941; *Illinois Alumni News*, July 1, 1941; Oscar Mayer to A.J. Janata, August 28, 1941, RS 2/9/1–53.

11. *Chicago Tribune*, June 27–28, 1941; Athletic Association Board of Directors Minutes, June 12, 1941, George Goble Papers, RS 14/2/20–6..

12. *Daily Illini*, May 16, 28, 1941, June 3, 25, 28–29, 1941, July 9, 1941.

13. *Daily Illini*, July 15–16, 1941; "Report by the ... Committee on Athletic Activities," July 15, 1941, RS 16/1/50–1; *Board of Trustees 41st Report*, July 15, 1941, 380–385; *Champaign-Urbana Courier*, July 15, 1941; *Champaign-Urbana News-Gazette*, July 18, 1941.

14. *Champaign-Urbana Courier*, July 15, 1941; *Champaign-Urbana News-Gazette*, July 18, 1941; *Chicago Tribune*, June 27, 1941.

15. Athletic Association Records, 1941; Disks 633, October 9, 1941 and 845, October 31, 1941, Sound Recordings, RS 13/6/5; Zuppke to Jason Roberts, November 13, 1941.

16. Zuppke to Way Woody, November 25, 1941; *Board of Trustees 41st Report*, November 18, 1941, 699; December 30, 1941, 735; *Champaign-Urbana News-Gazette*, November 18, 23, 1941; Zuppke to Al Fuller, March 16, 1938, RS 28/3/20–2; Athletic Association Record Books, November 22, 1941.

Chapter 21

1. North American Newspaper Alliance, Grantland Rice, "The Sportlight," November 22, 1941; Zuppke to Rice, December 19, 1941.

2. Zuppke to Frank Wilton, November 26, 1941; *Portland Oregonian*, November 18, 1941.

3. *Illinois State Journal*, November 18, 1941; *Moline Daily Dispatch*, November 18, 19, 21, 1941; *Rock Island Argus*, November 20, 24, 1941; *Los Angeles Times*, November 18, 1941; *New York Times*, November 18, 1941; *Philadelphia Evening Bulletin*, November 18, 1941; *St. Louis Post-Dispatch*, Novemeber 18,

1941; *Chicago Daily News*, November 21, 1941.

4. Zuppke to C.F. Williams, December 10, 1941; Zuppke to Nora E. Williford, December 10, 1941; Notes for conference with Arthur C. Willard, July 1941; Zuppke to Ernest E. Bearg, December 19, 1941; *Board of Trustees 41st Report*, December 30, 1941, 735.

5. Harold Pogue to Zuppke, January 21, 1942; *Detroit Free Press*, January 1, 1942.

6. Zuppke to Harrison E. Cunningham, January 9, 1942; Cunningham to Zuppke, January 14, 1942, RS 1/1/1–26; Frank A. Bush to Zuppke, June 21, 1942; M.E. Davenport to Zuppke, June 15, 1942; Zuppke to R.A. Stipes, March 9, 1942; Harry Stuhldreher to Zuppke, May 2, 1942; Frank Bush to Zuppke, June 21, 1942; M.E. Davenport to Zuppke, June 15, 1942.

7. Halas, George S., *Halas: An Autobiography* (Chicago, IL: Bonus Books, 1986), 202–203; Arch Ward to Zuppke, March 5, 1943, April 27, 1942, June 6, 1942. The Halas book was originally published as *Halas by Halas.*

8. *Chicago Tribune*, August 16–29, 1942.

9. *Chicago Herald-American*, August 30, 1943, October 31, 1943, November 10, 1943; *Champaign-Urbana Courier*, October 7, 1943, November 9, 1943; *Chicago Daily News*, November 9, 1943.

10. Esther M. Ingle to Zuppke, May 27, 1942; *Champaign-Urbana News-Gazette*, June 28, 1944, November 10, 1944; *Champaign-Urbana Courier*, July 2, 1944, October 17, 1944.

11. Zuppke to Middle West Sports Writers, April 28, 1944; Arch Ward to Zuppke, May 10, 1944; *Chicago Daily News*, November 4, 1944; *Chicago Tribune*, October 12, November 25, 1944; *Champaign-Urbana News-Gazette*, June 18, 28, 1944; *Champaign-Urbana Courier*, July 2, 1944, October 12, 17, 1944.

12. *Chicago Daily News*, July 3, 1945; *Champaign-Urbana News-Gazette*, July 19, 1942, September 27, 1942; July 2, 1945; November 26, 1945; April 11, 12, 1946, July 3, 1947; *Illinois Alumni News*, March 1940, 11; *Champaign-Urbana Courier*, October 7, 1943; September 27, 30, 1945, April 22, 1946, September 11, 1946; Zuppke to Allison Danzig, November 17, 1956; Zuppke to Eddie T. Jones, November 1945; Zuppke to Ernest Hemingway, October 3, 1950.

13. *Champaign-Urbana News-Gazette*, April 6, 1946; *Illinois Alumni News*, March 2, 1942; Champaign-Urbana newspaper clipping, January 1947.

14. *Champaign-Urbana New-Gazette*, April 11–12, 1946, September 3, 11, 1946, October 22, 1946; *Champaign-Urbana Courier*, April 22, 1946, September 22, 1946; George Halas to Zuppke, July 1, 1947; Al Fuller to Zuppke, August 16, 1947; Whittingham, *Chicago Bears*, 128, 130.

15. *Champaign-Urbana Courier*, September 3, 1946.

16. Zuppke to Grange, May 2, 1947; Zuppke to Cleveland, September 18, 1947.

17. George Halas to Zuppke, July 1, 1947; Al Fuller to Zuppke, August 16, 1947; Zuppke to Carl Voyles, January 29, 1948; Voyles to Zuppke, November 26, 1948; *Champaign-Urbana News-Gazette*, September 11, 1950; *Chicago Herald-American*, September 20, 1950; Zuppke to Branch Rickey, April 8, 1950.

18. Arthur L. Evans to Zuppke, August 16, 1949; Testimonial Dinner Program, October 27, 1949; Disk T595, Sound Recordings, RS 13/6/5; Ernie Lovejoy to Robert Cromie, December 14, 1957; *Champaign-Urbana News-Gazette*, June 16, 1949, October 28, 1949; *Champaign-Urbana Courier*, October 28, 1949; Bill Stern to Zuppke, September 12, 1949; Chick Meehan to Gordon Bilderback, November 1949; Arthur E. French to Zuppke, December 1, 1949; Muskegon Sports Hall of Fame Biography, June 9, 1990; Clark J. Buswell to Zuppke, January 24, 1950.

19. Draft Zuppke letter, 1951; Zuppke to Edwin Pope, April 8, 23, 1955; Nelson, *The Anatomy of the Game*, 84, 162, 212.

20. *Chicago American*, July 6, 1953; *Champaign-Urbana News-Gazette*, October 1, 7, November 3, 1950; September 16, 1953; *Milwaukee Journal*, January 17, 1951; Robert Russell to Zuppke, 1951, annotated.

21. *Christian Science Monitor*, November 21, 1951; *Chicago American*, July 6, 1953; Zuppke to Eddie Jacquin, November 27, 1956.

22. Biographical Manuscript, ca., 1956; Zuppke to Fred H. Young, August 8, 1955; *Chicago Tribune*, October 31, 1952; *Champaign-Urbana News-Gazette*, September 16, 1953; Biographical Manuscript. ca. 1956.

23. Ernie Lovejoy to Zuppke, January 4,

1957; Merritt Schoenfeld to Zuppke, March 1, 1957; Jack Watson to Zuppke, April 4, 1957; "Memorandum on Grants-in-Aid Program," November 20, 1959, RS 32/1/1.

Chapter 22

1. University of Wisconsin Commencement Program, June 22, 1905, 20; Peter Murry and Linda Murray, *The Art of the Renaissance* (New York: Oxford University Press, 1963), 29; Alice Hawkins, "Football and the Art Game," *The School Arts Magazine,* March 1932, 387–393; Robert C. Zuppke, "Portraits in Pigskin," *Esquire,* October 1936, 150. Eleven paintings held by Division of Intercollegiate Athletics; *St. Louis Post-Dispatch,* December 8, 1937; *Washington Evening Star,* November 25, 1937.

2. *Daily Illini,* July 26, 1917, April 22, 1920, January 19, 1921, May 16, 21, October 19, December 13, 1922, September 15, 1923; Chicago Society of Artists invitation, February 1, 1912; *Chicago Tribune,* December 13, 1912; *St. Louis Post-Dispatch,* December 8, 1937; Hawkins, "Football and the Art Game," 388; *Daily Illini,* July 16, 1926; *Chicago Evening Post,* December 1, 1932.

3. *Chicago Tribune,* March 1, 1931; *Chicago Evening Post,* October 1, 1932; Hawkins, "Football and the Art Game," 387–393; "Art and Athletics," *Everyday Art* (March-April 1932), 7–10; *Phoenix Gazette,* January 26, 1935; *St. Louis Post-Dispatch,* December 8, 1937; Zuppke to Julia Theola, June 12, 1934, RS 28/3/1; 10th, 11th, 12th, 13th and 14th Faculty Art Exhibit Programs, 1934–38, RS 12/3/805–2.

4. Business Men's Art Club of Chicago, *Yearbook, 1925,* 11; Hawkins, "Football and the Art Game," 387–388; *Esquire,* October 1956, 64, 122, 143; Grange, *Zuppke,* 92, 144; *Literary Digest,* June 26, 1937; *Chicago Evening Post,* October 1, 1932.

5. *Champaign-Urbana News-Gazette,* May 25, 1937; Zuppke to Frank A. Almy, August 26, 1937; Almy to Zuppke, October 19, 1937; Al Fuller to Zuppke, March 15, 1938; Zuppke to Fuller, April 3, May 12, 16, 1938; Ralph Cannon to Zuppke, April 7, 1938; Zuppke to George Carr, April 27, 1938; Zuppke to Charles Nevada, November 11, 1941; *Chicago Tribune,* May 11, 1938; *Chicago Daily News,* May 14, 1938.

6. *New York Times,* November 26, 1937; *Washington Star,* November 25, 1937.

7. *Champaign-Urbana News-Gazedtte,* October 7, 1943; Zuppke to Hemingway, ca. 1948.

8. Zuppke to Samson Raphaelson, November 25, 1946.

9. Zuppke to Frank Riebull, November 12, 1947; James Easterbrook to Zuppke, February 20, 1947; Millicent Easter to Zuppke, December 1, 1947; Walter Barber to Zuppke, April 12, 1950: Galesburg Civic Art League Program, 1953–54; Zuppke to Clifton Adams, November, 1953; Arts Comments, Notes and Sketches, 1953.

10. Jess M. Dowell to Zuppke, December 19, 1939 and Equitable Life Insurance to Zuppke, July 8, 1941, 250:176 and 257:26, Grantee Index, 1928–75, Champaign County Recorder's Office; Zuppke to Henry Swartz, June 27, 1947 and Zuppke to Fred Conrad, October 11, 1941, 285:290 and 289:306, Grantor Index, 1928–75; *Chicago Daily News,* May 9, 1942; *Chicago Tribune,* October 8, 1940, March 13, 1943, October 31, 1952; *Prairie Farmer,* December 11, 1943; James Capel to Zuppke, October 17, 1947, Edna to Zuppke, December 1947.

11. Zuppke to Burt Hurd, August 7, 1954; Zuppke to Polly Predmore, May 13, 1938; Zuppke to Charles J. Moynihan, June 6, 1938, RS 28/3/20–2; Claire Calvert to Zuppke, July 16, 1947; Burt Hurd to Zuppke, September 8, 1947; Hurd to Zuppke, September 3, 1948; *Milwaukee Journal,* December 27, 1939; Harry Hall to Zuppke, January 21, 1948; D.C. Ahrens to Zuppke, June 28, 1950; Suzanne Peterson to Zuppke, May 9, 1948; Zuppke to Ednyfed H. Williams, April 7, 1950; *Chicago Daily News,* October 13, 16, 1950; *Champaign-Urbana Courier,* November 20, 1950; Charles Moynihan to Zuppke, January 23, 1951; Jack Stewart to Zuppke, February 5, 1951; Burt Hurd to Zuppke, January 12, 1952; Zuppke to Allison Danzig, May 15, 1951; *Champaign-Urbana News-Gazette,* September 20, 1951; Zuppke to Charles Moynihan, October, 8 1952; *Grand Rapids Herald,* July 19, 1953; *The Milwaukee Eagle,* September 28, 1953; Robert Cannon to Zuppke, September 22, 1953.

12. Mike Tobin to Max Friedman, January 10, 1934, RS 28/3/1; *Daily Illini,* April 5, 1922, July 20, 1923 Zuppke to Paul F. Zup-

pke, June 30, 1924, RS 28/3/1; *Illinois Alumni News*, July 1937, 25; Zuppke to Mac Schoenfeld, April 14, 1938; *Muskegon Chronicle*, August 11, 1953; *Grand Rapids Herald*, July 19, 1953.

13. Zuppke to Marajen Chinigo, ca. February 1954; George Halas to Zuppke, February 19, 1954; Paul Pohle to Zuppke, February 23, 1954, March 10, 29, 1954; Zuppke to Pohle, April 2, 1954; Lou Marks to Zuppke, June 11, 1954; Bob Reitsch to Zuppke, September 24, 1954; Lou Cotie to Zuppke, July 20, 1954; Charles Carney to Zuppke, November 11, 1954; Jim Peterson to Zuppke, August 24, 1954; Christy Walsh to Zuppke, September 10, 1954; Grantland Rice Memorial, October 31, 1954.

14. Zuppke to Edwin Pope, April 8, 24, 1955; *Champaign-Urbana Courier*, June 6, 14, 1955, September 14, 1955, November 22, 1955, December 20, 24, 25, 1955; *Champaign-Urbana News-Gazette*, October 13, 15, 1955.

15. *Chicago Daily News*, September 8, 1950; *Muskegon Chronicle*, August 11, 1953; Zuppke to Potter, February 26, 1954.

16. *Who's Who in the Midwest, 1941*, 1353; *Champaign-Urbana News Gazette*, August 1, 1936, December 26, 30, 1957; Still, *Milwaukee*, 419.

17. Check Stub Book, March 2 to November 15, 1956; Leona Zuppke to Bob Scott, October 20, 1951; *Champaign-Urbana News-Gazette*, July 2, 1953, September 12, 1956, December 23, 1957; Leona Zuppke to Ella and Jack Watson, August 23, 1957; Leona Zuppke to Milwaukee Press Club, November 14, 1957; *Champaign-Urbana Courier*, December 23, 1957.

18. *Champaign-Urbana News-Gazette*, December 24, 1957.

19. *Champaign-Urbana News-Gazette*, December 23, 24, 1957; *Chicago Tribune*, December 23, 1957.

20. *Champaign-Urbana News-Gazette*, October 29, 1949; Zuppke to Carl Keith, June 22, 1940.

21. Ray Eliot and Douglas R. Mills, Memorial Tributes, December 1957.

22. *Champaign-Urbana News-Gazette*, December 23, 24, 1957; *Board of Trustees 39th Report*, February 27, 1937, 182; *Champaign-Urbana Courier* and *Champaign-Urbana News-Gazette*, April 4, 1958; *Chicago Daily News*, December 30, 1957.

Chapter 23

1. *Illinois Football Guide, 1991*, 30.

Bibliography

Archival Sources

University of Illinois Archives (Record series number and title)

0/1/801	University of Illinois Material, 1851–
1/1/1	Trustees Correspondence, 1919–63
1/1/802	Trustees Reports, 1867–
2/5/3	Edmund James General Correspondence, 1904–19
2/5/5	James Subject Files, 1904–18
2/5/6	James Faculty Correspondence, 1904–15
2/5/15	Staff Appointments File, 1905–
2/5/21	Vergil Phelps Papers, 1882–1968
2//6/1	David Kinley General Correspondence, 1919–30
2/6/21	Albert Lee Papers, 1912–28
2/6/3	Legislative Campaign Material, 1921–29
2/6/805	Stadium Drive Publications, 1921–27
2/7/5	Harry Chase Subject File, 1930–33
2/9/1	Arthur Willard General Correspondence, 1934–46
3/1/1	Council of Administration Minutes, 1894–1931
4/2/12	Athletics Committee & Faculty Representatives File, 1907–68
4/5/12	Educational Organization & Administration Committee File, 1930–31
5/1/21	Coleman Griffith Papers, 1919–63
6/3/11	Athletic Association Audit and Financial Records, 1931–40
12/3/805	Art & Design Exhibit & Lecture Announcements & Catalogs, 1876–
13/6/5	WILL Sound Recordings, 1936–
14/2/20	George Goble Papers, 1918–57
16/1/21	George Huff Papers, 1883–1947
25/2/801	Admissions Publications, 1879–
26/1/2	Alumni Association Minutes, 1912–73
26/1/20	Carl Stephens Papers, 1912–51
26/4/1	Alumni Morgue, 1882–1989
26/20/30	Stewart Howe Collection, 1923–92
26/20/37	Avery Brundage Collection, 1908–75
26/20/38	Samson Raphaelson Papers, 1921–76
28/1/3	Athletic Association Board of Directors Minutes, 1908–40
28/1/10	Athletic Association Director's Scrapbooks, 1930–76
28/2/20	Frank Murphy Papers, 1969
28/3/1	Football Coaches Correspondence, 1933–34
28/3/10	Course in Athletic Coaching File, 1926–30

28/3/20	Robert C. Zuppke Papers, 1900–57
28/3/21	Burt Ingwersen Papers, 1967
28/5/805	Football Publicity Materials, 1911–65
28/5/811	Football Programs, 1912–41
32/1/804	Foundation Annual Meetings File, 1935–63
37/7/7	Illinois Union Records, 1931–41
39/1/1	Public Information Subject File, 1919–84
41/1/20	Fred Turner Papers, 1918–75
41/20/94	Edith Lemarr Scrapbook, 1923
41/20/165	Jacob Goldstein Papers, 1929
41/20/172	Guy Thompson Scrapbook, 1928–29
41/71/812	Alpha Sigma Phi Illini Eta-Gram, 1930–45
41/71/834	Delta Tau Delta Beta Upsilon Booster, 1911–66

University of Illinois, Division of Intercollegiate Athletics, Athletic Association. Record Books, 1913–41

Illinois Historical Survey, George Chapin Papers

Published Sources

Allen, Charles L., ed. *Illinois' Greatest Football* Game. 1925. Pennsylvania game press clippings.

Angell, James R. "The Over Population of the Colleges." *Harpers*, October 1927.

Baker, Ira O., and Everett King. *A History of the College of Engineering of the University of Illinois, 1868–1945*. 2 vols. Urbana: University of Illinois, 1945.

Baldwin, Douglas O., ed. *Sports in North America*. Gulf Breeze, FL: Academic International Press, 2000.

Barber, William J. *George Huff: A Short Biography*. Privately printed, 1951.

Bennis, Chuck, and Jim Barnhart, *Illinois, Zup and I*. N.p., IL: Smith Printing, 1991.

Burford, Cary C. *We're Loyal to You, Illinois*. Danville, IL: Interstate, 1952.

Business Men's Art Club of Chicago, *Yearbook, 1925*.

Cannon, Ralph. "Football's Forgotten Men." *Esquire*, October 1936.

Carr, George R. "Robert C. Zuppke, Coach." *Alumni Quarterly*, January 1913.

Carroll, John M. *Red Grange and the Rise of Modern Football*. Urbana: University of Illinois Press, 1999.

———. "The Rise of Organized Sports." In *Sports in Modern America,* edited by William Baker and John Carroll. St. Louis: River City Publishers, 1981.

Chu, Donald. *The Character of American Higher Education & Intercollegiate Sports*. Albany: State University of New York Press, 1989.

Clark, Thomas A. *The Sunday Eight O'Clock*. Urbana: Illini, 1916.

Curti, Merle, and Vernon Carstensen. *The University of Wisconsin*. Madison: University of Wisconsin Press, 1949.

Danzig, Allison. *The History of American Football*. Englewood Cliffs, NJ: Prentice-Hall, 1956.

Dilliard, Irving. "Robert Carl Zuppke." In *Dictionary of American Biography, Supplement Six, 1956–1960,*). Edited by John Garraty, 728. New York: Charles Scribner's Sons, 1980.

Ebert, Roger, ed. *An Illini Century*. Urbana: University of Illinois Press, 1967.

Ellis, Griffith O. *American Boy Short Stories*. New York: Sun Dial Press, 1937.

Eubanks, Lon. *The Fighting Illini*. Huntsville, AL: Strode Publishers, 1976.

Evensen, Bruce. "George Halas." In *The Scribner Encyclopedia of American Lives, Sports Figures*. Edited by Arnold Markoe. Vol. 1. New York: Charles Scribner's Sons, 2002.

Falla, Jack, *NCAA: The Voice of Collegiate Sports.* Mission, KS: National Collegiate Athletic Association, 1981.

Flexner, Abraham. *Universities: American, English and German.* New York: Oxford University Press, 1930.

Fullerton, Hugh. "All-American Football Coaches." *Liberty,* February 12, 1927.

Gallagher, Robert S. "The Galloping Ghost." *American Heritage,* December 1974.

Grange, Harold E. *Zuppke of Illinois.* Chicago: A.L. Glaser, 1937.

Griffith, John L., ed. *The Big Ten Book of Athletic Events.* Chicago: C.D. Hodson, 1929.

Halas, George (with G. Morgan and A.Veysey). *Halas by Halas.* Chicago: McGraw-Hill, 1979.

Hawkins, Alice. "Football and the Art Game" in *The School Arts Magazine,* March 1932.

Hindsley, Mark. *My Bands and I.* Urbana: privately printed, 1984.

Hoddeson, Lillian, ed. *No Boundaries.* Urbana: University of Illinois Press, 2004.

Holden, Albon. "Ten Personalities in the Football Coaching Game." *Big Ten Weekly,* September 30, 1926.

Hyman, Mervin D., and Gordon S. White, *Big Ten Football.* New York: Macmillan, 1977.

Johnson, Henry C., and Erwin Johanningmeier. *Teachers for the Prairie.* Urbana: University of Illinois Press, 1972.

Kinley, David. *The Autobiography of David Kinley.* Urbana: University of Illinois Press, 1949.

Leckie, Robert. *The Story of Football.* New York: Random House, 1965.

Leland, Leland F. *The Golden Book of Tau Kappa Epsilon 1899–1940.* St. Paul, MN: Fraternity Press, 1949.

Lester, Robin. "Michigan-Chicago 1905," *Journal of Sport History* (Summer 1991).

_____. *Stagg's University.* Urbana: University of Illinois Press, 1995.

Levine, David O. *The American College and the Culture of Aspiration 1915–1940.* Ithaca, NY: Cornell University Press, 1986.

Levy, Alan H. *Tackling Jim Crow.* Jefferson, NC: McFarland, 2003.

McCallum, John D. *Big Ten Football Since 1895.* Radnor, PA: Chilton Book, 1976.

Morton, Ira. *The Galloping Ghost.* Wheaton, IL: Dupage Heritage Gallery, 1981.

Murray, Peter, and Linda Murry. *The Art of the Renaissance.* New York: Praeger, 1963.

Nelson, David N. *The Anatomy of the Game.* Newark: University of Delaware, 1994.

Oriard, Michael. *King Football.* Chapel Hill: University of North Carolina Press, 2001.

_____. *Reading Football.* Chapel Hill: University of North Carolina Press, 1993.

Pearson, Mike. *Illini Legends & Lore.* Champaign, IL: Sports Publishing, 2002.

_____. *Illini Legends Lists & Lore.* Champaign, IL: Sagamore Publishing, 1995.

Pencak, William. *For God & Country: The American Legion 1919–41.* Boston: Northeastern University Press, 1989.

Peterson, James A. *Grange of Illinois.* Chicago: Hinckley & Schmitt, 1956.

Pierson, George W. *Yale College 1871–1921.* New Haven: Yale University Press, 1952.

Pope, Edwin. *Football's Greatest Coaches.* Atlanta: Tupper and Love, 1955.

Raphaelson, Samson. *Story of the Stadium.* University of Illinois, Urbana, IL, 1922.

Revised Handbook for Boys. 3rd ed. New York: Boy Scouts of America, 1927.

Roberts, Howard. *The Chicago Bears.* New York: Putnam, 1947.

Rosenthal, Michael. *The Character Factory.* New York: Pantheon Books, 1986.

Savage, Howard J. *American College Athletics.* Carnegie Foundation for the Advancement of Teaching, Bulletin 23. New York, 1929.

_____. *Fruit of an Impulse.* New York: Harcourt, Brace, 1953.

Schlereth, Thomas J. *The University of Notre Dame.* Notre Dame, IN: University of Notre Dame Press, 1976.

Smith, Ronald A. "Athletics in the Wisconsin State University System, 1867–1913." *Wisconsin Magazine of History,* Autumn 1971.

_____. *Play by Play.* Baltimore: Johns Hopkins University Press, 2001.

Solberg, Winton U. *The University of Illinois, 1867–1894*. Urbana: University of Illinois Press, 1968.

_____. *The University of Illinois, 1894–1904*. Urbana: University of Illinois Press, 2000.

Sperber, Murray. *Shake Down the Thunder*. New York: Henry Holt, 1993.

Stephens, Carl. *Illini Years: A Picture History*. Urbana: University of Illinois Press, 1950.

Stewart, Alva W. *College Football Stadiums*. Jefferson, NC: McFarland, 2000.

Still, Bayrd. *Milwaukee*. Madison: State Historical Society of Wisconsin, 1965.

Thelin, John R. *Games Colleges Play*. Baltimore: Johns Hopkins University Press, 1994.

Toma, J. Douglas. *Football U.: Spectator Sports in the Life of the American University*. Ann Arbor: University of Michigan Press, 2003.

Treat, Roger. *The Encyclopedia of Football*. New York: A.S. Barnes, 1979.

Turner, Fred H. "Athletes Lead in Brains." *Big Ten Weekly*, April 1, 1926.

Umphlet, Wiley L. *Creating the Big Game*. Westport, CT: Greenwood, 1992.

University of Illinois Alumni Year Book. Chicago: Rockwell F. Clancy, 1935.

Visher, Stephen S. *Scientists Starred 1903–1943 in "American Men of Science."* Baltimore: Johns Hopkins University Press, 1947.

Voltmer, Carl A. *A Brief History of the Intercollegiate Conference of Faculty Representatives*. New York: George Banta, 1935.

Walsh, Christy. *Adios to Ghosts*. New York: privately printed, 1935.

Watterson, John S. *College Football*. Baltimore: Johns Hopkins University Press, 2000.

Whittingham, Richard, *The Chicago Bears*. Chicago: Rand McNally & Co., 1979.

_____. *What a Game They Played*. New York: Simon & Schuster, 1984.

Williamson, Harold F., and Payson Wild, *Northwestern University 1850–1975*. Evanston, IL: Northwestern University, 1976.

Wilson, Kenneth L., and Jerry Brondfield. *The Big Ten*. Englewood Cliffs, NJ: Prentice-Hall, 1967.

Yost, Fielding H. *Football for Player and Spectator*. Ann Arbor, MI: University Publishing, 1905.

Zuppke, Robert C. *Coaching Football*. Champaign, IL: Bailey & Himes, 1930.

_____. *Football Technique and Tactics*. Champaign, IL: Bailey and Himes, 1924.

_____. *Football Technique and Tactics*. Champaign, IL: Zuppke and Bearg, 1922.

_____. "Portraits in Pigskin." *Esquire*, October 1936.

_____. *10 Things a Boy Should Know How to Do!* (1934).

_____. "Will Illinois Repeat?" *Illinois Magazine* 7, no. 1 (October 1915): 5–6.

Other Sources

Milwaukee Historical Society and Public Library

Muskegon, Michigan Hackley Library

Northwestern University Archives, Zuppke letter, 1919

Notre Dame University Archives, Director of Athletics File, 1909–29

Directories, newspapers, dissertations, internet postings and papers presented at professional meetings are cited in the endnotes.

Index